Audit Quality

Jonas Tritschler

Audit Quality

Association between published reporting errors and audit firm characteristics

Foreword by Univ.-Prof. Dr. Rudolf Steckel
and Univ.-Prof. Dr. David Manry

Springer Gabler

Jonas Tritschler
Innsbruck, Austria

PhD Thesis University of Innsbruck, 2013

ISBN 978-3-658-04173-1 ISBN 978-3-658-04174-8 (eBook)
DOI 10.1007/978-3-658-04174-8

The Deutsche Nationalbibliothek lists this publication in the Deutsche Nationalbibliografie; detailed bibliographic data are available in the Internet at http://dnb.d-nb.de.

Library of Congress Control Number: 2013952721

Springer Gabler

Printed on acid-free paper

Springer Gabler is a brand of Springer DE.
Springer DE is part of Springer Science+Business Media.
www.springer-gabler.de

Foreword

We are delighted to present Jonas Tritschler's dissertation on Audit Quality. Auditing remains a very active research area in financial economics and accounting. Much of the research focuses on audit quality, materiality, error rates, audit partner tenure, and auditor experience. Although there has been a convergence of thought among regulators and enforcement agencies on characteristics of audit quality, there is no widely-held operational definition of audit quality in the research literature. Moreover, most audit research on German firms has not made use of actual audit errors reported in the German Federal Gazette.

Arising from the author's experience as a practicing CPA in a "Big Four" audit firm, this book is quite different from other research in this field, as it confronts the subject of audit quality from a pragmatic perspective. The approach the author adopts is based on the very origins of quality considerations, and does not rely on the seemingly-ubiquitous earnings management approach.

In the 1940s, manufacturing quality was usually measured by the number of defects per thousand units of finished products. The researcher uses a similar approach to measure audit quality at the audit firm level. Since 2005, public interest entities have been required to publish their material reporting errors in the German Federal Gazette. Actual published audit failures, the remaining material misstatements identified in audited financial statements by regulatory authorities, thus comprise the data points used in this research to measure audit quality.

Auditing is a people business, with human resources as production factors. Quantified audit input factors, such as competence and experience, provide variables to explain performance differences in audit service quality. Favorable input factors, associated with low auditor failure rates (the number of absolute reporting errors divided by the auditor's number of clients in the public market), suggest causality.

In essence, this is a study that focuses on the audit quality of German audit firms and the unique aspects of the German regulatory framework. It includes a wealth of institutional detail on German enforcement authority (FREP) examination triggers, as well as on how these fit into EU securities markets oversight.

International accounting standards are converging over time. Much contemporary research covers similarities and differences among developed nations.

Given the scarcity of empirical research into auditors of German public companies and their regulatory environment, the focus and encyclopedic detail of this book mark it as authoritative, innovative, and significant.

Last but not least, we believe that a periodic disclosure of audit quality would increase audit quality over time. Thus, research on the development of a transparent audit quality measure at the audit firm level in Germany (or even world-wide) would be an important first step towards creating competition in both audit fees and audit quality. This in turn could lead to a win-win situation for capital markets, regulators, and economies in general.

Because of the somewhat unusual but interesting and very relevant content, we are confident that this research work will appeal to a wide selection of academic and professional readers. Students, researchers, practitioners, and regulators will find this book useful for further study and additional research.

Innsbruck — Univ.-Prof. Dr. Rudolf Steckel
New Orleans — Univ.-Prof. Dr. David Manry

Acknowledgements

First of all, I want to thank my doctoral advisors, Rudolf Steckel, University of Innsbruck and David Manry, University of New Orleans. Rudolf Steckel liked my research idea from the very beginning, which kept me motivated throughout a long and challenging period of time. His continuous guidance, valuable advice, and constant encouragement made it possible to finish my dissertation within three years of research.

I am very proud and grateful for having David Manry as my advisor. I will not forget the stimulating discussion when we first met in New Orleans (he almost missed his Wednesday-3pm-lecture because of our lively discussion!). His ideas and his advices helped much to concretize my research model, and his dedicated review and feedback encouraged me to continue as a researcher and to develop further models on audit quality measurements.

I am also very grateful to a former colleague at work and a friend, Josef McGuigan, who critically reviewed and commented on my pre-draft version (before handing it in to my advisors). His excellent comments helped a lot to improve the quality of my research paper. I am sure that he could become an exceptional researcher in accounting and auditing if only he wanted. It is a pity that he did not choose a research career!

Further thanks go to Ellen Palli, who manages the Austrian-Student-Program. The program, in connection with Walter Lane (by the way, I liked his lectures in economics very much!), built the transatlantic bridge from Innsbruck to New Orleans, which helped me to get in touch with David Manry.

I say also thanks to Rudolf Steckel's research team in the Department of Accounting, Auditing and Taxation, especially to Julia Baldauf and Marcel Steller, for allowing me the opportunity to present and discuss my research idea – even though it was quite vague and half-baked in the beginning.

Last but not least, I would like to thank Irene Thaler, who organized and scheduled most of the meetings with Rudolf Steckel and who managed the administrative hurdles such as the formal research proposal acceptance at the registrar's office (bureaucracy sometimes can be even as challenging as research work itself!).

I owe all of you my sincere and deepest gratitude – thank you very much indeed!

Innsbruck　　　　Jonas Tritschler

Table of Contents

Foreword V
Acknowledgements VII
List of Figures XV
List of Tables XIX
Abbreviations XXI
List of Symbols XXIII

1 Introduction 1
1.1 Problem Statement 1
1.2 Research Objective 3
1.3 Research Data and Methodology 4
1.4 Basic Assumptions and Hypothesis 5
1.5 Outline of this Study 6

2 Literature Review and Current Issues 7
2.1 Agency Theory and Audit Services 7
2.2 Definitions of Audit Quality 10
2.2.1 Two Main Schools of Thoughts 10
2.2.1.1 DeAngelo's Definition of Audit Quality 10
2.2.1.2 Level of Compliance with Standards 10
2.2.1.3 Financial Reporting Quality and Compliance with Auditing Standards 11
2.2.1.4 Francis Framework on Audit Quality Research 13
2.2.2 Regulatory Definitions and Frameworks on Audit Quality 14
2.2.2.1 Directive of the European Union 14
2.2.2.2 PCAOB's Definition of Audit Quality 14
2.2.2.3 International Standard on Quality Control (ISQC 1) 15
2.2.2.4 IAASB Framework on Audit Quality 18
2.2.2.5 UK Financial Reporting Council's Framework on Audit Quality 24

2.2.2.6 Overview of Important Institutions Concerned with Audit Quality 24
2.3 Determinants of Audit Quality 25
2.3.1 Overview 25
2.3.2 Independence 27
2.3.2.1 Prerequisite for Professional Judgment 27
2.3.2.2 Threats to Independence 30
2.3.3 Audit Firm Size 40
2.3.4 Audit Fees 41
2.3.5 Provision of Non-Audit Services 48
2.3.6 Audit Tenure 50
2.3.7 Legal Liability 53
2.3.8 Accounting and Audit Knowledge 54
2.3.9 Client, Industry and Audit Experience 58
2.3.10 Audit Effort and Resource Mix 59
2.3.11 Audit Methodology and Tools 60
2.4 Criticism on Selected on Audit Quality Measures 61
2.4.1 Earnings Management 61
2.4.2 Restatements 65
2.4.3 Going-Concern Reporting 66
2.5 Conclusion and Knowledge Gap 67

3 Audit Quality Measure Based on Reporting Errors 69
3.1 Overall Audit Objectives and Audit Failures 69
3.1.1 Overall Objectives of the Auditor 69
3.1.2 Material Misstatements 70
3.1.2.1 Misstatements in Financial Statements 70
3.1.2.2 Materiality 71
3.1.2.2.1 Concepts of Materiality 71
3.1.2.2.2 Quantitative Considerations of Materiality 76
3.1.2.2.3 Qualitative Considerations of Materiality 77
3.1.2.3 Audit Risk and Materiality 79
3.1.2.4 Consequences 80
3.1.3 Audit Failures 80
3.1.3.1 Definitions 80
3.1.3.2 Indicators of Audit Failures 83
3.1.3.2.1 Significant Audit Engagement Deficiencies 83

3.1.3.2.2 Restatements 86
3.1.3.2.3 Litigations 89
3.1.3.2.4 Accounting Enforcement Releases 90
3.2 Accounting Enforcement in Germany 91
3.2.1 Legal Basis 91
3.2.2 Examination Triggers 93
3.2.2.1 Examination with Cause (Concrete Indicators) 94
3.2.2.2 Examination on Request by BaFin (Certain Indicators) 94
3.2.2.3 Examination by Random Sampling (no Indicators) 95
3.2.3 Enforcement Process 101
3.2.3.1 Examination Commencement 101
3.2.3.2 Examination Process 103
3.2.3.3 Process for Publication 104
3.2.3.4 Materiality in the Enforcement Process 106
3.2.4 Summary of Enforcement Results 108
3.2.4.1 Error Rate Trend 108
3.2.4.2 Error Categories 109
3.2.4.3 Causes of High Error Rates 111
3.2.5 Evaluation of the Enforcement Methodology 112
3.2.5.1 Evaluation Criteria 112
3.2.5.2 Evaluation by Criteria 116
3.2.5.2.1 Objectivity 116
3.2.5.2.2 Reliability 119
3.2.5.2.3 Validity 121
3.2.5.2.4 Transparency 122
3.2.5.2.5 Adequacy 122
3.2.5.2.6 Reflexivity 123
3.2.5.2.7 Discussion of Limitations 124
3.2.5.2.8 Triangulation 125
3.2.5.2.9 Evaluation Summary 125
3.3 Published Reporting Errors as Audit Quality Indicator 128
3.3.1 Audit Failure Rates Definitions 128
3.3.1.1 Auditors' Absolute Failure Frequency 128
3.3.1.2 Auditors' Relative Failure Frequency 129
3.3.2 Data Description 130
3.3.2.1 Data Basis 130

3.3.2.2 Distribution of Absolute Failure Frequencies 131
3.3.2.3 PIE Market Concentration 132
3.3.2 Data Analysis 134
3.3.2.1 Absolute Failure Frequencies 134
3.3.2.2 Relative Failure Frequencies 136
3.3.2.3 Big vs. Small Audit Firms 142
3.3.3 Conclusions 144

4 Reporting Errors and Audit Firm Characteristics 147
4.1 Audit Service Production Models 147
4.1.1 Audit Production Function 147
4.1.2 A Modified Audit Production Framework 149
4.2 Audit Input Factors 150
4.2.1 Audit Input Factors Overview 150
4.2.2 Auditor's Competence and Audit Effort 151
4.2.2.1 Cost-Optimization Model 151
4.2.2.2 Optimization Model for the Input Factors Audit Time and Experience 154
4.2.2.3 Auditor's Competence 156
4.2.2.4 Audit Effort 158
4.2.3 Audit Methodology 159
4.2.4 Audit Support Systems 161
4.3 Preparing and Auditing Financial Statements 164
4.3.1 Process Overview 164
4.3.2 Financial Statement Preparation 165
4.3.3 Audit Process 165
4.3.4 Interactions and Iterative Process 166
4.4 Audit Firm Structure and Audit Firm Characteristics 167
4.4.1 Multinational Audit Firms and SMP 167
4.4.2 Organizational Levels of Multi-National Audit Firms 168
4.4.3 Structure of Audit Firm's Organization 170
4.4.4 Audit Engagement Team Structure 171
4.4.5 Employee Specialization 172
4.4.6 Accessible Audit Firm Characteristics 173
4.5 Audit Firm Characteristics and Financial Reporting Errors 174
4.5.1 Working Hypothesis 174
4.5.2 Research Model 175

4.5.3 Research Data ... 175
4.5.4 Certified Audit Professionals Ratio ... 175
4.5.5 Employee Experience ... 179
4.5.5.1 Average of Experience per Employee ... 179
4.5.5.2 Total Years of Experience of all Employees ... 184
4.5.6 Client-Specific Experience ... 186
4.5.7 Results Summary ... 190

5 Summary and Conclusions ... 193
5.1 Conclusions on Literature Review and Current Issues ... 193
5.2 Summary and Conclusions on Empirical Study ... 194
5.3 Limitations and Further Research ... 196

Appendix ... 199
Appendix A: Published Reporting Errors ... 199
Appendix B: Involved Audit Firms ... 204
Appendix C: Data Basis for Certification Rate Calculation ... 206
Appendix D: Example Calculation of Isoquality Curves ... 210
Appendix E: Derivation of Formulas ... 216

References ... 219

List of Figures

Figure 2.1: Shareholder-Management-Relationship including the Auditor ... 9
Figure 2.2: Audit Quality: School of thoughts ... 12
Figure 2.3: IAASB Perspectives on Audit Quality ... 19
Figure 2.4: Overview of Important Institutions Concerned with Audit Quality ... 25
Figure 2.5: The Globe of Audit Quality: Cause-Effect-Diagram ... 26
Figure 2.6: Relationship between Low Quality Accounting, High Risk Engagements and igher Audit Fees ... 43
Figure 2.7: Low Balling According to DeAngelo's Audit Cost Model ... 45
Figure 2.8: Cumulative View on DeAngelo's Model ... 46
Figure 2.9: Audit Analytics, Audit Fees and Non-Audit Fees – A Seven Year Trend ... 49
Figure 2.10: Audit Quality and Audit Tenure Relation ... 51
Figure 2.11: Professional Accountants Education Framework According to IESBA 2010 ... 56
Figure 2.12: A Standard "Audit Engagement Team Structure" ... 57
Figure 2.13: Management's and Auditor's Accounting Biases ... 63
Figure 3.1: Misstatements in Financial Statements ... 71
Figure 3.2: Concepts of Materiality: Framework 1989 and Conceptual Framework 2010 ... 73
Figure 3.3: Line of Materiality Thresholds ... 75
Figure 3.4: Definitions of Audit Deficiency, Significant Audit Deficiency and Audit Failure ... 82
Figure 3.5: Trends in Audit Deficiencies ... 84
Figure 3.6: Total Number of Restatements of U.S. Stock Exchange Listed Firms ... 87
Figure 3.7: Accounting Enforcement in Germany ... 92
Figure 3.8: Applied Risk Function on Financial Statements Examinations ... 99
Figure 3.9: Guidance on Appropriate and Non-Appropriate Selection ... 100
Figure 3.10: Commencement Process ... 103
Figure 3.11: Examination Process ... 104

Figure 3.12: Process for Publication ... 105
Figure 3.13: Completed Examinations, Error Rate Trend ... 109
Figure 3.14: Most Frequently Identified Errors ... 110
Figure 3.15: Error Frequencies per Index ... 111
Figure 3.16: Detected Errors vs. Published Errors ... 130
Figure 3.17: Distribution of Absolute Failures Frequencies (AFF) ... 132
Figure 3.18: Concentration in the PIE Audit Market ... 134
Figure 3.19: Absolute Failure Frequencies per Audit Firm (AFF $\geq$ 3) ... 135
Figure 3.20: AFRs of Audit Firms Having more than or Equal to 10 PIE Clients since 2008 on Average ... 142
Figure 3.21: Audit Failure Rates Compared BigN to Non-BigN ... 144
Figure 4.1: Audit Quality in Terms of Assurance Level ... 149
Figure 4.2: A modified Audit Production Framework ... 150
Figure 4.3: Audit Inputs, Criteria, and Indicators ... 151
Figure 4.4: Isoquality Curves at Different Assurance Levels ... 153
Figure 4.5: Isoqualty, Isocost, and Optimal Input Combination ... 153
Figure 4.6: Optimal Relation between Time Spent on Operative Audit and Quality Assurance ... 159
Figure 4.7: PwC Audit Approach ... 161
Figure 4.8: Audit Support System Design Principles Enabling Audit Process Quality ... 163
Figure 4.9: Financial Reporting Preparation and Auditing ... 164
Figure 4.10: Outcome of Auditing: a Continuous Improvement of Assurance Level ... 167
Figure 4.11: Typical Multi-National Audit Firm's Organizational Levels . 169
Figure 4.12: Typical Matrix Organization Example of a Big Audit Firm ... 170
Figure 4.13: Typical Organizational Dimensions of Big Audit Firms ... 171
Figure 4.14: Employee Specialization ... 172
Figure 4.15: Certification Rates of Top 7 Audit Firms ... 177
Figure 4.16: Correlation of Certification Rates with Auditor's Failure Rate of Top 7 Audit Firms ... 178
Figure 4.17: Average Experience in Years (Big4) ... 182
Figure 4.18: Correlation of Average Experiences in Years with Auditor's Failure Rate (Big4) ... 183
Figure 4.19: Total Years of Experience (Big4) ... 185
Figure 4.20: Correlation of Total Years of Experience with Auditor's Failure Rate (Big4) ... 185
Figure 4.21: Client Fluctuation Rates ... 188

Figure 4.22: Correlation of Client Fluctuation Rate with Auditor's Failure Rate 189
Figure 4.23: Correlation of Average Rank with AFR 191
Figure D.1: Isoquality Curve Based on Table E.1 211
Figure D.2: Isocost Curves 213
Figure D.3: Determining the Cost-Minimum Point 214
Figure E.1: Developing the Measure "Years of Experience" in an Audit Firm 216

List of Tables

Table 2.1: Audit Quality Attributes According to IAASB's Framework... 20
Table 2.2: The Relative Importance of Audit Quality Attributes 27
Table 2.3: Audit Fees Threshold in Relation to Audit Firms Total Revenues 32
Table 2.4: Specific Auditor Rotation Requirements of Selected European Countries 39
Table 3.1: Quantitative Approaches of Materiality Thresholds 76
Table 3.2: QMF According to ISA 450.A16 78
Table 3.3: Principles of Enforcement According to CESR Standard No. 1 96
Table 3.4: Main Causes for Errors 112
Table 3.5: Summary of the Assessment of the Enforcement Methodology 126
Table 3.6: PIE Auditors and PIE Clients in the German Audit Market ... 133
Table 3.7: Data Preparation for Further Analysis 139
Table 3.8: Auditors' Failure Rates (Audit Firms with more than or equal to 10 PIEs Clients on Average since 2008) 141
Table 3.9: Audit Failure Rates compared BigN to the Remainder........... 143
Table 4.1: Example of Optimal h^* at Minimum Cost, Generating an Assurance Level q 148
Table 4.2: Cognitive Biases likely to Affect the Auditor's Professional Judgment 158
Table 4.3: Calculation of the Certification Rate 176
Table 4.4: AFR and Certification Rate 177
Table 4.5: Number of Total Employees, Hires, Separations 181
Table 4.6: Employee Attrition Rate and Average Years of Experience ... 182
Table 4.7: PIE Client Fluctuation Rates 187
Table 4.8: AFR and Client Fluctuation Rate 188
Table 4.9: Linear Regressions Results Summary 191
Table A.1: 186 Reporting Errors Published between February 3, 2006 and December 31, 2012 199
Table A.2: Audit Firms and Legal Entities in Context with PRE 203
Table B.1: Involved Audit Firms 204

Table C.1: Certified Audit Professionals per Audit Firm 206
Table C.2: Number of Employees per Audit Firm 207
Table C.3: Certified Audit Professionals per Audit Firm 208
Table C.4: PIE Clients per Audit Firm 208
Table C.5: Break down of BDO PIE Clients into BDO and AWT Clients 208
Table C.6: Break down of ESMB PIE Clients into ESM and BACHEM Clients 209
Table C.7: Break down of PKF PIE Clients into PKF Deutschland and PKF Fasselt Clients 209
Table D.1: Isoquality Values: Experience in Years and Audit Time in Hours 211
Table D.2: Isoquality Curves at Different Assurance Levels.................. 213
Table D.3: Total Audit osts for the Given Example 215

Abbreviations

AFF	Absolute Failure Frequency
AFR	Auditor's Failure Rate
APAK	Abschlussprüferaufsichtskommission (German Audit Oversight Commission)
ASC	Accounting Standard Codification (U.S. GAAP)
BaFin	Bundesanstalt für Finanzdienstleistungsaufsicht (Federal Financial Supervisory Authority)
BDO	Binder, Dijker, Otte & Co
CAPM	Capital Asset Pricing Model
CESR	Committee of European Securities Regulators (since 2011: ESMA)
CPA	Certified Public Accountant
DStR	Deutsches Steuerrecht (Journal)
EBA	European Banking Authority
EBIT	Earnings before interest and taxes
EECS	European Enforcers Coordination Sessions
EIOPA	European Insurance and Occupational Pensions Authority
ESA	European Supervisory Authorities
ESMA	European Securities and Markets Authority
ESMB	Ebner, Stolz, Mönning & Bachem
et seq.	et sequens (and the following)
EU	European Union
EVA	Economic value added
E&Y	Ernst & Young
FRC	UK Financial Reporting Council
FREP	Financial Reporting Enforcement Panel (German: DPR – Deutsche Prüfstelle für Rechnungslegung e.V.)
GAAP	Generally Accepted Accounting Principles
GAO	U.S. Government Accountability Office
HGB	Handelsgesetzbuch (German Commercial Code)
IAASB	International Auditing and Assurance Standards Board
IAESB	International Accounting Education Standards Board
ICAEW	Institute of Chartered Accountants in England and Wales
ICAI	Institute of Chartered Accountants of India

IESBA	International Ethics Standards Board for Accountants
IFAC	International Federation of Accountants
ISA	International Standards on Auditing
IFRS	International Financial Reporting Standards
IDW	Institut der Wirtschaftsprüfer (German Institute of Auditors)
IMA	Institute of Management Accountants
KPMG	Klynveld, Peat, Marwick & Goedeler
KWG	Gesetz über das Kreditwesen (German Banking Act)
MDA	Management Discussion and Analysis
NAS	Non-audit services or non-assurance services
NASBA	National Association of State Boards of Accountancy
OLS	Ordinary Least Squares
OLG	Oberlandesgericht (Higher Regional Court)
PCAOB	Public Company Accounting Oversight Board
PIE	Public Interest Entity
PRE	Published Reporting Error ("Fehlerbekanntmachung")
PublG	Publizitätsgesetz (Public Disclosure Act)
PwC	PricewaterhouseCoopers
SAG	Standing Advisory Group (Part of PCAOB)
SEC	Securities and Exchange Commission
Sec.	Section
SME	Small and medium-sized enterprises
SMP	Small and medium-sized practices (accountancy practitioners)
SOX	Sarbanes-Oxley Act of 2002
StBG	Steuerberatungsgesellschaft
StBGebV	Steuerberatergebührenverordnung (tax adviser fee ordinance)
TR	Transparency Report
UGB	Unternehmensgesetzbuch (Austrian Commercial Code)
UK	United Kingdom
U.S.	United States of America
VAG	Versicherungsaufsichtsgesetz (German Insurance Supervision Act)
WiPrPrüfV	Wirtschaftsprüferprüfungsverordnung (Public Accountants Certification Ordinance)
WPG	Wirtschaftsprüfungsgesellschaft
WPK	Wirtschaftsprüferkammer (English: German Chamber of Public Accountants)
WPO	Wirtschaftsprüferordnung (Public Accountants Act)
WpHG	Wertpapierhandelsgesetz (Securities Trading Act)

List of Symbols

¬	Not sign / negation
>	Less than
<	Greater than
=	Equals
≡	Exactly identical to
≥	Less than or equal to
≤	Greater than or equal to
∅	Average
α	Alpha / coefficient
β	Beta / coefficient
Σ	Sigma / sum
Ω	Omega / population
€	Euro
$	Dollar
&	And
∈	Element of
ℕ	Natural number

1 Introduction

1.1 Problem Statement

In the beginning of the 21st century, the global economy has faced immense challenges concerning the regulations of the global capital and financial markets. As a consequence of the rising number of accounting scandals of famous global players such as Enron, Worldcom and Parmalat, the credibility of top managers and auditors had been questioned. Surprisingly all firms mentioned above had received an unqualified opinion by their auditors until the very last moment of existence. This fact provokes a renewed discussion about the overall quality of financial reporting and the performance of audit firms, which assure the accuracy and completeness of financial reports. Fueled by these occurrences, academic researchers, regulators and professional institutions focused their work on the analysis of auditors' performance in terms of quality.

A new level of mistrust had been reached in the financial crises 2008 and 2009. The fall of Lehman Brothers triggered a chain reaction which almost led to a collapse of the complete banking sector worldwide. Only governments could save their banks with granting guarantees in billions of euro. Once more the causes had been discussed and investigated. The question "who is able to detect and report risks in an early stage?" has been raised and discussed plenty of times. It is no wonder that, along with management and supervisory board of the banks, the auditors had been in focus again. It is evidently the independent auditor who has to review the valuation of financial assets and who has to assess the going concern issue on a regular basis. PCAOB and some newspapers named the auditors "watchdogs that didn't bark".[1] Instead, rating agencies have been playing more and more the role of reporting going concern opinions by pre-announcing downgrades of credit risks of affected firms, banks and countries. As a consequence, the European Commission released a Green Paper in 2010 which includes dedicated countermeasures in order to ensure auditors independence, reliability and to improve the quality of the work of financial statement auditors.[2]

---

1 http://pcaobus.org/News/Events/Documents/03162011_IAGMeeting/The_Watchdog_That_Didnt_Bark.pdf.

2 European Commission (2010): Green Paper "Audit Policies: lessons learned from the crises".

Auditors' performance and audit quality itself had been in a research focus for more than 30 years. In 2010, IAASB stated about audit quality: "There have been a number of attempts to define audit quality in the past. However, none of them has resulted in a definition that achieved universal recognition and acceptance. Audit quality is, in essence, a complex and multi-faceted concept".[3]

The ongoing challenge is how to operationalize audit quality and what measurements are most appropriate. Contemporary approaches all end up in measures which are derived from proxies (also called surrogates) such as auditors' size, client's tenure and ratio of non audit fees to total fees as well as the extent of discretionary accruals, the correctness of going concern opinions, occurrences of financial restatements and auditors' lawsuits and litigations. Hundreds of studies result in different and sometimes contradictory conclusions. Only some work had been done on operationalizing input based indicators such as auditors' skills (mainly competence and experience), deployed audit time (effort), audit methodology or audit firm culture.

Another knowledge gap is taken from the fact that only some research had been performed in the field of published financial reporting errors of German public interest entities.

In this regard, this study raises the following questions:

- Can an audit quality measurement be developed on audit firm level based on published financial reporting errors?
- Can input factors such as competence, experience and audit effort be operationalized in the way that public data can be used and do they explain differences in audit quality on audit firm's level?
- Is there a measurable correlation between audit quality and selected audit input factors?
- Are audit input factors substitutable as any production factors according to the production function theory?

3 IAASB (2011), p. 3.

1.2 Research Objective

Derived from the research questions above, the following research objectives determine the structure of this thesis. It has four main objectives:

- Establishing of a measurement called "Auditor's Failure Rate" (AFR) based on published financial reporting errors as audit quality indicator,
- Defining measurable proxies for input factors such as audit competence and audit experience,
- Testing of direct correlation between input factors and audit quality levels,
- Explaining audit quality differences on audit firm level by discussing selected audit firm characteristics.

To reach these objectives, this study develops an audit quality measurement which is based on financial reporting errors of German public interest entities published in the German Federal Gazette. Further, it examines the association between published reporting errors and audit firm characteristics in the context of audit quality in Germany.

This study contributes to the existing literature in two perspectives. First, a new audit quality measurement on audit firm level ("Auditor's Failure Rate") is developed from the basis of revealed accounting errors by the by the Financial Reporting Enforcement Panel[4] (FREP) in Germany. Second, the study defines proxies in order to measure input factors such as auditors' competence and experience on audit firm level and deployed audit time on audit engagement level. These proxies are used as independent variables in a set of regression models with the purpose of testing the correlation with a given auditor's failure rate (dependent variable).

4 Deutsche Prüfstelle für Rechnungslegung e.V. (DPR).

1.3 Research Data and Methodology

From January 2006 to November 2012 the Financial Reporting Enforcement Panel (FREP) together with the German Federal Financial Supervisory Authority[5] (Bundesanstalt für Finanzdienstleistungsaufsicht, short: BaFin) have detected and enforced the release of 186 accounting errors in the financial statements of public interest entities (PIEs) in Germany. [6] Assuming that all published reporting errors can be classified as material misstatements implies that in these cases not only financial reporting failures but also audit failures may have incurred. At least the reported enforcements can be seen as an outcome of low audit quality, since those financial reporting errors had not been detected and reported by the auditor in the course of the audit.[7]

All audit firms involved in the above mentioned accounting enforcements are analyzed on selected audit firm and audit engagement characteristics. These characteristics do not cover the typical proxies such as Big4 or NonBig4, size, and auditor's tenure; instead, they are based on input factors indicators such as ratio of certified audit professionals to the total number of employees of the audit firm (certified audit professionals rate), average years of experience of an employee, and client fluctuation.

Testing the correlation of selected audit firm characteristics (such as certification rate of audit professionals or audit experience in years of an average employee) with previously determined auditor's failure rate (ratio of the number of reported financial reporting errors in relation to the total number of PIE clients of the audit firm[8]) shall give evidence of whether or not lower levels of input factors by audit firms causes accounting errors.

---

5 The enforcement procedure in Germany works on two levels. At the first level the German Financial Reporting Enforcement Panel (FREP) examines individual and consolidated annual financial statements on a random sampling basis, with cause if there are concrete indications of an infringement of financial reporting requirements or at the request of BaFin. In case a company does not participate voluntarily in the examination or does not agree with the findings of the examination or if there are substantial doubts about the findings or the conduct of the examination, BaFin comes in at the second level. In case it serves the public interest, BaFin can force the company to publish the errors, as it has the right to take supervisory measures (www.bafin.de)..

6 http://www.bundesanzeiger.de/.

7 Compare to the audit quality definition of DeAngelo (1981a): "audit quality … is the market-assessed joint probability that a given auditor will both (a) discover a breach in the client's accounting system and (b) report the breach.", p. 186.

8 The best reference basis for auditor's failure rate is obviously not the total numbers of PIE clients, but the number of PIE clients, which have been examined. Unfortunately, the number of

1.4 Basic Assumptions and Hypothesis

In order to develop the mentioned audit quality measurement the following assumptions are discussed and researched:

A1: Material misstatements remaining in audited financial statements are not only financial reporting failures but implicitly also audit failures and therefore an indicator of low audit quality.

A2: Companies are required by FREP/BaFin to correct financial statements because the revealed financial reporting failure is material (material misstatement).[9] Hence published reporting errors are the result of detected material misstatements by FREP/BaFin.

A3: The enforcement procedure produces objective, reliable and valid results (particularly in the long run) and the enforcers' methods are transparently documented, adequately applied.

Having discussed the assumptions in chapter 3, the following hypotheses are tested by an empirical study in chapter 4:

[Certified audit professionals]
H1: The certified audit professional ratio has an inverse relationship to the auditor's failure rate: The lower the ratio of the number of certified audit professionals to the estimated number of employees in audit services, the higher the auditor's failure rate.

[Experience: employee's working experience and client-specific experience]
H2: Years of experience has an inverse relationship to the auditor's failure rate, the lower the years of experience of an auditor, the higher the auditor's failure rate, and
H3: Auditor turnover has a direct relationship to the auditor's failure rate: the less frequent a client changes auditors, the lower the auditor's failure rate.

PIE clients, which have been examined is not know. Hence, the mentioned reference basis is a surrogate (chapter 3.3.3.2).

9 This assumption is based on a statement of FREP's president, Prof. Dr. Edgar Ernst. According to him all published errors are material; immaterial ones are not published (refers to a speech at the "11. Fachtagung 2011: Das Rechnungswesen im Konzern", Frankfurt a. M., November 25, 2011).

1.5 Outline of this Study

After giving an introduction over the objectives, assumptions and hypotheses of this study in chapter one, chapter two reflects a comprehensive literature review in the field of audit quality research of the last 30 years.

In chapter three, an audit quality measurement on audit firm level is developed. Financial reporting errors, as detected by the German enforcement institutions during examinations, which subsequently are published in the Federal Gazette by the involved companies, are the basis for this measurement.

Chapter three begins with discussing terms such as material misstatement, the overall objective of audits, audit deficiencies and audit failures. It then describes the enforcement procedure in Germany starting with the selection process, continuing with the examination process and ending with the error publication in the German Federal Gazette. It challenges the question whether the examination results of the German enforcers can be used as an audit quality measurement by evaluating the methods used in the selection and examination process. In the end of chapter three, a quality measurement is developed and applied to analyze the audit quality of PIE auditors[10] in Germany.

Chapter four introduces the theory about input factors and aims to connect the developed audit quality measurement with selected audit firm characteristics in order it explain quality differences of public interest entities auditors in Germany.

Chapter five summarizes the main outcomes of the dissertation and draw conclusions from the empirical studies performed. It provides also an outlook to potential further research in this field.

10 The terms “audit firm”, “accounting firm”, and “auditor” are synonymously used in this study..

2 Literature Review and Current Issues

2.1 Agency Theory and Audit Services

Before discussing the quality of audit services, it is essential to understand the need of and the demand for audit services. On the one hand, financial statement audits are required by law and depend in most jurisdictions on both the company's legal structure and the company's size, such as total assets, turnover, and/or number of employees.[11] On the other hand, the principal-agent problem delivers the economic reasoning for a financial audit. It is based on the dilemma of different interests of both parties – the principal and the agent. Although the agent is hired by the principal and has a mission to fulfill according to the principal's interest, the agent tends to follow his own interest and to maximize his own benefit, whenever there is the opportunity. Such opportunities are given in situations of asymmetric information. Having less information than the agent, the principal cannot ensure that the agent is always acting in the principals' best interests.

The Agency Theory provides approaches to tackle the problem.[12] For this purpose, it categorizes three types of asymmetric information: hidden characteristics, hidden action/information, and hidden intention.

Hidden characteristics are characteristics of the agent itself or characteristics of the agent's services and goods. These characteristics are not known before the contract between the principal and the agent is signed. If the principal knew the hidden characteristics, he probably would not have signed the contract. Hence, the principal always faces the risk of adverse selection. One of the first research papers on adverse selection was composed by Akerlof (1970) in his paper "The Market for Lemons: Quality Uncertainty and the Market Mechanism". The counteracting institutions to avoid adverse selections are signaling and screening.[13] Signaling is the action of the agent, who signals that information provided are

---

[11] Compare to the mandatory audit requirements in Germany: mid-sized and big corporate companies (mittelgroße und große Kapitalgesellschaften) have to undergo an annual financial audit (Sec. 316 of the HGB); non-corporate companies have to undergo also annual financial audits, if they are subject to the German Disclosure Act (Publizitätsgesetz).

[12] The approaches to encounter the principal-agent dilemma are always connected to additional costs either for the principal or the agent, the so-called agency costs.

[13] Akerlof, George A. (1970), p. 492.

credible.[14] The agent may take costly actions in an attempt to convey the information (a car seller as agent offers a warranty).[15] Screening is the action of the principal. The principal attempts to elicit information from the agent by letting him choose, for instance, the type of contract.[16]

Hidden actions or hidden information occur only after the contract between the principal and the agent is signed. Hidden action means that the agent has an arbitrary leeway, which the principal cannot fully observe.[17] Examples for hidden actions exist in employer-employee relationship, car repair services, and all kinds of insurance relationships.

Hidden information exists where the principal can indeed observe the actions, but cannot estimate the quality of them (e.g. due to the lack of expertise).[18] Examples where hidden information occurs typically are seller-buyer relationships, physician-patient relationships, and all kinds of experts' consultations. The principal's risk in both cases is referred to moral hazard.[19] One approach to mitigate moral hazard is a (strict) monitoring over the agent, which is not always possible. Another approach is to provide incentives to influence the agent's interest.

Hidden intention is similar to hidden characteristics as the hidden intention may exist already before the contract between the principal and agent is signed. Even if the principal has all the transparency and control over the agent's actions (this means there is neither a hidden action nor hidden information), it may still be the case that the unknown intention of the agent causes conflicts. In cases, where the agent makes an irreversible investment and the principal relies on the good will of the agent, the principal may get caught in a dependency relationship with the agent, because of the irreversible investment. Literature speaks in these cases from a hold-up risk for the principal, if the agent can exploit the situation.[20] Approaches to resolve such problems are based on attempt in aligning and harmonizing the interests of both parties. This can be reached by adding contractual

---

14 Varian (1992), p. 469.

15 Varian (1992), p. 469; Kessler (2012), p. 14.

16 Kessler (2012), p.25.

17 Arrow (1985), p. 38.

18 Glossary of the Department Business Administration, University of Muenster, Germany, http://www.wiwi.uni-muenster.de/06/toplinks/glossar/glossar.php?begriff=2 (December 15, 2012, 15:00 CET).

19 Herzig/Watrin (1995), p. 750; Picot/Dietl/Frank (2005), p. 75.

20 For instance, Herzig/Watrin (1995), p. 792; Picot/Dietl/Frank (2005), pp. 79 et seq.

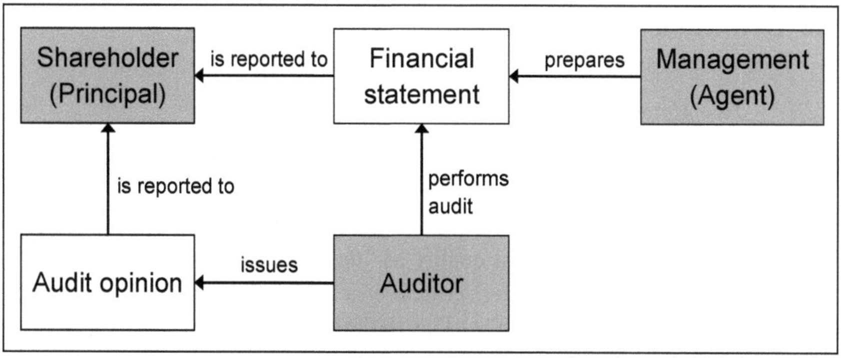

Figure 2.1: Shareholder-Management-Relationship including the Auditor (source: chart based on Messier 2003[21])

penalties for such cases to the contract or by requesting (supplementary) collateral from the agent.[22]

In context of the shareholder-management relationship, all three types of asymmetric information may occur; however, hidden information and hidden actions are the predominant risks (moral hazard) in this relationship. In order to dissolve the information asymmetry of (financial) information between the shareholders (principal) and the management (agent), auditors are engaged to ensure the completeness, accuracy and reliability of financial information. Audits, in general, are a tool to review management's actions and management's reporting on a regular basis, which decreases the information deficit of the principal. Figure 2.1 shows the principal-agent-relationship between shareholder and management, including the auditor.

---

21 Messier (2003), p. 6.

22 Herzig/Watrin (1995), p. 792; Picot/Dietl/Frank (2005), pp. 79 et seq.

2.2 Definitions of Audit Quality

2.2.1 Two Main Schools of Thoughts

2.2.1.1 DeAngelo's Definition of Audit Quality

Indisputably, the most cited definition of audit quality stems from DeAngelo (1981a). DeAngelo defines audit quality as "the market-assessed joint probability that a given auditor will both (a) discover a breach in the client's accounting system, and (b) report the breach".[23] This definition contains two aspects of audit quality: (1) the competence of the auditor for detecting misstatements and (2) the independence of the auditor for reporting such misstatements. Although this is the most cited definition of audit quality, the problem is that audit quality according this definition cannot be observed let alone measured.[24] Hence audit quality measures based on this definition are indirect methods of measuring audit quality with the aid of indicators.[25] Probably the most used proxy in audit quality research studies is the statistical estimation of discretionary accruals in financial statements. The assumption is that companies' representatives attempt to manage the annual results such they benefit the most. Audit quality in this sense means how well the auditor can prevent discretionary accruals in the financial statement. Others proxies for audit quality based on DeAngelo's definition for example are restatements, accounting (and auditing) enforcement releases and going concern reports.

2.2.1.2 Level of Compliance with Standards

Another approach how to define audit quality is a more normative way of thinking. The auditor performs with excellent quality if he/she complies completely with all relevant standards.[26] In this perspective, the level of compliance with auditing standards reflects the level of audit quality. Peer review findings, inspection results of oversight boards (such as the PCAOB in USA and the APAK in Germany) as well as lawsuits against auditors are in this case the best indicators for audit quality. Criticism of this approach is evident. The overall objective

---

23 DeAngelo (1981a), p. 186.

24 Knechel, W. R. (2009), p. 2.

25 In contemporary research, in cases where indirect measures of audit quality are discussed, indicators are also referred to surrogates or proxies.

26 Krishnan, J. and Schauer P. C. (2001), p. 85.

of an audit is not to comply best as possible with relevant standards, instead it is to ensure high quality financial reporting. The European Commission explicitly stated in its green paper "Audit Policies: lessons learned from the crises" that "more substance over form" is needed not only in IFRS accounting but also in financial statement auditing as the following citation describes:

> "From a user perspective, auditors should provide a very high level of assurance to stakeholders on the components of the balance sheet and the valuation of those components at the balance sheet date. The Commission wishes to explore the case for 'going back to basics' with a strong focus on substantive verification of the balance sheet and less reliance on compliance and systems work i.e. tasks that should primarily remain the responsibility of the client and in the main be covered by internal audit. Auditors could disclose which components were directly verified and which were verified on the basis of professional judgment, internal models, hypotheses and management explanations. To provide a 'true and fair view', auditors should ensure that substance prevails over form."[27]

2.2.1.3 Financial Reporting Quality and Compliance with Auditing Standards

DeAngelo's definition connects audit quality one to one with financial reporting quality. A financial report where all accounting breaches have been detected and reported by the auditor represents high audit quality. Hence, the level of assurance that no material error remains undetected and unreported is the metric of audit quality in DeAngelo's definition. Followers of this thought of school, for instance, are, Palmrose (1988) "the probability that an auditor detects and reports misstatements"[28], Titman/Trueman (1986) "accuracy of information auditors provide to investors"[29], Leffson (1988) "Urteilsfähigkeit, Urteilsfreiheit und sachgerechte Urteilsbildung (judgment capacity or competence, judgment freedom or independence, and proper judgment development)"[30] and Knechel (2009) "Audit quality is the achieved assurance level".

The other approach where audit quality goes along with the level of compliance with auditing standards is represented, for instance, by Copley/Doucet (1993), Krishnan/Schauer (2001), McConnell/Banks (1998), Aldhizer/Miller/Moaglio (1999) and Niemann (2004).[31]

---

27 European Commission (2010), p. 7.
28 Palmrose (1988), p. 55.
29 Titman/Trueman (1986), pp. 159 et seq.
30 Leffson (1988), pp. 66-67.
31 Wiemann (2011), p. 43.

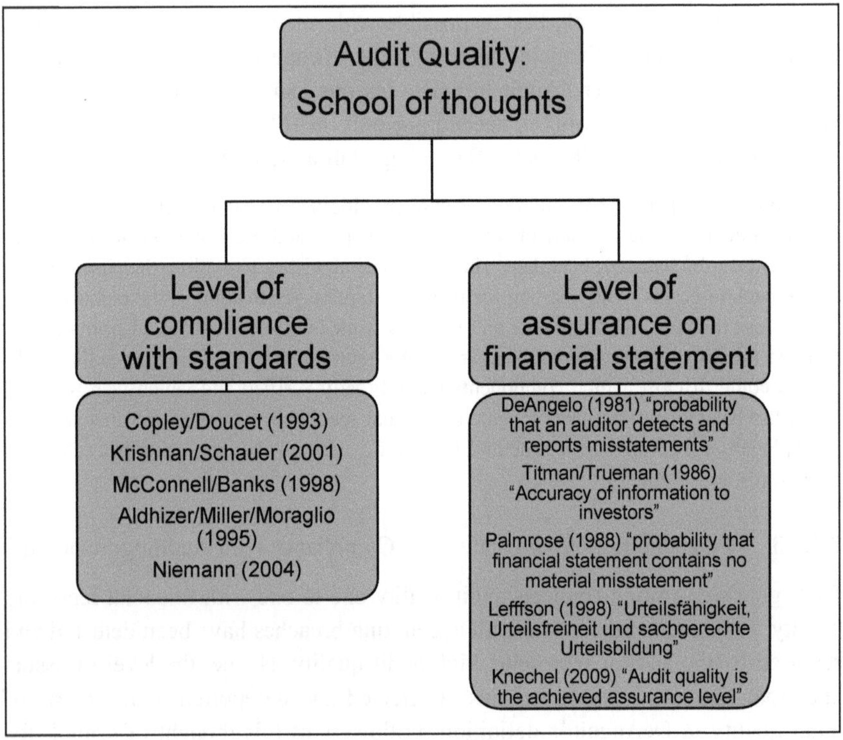

Figure 2.2: Audit Quality: School of Thoughts
(source: own development based on Wiemann 2012[32])

The hierarchy in figure 2.2 summaries the school of thoughts in audit quality research.

GAO (2003) combines both aspects (level of compliance with standards and level of assurance on financial statement) in its definition of (high) audit quality.[33] According to GAO (2003) a high quality audit is performed "(1) in accordance with generally accepted auditing standards (GAAS) to provide reasonable assurance that the audited financial statements and related disclosures are presented in accordance with generally accepted accounting principles (GAAP) and (2) are not materially misstated whether due to errors or fraud."[34]

32 Wiemann (2011), p. 43.
33 GAO (2003), p. 13.
34 GAO (2003), p. 13.

This definition shall also include not only the actual audit quality but also the perceived audit quality. It assumes that "reasonable third parties with knowledge of the relevant facts and circumstances would have concluded that the audit was conducted in accordance with GAAS and that, within the requirements of GAAS, the auditor appropriately detected and then dealt with known material misstatements by (1) ensuring that appropriate adjustments, related disclosures, and other changes were made to the financial statements to prevent them from being materially misstated, (2) modifying the auditor's opinion on the financial statements if appropriate adjustments and other changes were not made, or (3) if warranted, resigning as the public company's auditor of record and reporting the reason for the resignation to the SEC."[35]

2.2.1.4 Francis Framework on Audit Quality Research

Francis' framework has six dimensions, which affect audit quality: (1) audit inputs, (2) audit process, (3) accounting firms, (4) audit industry and audit markets, (5) institutions, and (6) economic consequences of audit outcomes.[36]

Apart from the financial statements and financial records which serve as well as inputs to the audit production Francis defines two *audit inputs*: (1) audit-testing procedures, and (2) engagement team personnel. The *audit process*, the second dimension of the framework, is the element where decisions and judgments are made by the engagement team with respect to the specific audit tests to be performed as well as the interpretation of evidence from these tests, and the ultimate engagement-level decision with respect to the audit report.[37]

According to Francis (2011) auditing takes place within the context of an *accounting firm*. Accounting firms issue audit reports together with client's financial statements. They hire, train, and compensate auditors and develop audit procedures.[38]

Providing audit services accounting firms constitute an *audit industry and an audit market*, which itself affect other markets and economic behavior. Last, auditing takes place within a larger *institutional context* that affects the incentives and behavior of individual auditors and accounting firms.[39]

---

35 GAO (2003), p. 13.
36 Francis, J. R. (2011), p. 125 et seq.
37 Francis, J. R. (2011), p. 125.
38 Francis, J. R. (2011), p. 126.
39 Francis, J. R. (2011), p. 126.

The audit report – the only observable audit outcome – affects clients and users of the audited accounting information leading to *economic consequences.*[40]

2.2.2 *Regulatory Definitions and Frameworks on Audit Quality*

2.2.2.1 Directive of the European Union

The European Commission defined audit quality implicitly while enacting a directive, which mandatorily constitutes a quality assurance system for auditors and audit firms. According to EU Statutory Audit Directive under Article 29 (1) (f) quality assurance reviews have to include the following components: (i) compliance with applicable auditing standards, (ii) independence requirements; (iii) quantity and quality of resources spent, (iv) audit fees charged, and (v) internal quality control system of the audit firm.[41] This legal definition identifies the antecedents of audit quality dimensions and it has been the fundament to implement peer reviews and later oversight board inspections in European jurisdictions.

2.2.2.2 PCAOB's Definition of Audit Quality

The Standing Advisory Group (SAG), which is a sub-group of the PCAOB, has defined the quality of an audit firm's work as follows:

"The quality of a firm's work ultimately depends on the

- integrity,
- objectivity,
- intelligence,
- competence,
- experience, and
- motivation

of personnel who

- perform,
- supervise,
- and review the work."[42]

---

[40] Francis, J. R. (2011), p. 126.

[41] European Parliament (2006a): Directive 2006/43/EC of the European Parliament and of the Council of 17 May 2006 on statutory audits of annual accounts and consolidated accounts..

[42] PCAOB (2011), QC Section 20.12, http://pcaobus.org/Standards/QC/Pages/default.aspx.

2.2.2.3 International Standard on Quality Control (ISQC 1)

ISQC 1 requires the audit firm (including sole practitioners) have to establish and maintain a system of quality control designed to provide it with reasonable assurance that the firm and its personnel comply with professional standards as well as with regulatory and legal requirements and that reports issued by the firm or engagement partner are appropriate in the circumstances.[43]

In order to ensure audit quality ISQC 1 sets out six areas which should be addressed by firm's quality control policies and procedures, and should be documented and communicated to the firm's personnel:[44]

- Leadership responsibilities for quality within the firm,
- Ethical requirements,
- Acceptance and continuance of client relationships and specific engagements,
- Human resources,
- Engagement performance and
- Monitoring.

Leadership Responsibilities for Quality within a Firm

The standard emphasizes that audit firm's management is responsible for the firm's system of quality control.[45] Management shall establish policies and procedures which promote a culture of quality within the organization. [46] Further, the standard stresses that "firm's leadership and the examples it sets significantly influence the internal culture of the firm".[47] Policies and procedures shall ensure that audit work complies with professional standards and applicable legal and regulatory requirements as well that reports issued are appropriate in the circumstances.[48]

Further, management shall also assign operational responsibility to persons, who have sufficient and appropriate experience and abilities for the firm's system of quality control in order to develop appropriate policies and procedures.[49]

---

43 IAASB (2012b), ISQC, Sec. 11 (Objective).
44 IAASB (2012b), ISQC, Sec. 16-17.
45 IAASB (2012b), ISQC, Sec. 18.
46 IAASB (2012b), ISQC, Sec. 18 and Sec. A4.
47 IAASB (2012b), ISQC, Sec. 18.
48 IAASB (2012b), ISQC 1, Sec. A4.
49 IAASB (2012b), ISQC 1, Sec. 19 and Sec. A6.

Relevant Ethical Requirements

According to IFAC, "the firm should establish policies and procedures designed to provide it with reasonable assurance that the firm and its personnel comply with relevant ethical requirements" such as the IESBA's Code of Ethics.[50]

The IESBA Code establishes the fundamental principles of professional ethics, which include:[51]

- Integrity (Code of Ethics, Sec. 110),
- Objectivity (Code of Ethics, Sec. 120),
- Professional competence and due care (Code of Ethics, Sec. 130),
- Confidentiality (Code of Ethics, Sec. 140); and
- Professional behavior (Code of Ethics, Sec. 150).

Acceptance and Continuance of Client Relationships and Specific Engagements

Auditors should consider the following factors when accepting or continuing audit relationships or engagements:

- Competence, Capabilities, and Resources (ISQC 1 Sec. 26a and Sec. A18),
- Integrity of Client (ISQC 1 Sec. 26c and Sec. A19),
- Continuance of Client Relationship (ISQC 1 Sec. 27a and Sec. A21),
- Withdrawal from engagement (ISQC 1 Sec. 28 and Sec. A19), and
- Considerations Specific to Public Sector Audit Organizations (ISQC 1, Sec. 26-28 and Sec. A23).

Human Resources

ISQC 1 requires audit firm to establish policies and procedures "designed to provide it with reasonable assurance that it has sufficient personnel with the competence, capabilities, and commitment to ethical principles".[52] Personnel issues relevant to the firm's policies and procedures related to human resources include, for instance:[53]

- "Recruitment,
- Performance evaluation,

50 IAASB (2012b), ISQC 1, Sec. 20.

51 IAASB (2012b), ISQC 1, Sec. 20 and Sec. A7; IESBA (2012), Sec. 100.5.

52 IAASB (2012b), ISQC 1, Sec. 29.

53 IAASB (2012b), ISQC 1, Sec. A24.

- Capabilities, including time to perform assignments,
- Competence,
- Career development,
- Promotion,
- Compensation and
- The estimation of personnel needs."

Competence can be developed through a variety of methods, such as professional education, continuing professional development (including training), work experience, coaching by more experienced staff, independence education for personnel who are required to be independent.[54]

Engagement Performance

ISQC 1 requires audit firm to establish policies and procedures "designed to provide it with reasonable assurance that engagements are performed in accordance with professional standards and applicable legal and regulatory requirements, and that the firm or the engagement partner issue reports that are appropriate in the circumstances".[55] Such policies and procedures shall contain:

- Matters relevant to promoting consistency in the quality of engagement performance (ISQC 1 Sec. 32a, and Sec. A32–A33);
- *Supervision* responsibilities (ISQC 1 Sec. 32b and Sec. A34);
- *Review* responsibilities (ISQC 1 Sec. 32c. and Sec. A35);
- Appropriate *consultation* take place and sufficient resources are available to enable appropriate consultation (ISQC 1 Sec. 34);
- Require an *engagement quality control* review of all audits of financial statements of listed entities (ISQC 1 Sec. 35-41); and
- *Documentation* of the engagement quality review (ISCQ 1 Sec. 42).

Monitoring

ISQC 1 requires audit firm to establish a monitoring process "designed to provide it with reasonable assurance that the policies and procedures relating to the system of quality control are relevant, adequate, and operating effectively".[56] This process shall:

---

[54] IAASB (2012b), ISQC 1, Sec. A25.

[55] IAASB (2012b), ISQC 1, Sec. 32-47.

[56] IAASB (2012b), ISQC 1, Sec. A24.

- Monitor the Firm's Quality Control Policies and Procedures (ISQC 1 Sec. 48);
- Evaluate and communicate deficiencies (ISQC 1 Sec. 49-54); and
- Deals appropriately with complaints and allegations (ISQC 1 Sec. 55-56).

2.2.2.4 IAASB Framework on Audit Quality

As research on audit quality is still unsatisfying, some non-academic institutions set up different frameworks. The latest framework (still in draft), an international one, have been conceived by the International Auditing and Assurance Standards Board (IAASB). In an overall approach IAASB considered all possible influences of audit quality which are categorized as: (1) Inputs, (2) Outputs, (3) interactions amongst key stakeholders and (4) contextual factors.[57]

The IAASB drafted the first version of its framework in a whitepaper in January 2011. The whitepaper states that "there have been a number of attempts to define audit quality in the past; however, none of those defintions has achieved an universal recognition and acceptance.[58] "Audit quality is, in essence, a complex and multi-faceted concept."[59] After several IAASB sessions, a sketch of the framework was developed capturing the relationships between the elements: context, inputs, outputs, and interactions (figure 2.3).

Inputs are categorized into three groups: "(a) the values, ethics and attitudes of individual auditors, (b) the knowledge and experience of auditors and the time allocated for them to perform the audit; and (c) the effectiveness of the audit process and quality control procedures".[60]

Outputs are "often determined by the context, including legislative requirements" and can be influenced by stakeholders; "for some stakeholders, such as investors in listed companies, the auditor's report is the primary output and this is relatively standardized".[61]

Interactions amongst Key Stakeholders include "both formal and informal communications", which will be "influenced by the context in which the audit is performed and allow a dynamic relationship to exist between inputs and outputs" elements of the framework.[62]

---

57 Refer to section 2.5.4 IAASB "Framework on Audit Quality".
58 IAASB (2011a), p.3.
59 IAASB (2011), p.3.
60 IAASB (2012a), p.10.
61 IAASB (2012a), p.11.
62 IAASB (2012a), p.11.

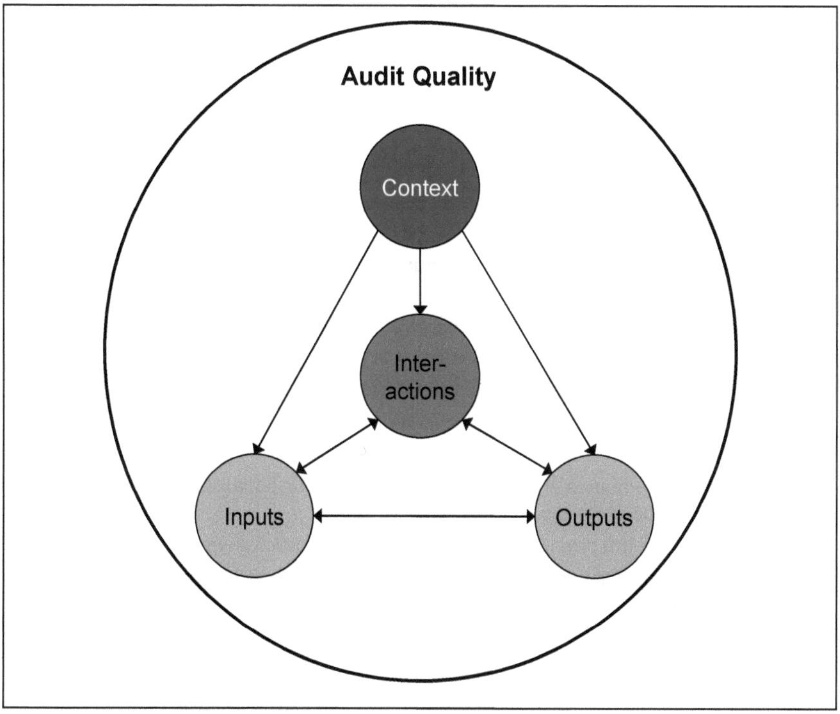

Figure 2.3: IAASB Perspectives on Audit Quality
(Source: IAASB 2012a)

The *contextual factors* include "corporate government requirements and the applicable financial reporting framework" as well as "legislative and regulatory requirements", which also "shape the interactions amongst key stakeholder".[63]

Within these framework elements, quality attributes are further developed considering different levels (engagement level, firm level, national level) and perspectives (auditor, entity, regulators, and user). The Audit Quality Framework of IAASB contains the following attributes (table 2.1).

[63] IAASB (2012a), p.11.

Table 2.1: Audit Quality Attributes According to IAASB's Framework (Source: IAASB 2012a[64])

Frame-work Element	Quality attributes
INPUTS – Values, Ethics, Attitudes	**Engagement Level** 1. The engagement team recognizes that the audit is performed in the wider public interest. 2. The engagement team exhibits professional skepticism. 3. The engagement team exhibits objectivity and integrity. 4. The engagement team exhibits professional competence and due care. 5. The engagement team is independent. **Firm Level** 1. Governance arrangements are in place that establish the appropriate "tone at the top." 2. The firm promotes the personal characteristics essential to audit quality. 3. Financial considerations do not drive actions and decisions that may have a negative effect on audit quality. 4. The firm provides partners and staff access to high quality technical support. 5. The firm promotes a culture of consultation on difficult issues. 6. Robust systems exist for making client acceptance and continuance decisions. **National Level** 1. Ethical requirements are promulgated which make clear both the underlying ethical principles and the specific requirements that apply. 2. Professional bodies are active in ensuring that the ethical principles are understood and the requirements are consistently applied. 3. Information relevant to client acceptance decisions is shared between audit firms.

64 IAASB (2012a), pp. 11-13.

Framework Element	Quality attributes
INPUTS – Knowledge, Experience and Time	**Engagement Level** 1. Partners and staff have the necessary competencies. 2. Partners and staff understand the entity's business. 3. Partners and staff make reliable professional judgments. 4. The audit engagement partner is actively involved in risk assessment, planning and supervising the work performed. 5. Staff performing detailed "on-site" work has sufficient experience, their work is appropriately directed, supervised and reviewed, and there is a reasonable degree of staff continuity. 6. Partners and staff have sufficient time to undertake the audit in an effective manner. 7. The audit engagement partner and other experienced members of the audit team are accessible to management and the audit committee. **Firm Level** 1. Partners and staff have sufficient time and resources to deal with difficult issues as they arise. 2. Engagement teams are properly structured and have sufficient time. 3. Partners and more senior staff provide less experienced staff with timely appraisals and appropriate coaching or "on-the-job" training. 4. Sufficient training is given to audit partners and staff on audit, accounting and, where appropriate, specialized industry issues. **National Level** 1. Robust arrangements exist for licensing audit firms/individual auditors. 2. Educational requirements for auditors are clearly defined and robust. 3. Arrangements exist for briefing auditors on current issues and for training them in new accounting, auditing or regulatory requirements. 4. The auditing profession is well positioned to attract and retain high quality individuals.

Frame-work Element	Quality attributes
INPUTS – Audit Process and Quality Control Procedures	**Engagement Level** 1. The engagement team complies with auditing standards and the firm's quality control procedures. 2. The engagement team makes proper use of information technology. 3. There is effective interaction with others involved in the audit including, where applicable, internal auditors. 4. There is engagement with management so as to achieve audit efficiency. 5. There is appropriate audit documentation. **Firm Level** 1. The audit process is adapted to developments in professional standards and to findings from internal quality control reviews and external inspections. 2. The audit methodology encourages individual team members to think creatively, apply professional skepticism and exercise appropriate professional judgment. 3. The methodology requires effective supervision and review of audit work. 4. The methodology requires appropriate documentation. 5. Audit quality is monitored and appropriate consequential action is taken. 6. Where required, effective engagement quality control reviews are undertaken. **National Level** 1. Auditing standards are promulgated which make clear both the underlying objectives as well as the specific requirements that apply. 2. Bodies responsible for external audit inspections consider relevant attributes of audit quality, both within audit firms and on individual audit engagements. 3. Effective systems exist for investigating allegations of poor audit quality and taking disciplinary action when appropriate.

Frame-work Element	Quality attributes
OUTPUTS	**From the Auditors** ■ The auditor's report on the financial statements and such other matters required by law and regulations ■ Reports from the auditor to those charged with governance ■ Reports from the auditor to management ■ Reports from the auditor to regulators ■ Transparency reports ■ Annual reports **From the Entity** ■ The audited financial statements ■ Reports from audit committees **From Audit Regulators** ■ Reports on the results of inspections of individual audits
INTER-ACTIONS	Effective Interactions between: ■ Auditors and management, audit committees, users, regulators ■ Management and audit committees, regulators, users ■ Audit committees and regulators, users ■ Regulators and users
CONTEX-TUAL FACTORS	■ Business practices and commercial law ■ Laws and regulations relating to financial reporting ■ The applicable financial reporting framework ■ Corporate governance ■ Information systems ■ Financial reporting timetable ■ Broader cultural factors

2.2.2.5 UK Financial Reporting Council's Framework on Audit Quality

A similar framework was set up four years earlier by the UK Financial Reporting Council. The Financial Reporting Council identified four main drivers for audit quality: (1) the culture within an audit firm; (2) the skills and personal qualities of audit partners and staff; (3) the effectiveness of the audit process; and (4) the reliability and usefulness of audit reporting.[65] These quality drivers are each explained by a list of indicators.

The focus in both frameworks (the UK FRC and the IAASB one) is on a process view of auditing where inputs are combined efficiently in order reach a certain outcome (assurance level), embedded in a specific contextual environment.

On a content view, the UK Financial Reporting Council covers the same elements and attributes like the IAASB does. However, the IAASB framework on audit quality is more comprehensive and detailed. Hence, the FRC's framework on national level will probably be obsolete soon and replaced by the pending international one from the IAASB.

2.2.2.6 Overview of Important Institutions Concerned with Audit Quality

Besides academia, the most important institutions which perform research on audit quality are accountancy professional institutions (such as IFAC, AICPA, CAQ, NASBA, ICAEW, and IDW), standard setters (such as the IASB, FASB, SEC, and PCAOB) and law makers (e.g. European Commission, U.S. Government).

Figure 2.4 depicts selected non-academic institutions in international, European and U.S. jurisdictions, which have performed research, have released papers or are generally concerned with audit quality.

---

65 FRC (2008a), p. 1.

Figure 2.4: Overview of Important Institutions Concerned with Audit Quality (source: own development)

2.3 Determinants of Audit Quality

2.3.1 Overview

Determinants of audit quality have been intensively researched in the last three decades. A very short but good audit research summary was compiled by Wooten (2003).[66] Based on DeAngelo's audit quality definition, Wooten explains all factors influencing audit quality and depicts them in its audit quality model. Inspired of his thoughts the "Globe of Audit Quality" has been developed (figure 2.5). It contains most of all researched determinations of audit quality in a cause and effect diagram that have been theoretically assumed and empirically furnished with correlation evidence.

66 Wooten (2003), pp. 48 et seq.

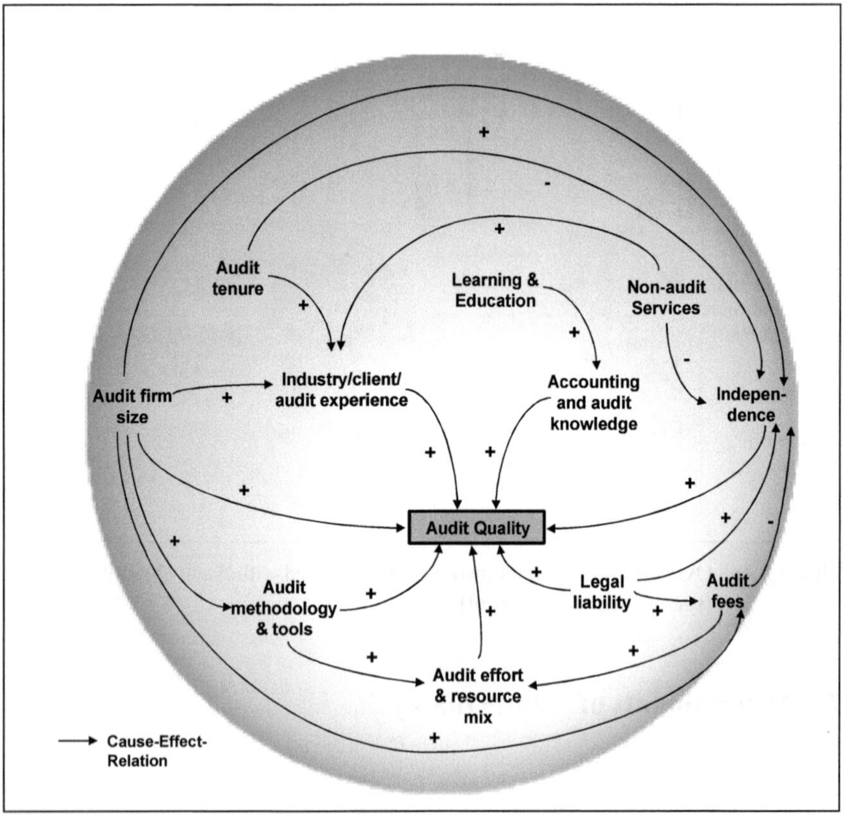

Figure 2.5: The Globe of Audit Quality: Cause-Effect-Diagram (source: own development)

The audit quality determinants of the "Globe of Audit Quality" and their relation to audit quality are explained in the subchapters from 2.3.2 to 2.3.9.

Indications about the relative importance of selected audit quality determinants were given by Kilgore et al. (2011).[67] In a questionnaire they asked 81 users of the relative importance (scores from 0 to 15) of ten selected audit quality attributes (audit firm size, audit partner tenure, provision of non-audit services, audit firm industry experience, audit quality-assurance review, partner/manager attention to audit, communication between audit team and client management,

67 Kilgore et al. (2011), pp. 153 et seq.

Table 2.2: The Relative Importance of Audit Quality Attributes (source: Kilgore et al. 2011)

Attribute	Relative Importance Score
Audit firm size	13.63
Partner/manager attention to audit	12.72
Senior manager/manager knowledgeable about client industry	11.04
Very knowledgeable audit team	10.65
Communication between audit team and client management	10.62
Audit firm industry experience	10.51
Partner knowledgeable about client industry	10.34
Provision of non-audit services	8.94
Audit partner tenure	6.39
Audit quality-assurance review	5.15

partner knowledgeable about client industry, senior manager/manager knowledgeable about client industry, very knowledgeable audit team). Apart from audit firm size, partner/manager's attention to the audit as well as audit manager's industry expertise had been the most important attributes (table 2.2).

2.3.2 Independence

2.3.2.1 Prerequisite for Professional Judgment

Independence is the fundamental prerequisite that auditors can exercise their professional judgment objectively and free from any influence. In regard to DeAngelo's (1981a) audit quality definition, the auditor's independence is the second component of her audit quality definition: Not only the technical ability to detect misstatements but also the willingness to report any detected breach are the basis for delivering high audit quality.[68]

Independence of the auditor has not only to exist in fact but also in appearance to third parties. This means that "the relationship between the auditor and his client should be such that firstly that he is himself satisfied about his independence" and secondly, no unbiased person could draw conclusions of an objective

68 Refer to chapter 2.1.1.1.

assessment of circumstances, that an impairment of the auditor's independence is likely.[69] Therefore IFAC distinguishes in its Code of Ethics between independence of mind (also referred to independence in fact[70]) and independence in appearance. According to Sec. 290.6 of the Code Ethics, the term "independence" is defined as follows: "Independence is:

a) The *independence of mind* is "the state of mind that permits the expression of a conclusion without being affected by influences that compromise professional judgment, thereby allowing an individual to act with integrity, and exercise objectivity and professional skepticism; and

b) *Independence in appearance* is the avoidance of facts and circumstances that are so significant that a reasonable and informed third party would be likely to conclude, weighing all the specific facts and circumstances, that a firm's, or a member of the audit or assurance team's, integrity, objectivity or professional skepticism has been compromised."[71]

In response to the Sarbanes Oxley Act of 2002 and its reinforced independence requirements such as the prohibition of the provision of certain non-audit services, the European Union drafted a recommendation paper including a framework on auditors' independence, where some major principles are set out concerning contingent fees, relative audit fees, overdue fees and provision of non-audit services.[72] In this recommendation paper, independence is defined similarly to the IFACs definition as:

"The requirement that a Statutory Auditor should be independent addresses both:

- independence of mind, i.e. the state of mind which has regard to all considerations relevant to the task in hand, but no others; and

69 ICAI (2005): Revised Guidance Note on Independence of Auditors, issued by the Council of the Institute of Chartered Accountants of India, Journal "The Charted Accountant", February 2005, p. 1090, http://www.icai.org/resource_file/10485feb051090-98.pdf (14:00 CET, October, 12 2012).

70 IESBA (2012), Sec. 290.6, and also referred to "actual independence" in contrast to "perceived independence" in diverse sources.

71 IESBA (2012): Code of Ethics, Sec. 290.6.

72 European Commission (2006b), p. 23 et seq.

- independence in appearance, i.e. the avoidance of facts and circumstances which are so significant that a reasonable and informed third party would question the Statutory Auditor's ability to act objectively."[73]

The European Commission also state in this paper that "independence is not an absolute standard which the Statutory Auditor must attain, free from all economic, financial and other relationships that could appear to entail dependence of any kind; such a state is manifestly impossible as everyone has some dependency or relationship with another person".[74] Hence, independence is relativized to a certain extent and some dependency is a normal occurrence.

The SEC maintains a brief definition of "independence in fact". In its final rule "Revision of the Commission's Auditor Independence Requirements", the Commission defines independence in fact as "the direct evidence of the auditor's mental state".[75] Whereas, the Commission states that independence of appearance can be "assessed only through observation of external facts; it thus provides that an auditor is not independent if a reasonable investor, with knowledge of all relevant facts and circumstances, would conclude that the auditor is not capable of exercising objective and impartial judgment".[76] A detailed comparison of independence definitions can be found in Bauer (2004).[77]

The independence definition is translated into requirements for the auditor in international and national professional and ethical codes. Independence is implicitly ensured when an auditor adheres to the principles of objectivity (Sec. 100, Code of Ethics), integrity (Sec. 100, Code of Ethics), confidentiality (Sec. 140, Code of Ethics) and professionalism (Sec. 130 and Sec. 150 of the Code of Ethics).[78]

In Germany those principles are codified in Sec. 43 (1) of the WPO (Public Accountants Act) and in the Sec. 2 (Unabhängigkeit = Independence), Sec. 3 (Verbot der Vertretung widerstreitender Interessen = prohibition of advocacy conflicts), Sec. 4 (Gewissenhaftigkeit = due care), Sec. 9 (Verschwiegenheitspflicht = confidentiality) Sec. 11 (Eigenverantwortlichkeit = personal responsibi-

73 European Commission (2002), p. 34.

74 European Commission (2002), p. 34.

75 SEC (2001), Section's headline "The Independence Standard", sentence 2.

76 SEC (2001), Section's headline "The Independence Standard", sentence 3.

77 Bauer (2004), pp. 32-48.

78 The fundamental principles according to the Code of Ethics are: integrity, objectivity, professional competence and due care, confidentiality and professional behavior (IESBA 2012, Sec. 100.5).

lity) and Sec. 13 (berufswürdiges Verhalten – professional behavior) of the "Berufssatzung der Wirtschaftsprüferkammer" (Professional Statutes of the Chamber of Auditors).

The responsibility of each auditor and audit firm is to ensure that all employees involved with a statutory audit adhere to these principles. Therefore the auditor / audit firm has to consider and document safeguards in terms of policies and procedure which negate or reduce any threats on independence to an acceptable level.[79]

2.3.2.2 Threats to Independence

Sec. 100.12 of IFAC's Code of Ethics identifies five types of threats to independence. These are: self-interest threat, self-review threat, advocacy threat, familiarity threat and intimidation threat.[80]

Self-Interest Threat

Self-interest threat is "the threat that a financial or other interest will inappropriately influence the professional accountant's judgment or behavior".[81] It occurs when an audit firm or its personnel could benefit from a financial interest in an audit client. Examples include (1) direct or indirect financial interest in an audit client, (2) loan or guarantee to or from the concerned client, (3) undue dependence on a client's fee and concerns about losing the client, (4) close business relation with an audit client, (5) potential employment with the client and (6) contingent fees for the audit engagement.[82]

The Code of Ethics also provides that a self-interest threat may occur when the fees generated from an assurance client represent a large proportion of the revenue from a single audit client.[83] It is apparent that this situation can lead to an economic dependency on the audit client: the bigger the importance of a single audit client, the higher the interest to hold the client in an economic point of view. This is particularly true in cases of material disagreements with the application of accounting principles between the two parties (audit firm and audit client) where an independent auditor would resign from the engagement. This is

79 IESBA (2012), Sec. 100.7-16; and European Commission (2002), p. 37.

80 IESBA (2012): Code of Ethics, Sec. 200.3.

81 IESBA (2012): Code of Ethics, Sec. 100.12 (a).

82 Compare to IESBA (2012), Code of Ethics, Sec. 200.5, further examples can be found there.

83 IESBA (2012): Code of Ethics, Sec. 290.220.

why some jurisdictions contain a percentage threshold of relative audit fees to total audit firm revenues generated by one client. Any percentage above the specific threshold would be considered to impair independence.

The Code of Ethics specifies a threshold for auditors of public interest entities. When audit fees from an audit client for two consecutive years represent more than fifteen per cent of the total fees received, the audit firm shall disclose to those in charge of governance.[84]

In Germany, regulators go one step further as they only allow audits where audit fees are below certain thresholds. The thresholds vary in terms of the company which is audited. In general for all companies, German public auditors are precluded from auditing financial statements if they or a person with whom they jointly practice their profession have in each of the last five years generated more than thirty per cent of their total income from professional activities from the corporation to be audited.[85] The mentioned threshold is reduced to only fifteen per cent, in case of audits of public interest entities.[86] These thresholds include fees from companies in which the corporation holds more than twenty per cent of the shares, and where this is also expected in the current year.[87] However, the Chamber of German Public Auditors may grant permission for temporary exceptions to avoid hardship.[88]

Also FRC, AICPA and the European Commission created rules and recommendations on the portion of audit fees to the total revenues of an audit firm. The most important are compiled in table 2.3.

Along with the potential economic dependency arising from a large portion of audit fee in relation to the total revenue of an audit firm, contingent fees and overdue fees jeopardize auditor's independence in a comparable way. Contingent fees are given, when auditors' remuneration is contingent upon the results of the service provided. They do directly raise both self-interest and advocacy threats, which are considered to bear an unacceptable level of independence risk.[89] Thus, contingent fee arrangements are prohibited according SEC/PCAOB rules, EU

---

84 IESBA (2012): Code of Ethics, Sec. 290.222.

85 Sec. 319 (3) of the HGB.

86 Sec. 319a (1) of the HGB.

87 Sec. 319 (3) of the HGB, Sec. 319a (1) of the HGB.

88 Sec. 319 (5) No. 5 of the HGB: "… zur Vermeidung von Härtefällen kann die Wirtschaftsprüferkammer befristete Ausnahmegenehmigungen erteilen = … in order to avoid hardship, the Chamber of German Public Auditors may grant permission for temporary exceptions".

89 IESBA (2012), Sec. 240.3, Sec. 290.225.

Table 2.3: Audit Fees Threshold in Relation to Audit Firms Total Revenues (source: own development)

<table>
<tr><th></th><th>For all audit clients</th><th>For clients in public interest</th></tr>
<tr><td>IFAC
Code of Ethics Sec. 290.220, Sec. 290.222</td><td>Independence concerned if audit fees from an audit client represent a large proportion of the total fees of the firm (self-interest or intimidation threat).
Code of Ethics Sec. 290.220</td><td>When audit fees from an audit client for two consecutive years represent more than 15% of the total fees received, the audit firm shall disclose to those in charge with governance.
Code of Ethics Sec. 290.222</td></tr>
<tr><td>PCAOB/AICPA
Code of Professional Conduct, ET Sec. 100.01.18(c)</td><td colspan="2">Threats and safeguards – firms should consider implementing policies and procedures to identify and monitor significant clients to help mitigate possible threats to a member's objectivity and independence
The Conceptual Framework for PCAOB/AICPA Independence Standards recognizes a financial self-interest threat to independence exists when there is "excessive reliance on the revenue from a single client."</td></tr>
<tr><td>European Commission Recommendation
2002/590/EC[90]</td><td colspan="2">The rendering of any (audit and non-audit) services by a Statutory Auditor, an Audit Firm or a Network to one Audit Client or its Affiliates should not be allowed to create a financial dependency on that Audit Client or client group, either in fact or in appearance.
Independence is impaired if firm or network receives from one audit client and its affiliates an unduly high percentage of total revenues in each year over a five year period.</td></tr>
<tr><td>UK FRC
APB Ethical Standard 4, Sec. 5-43</td><td>Independence impaired if audit fees represent more than 15% of total firm revenues from audit client and its subsidiaries.</td><td>Independence impaired if audit fees represent more than 10% of total firm revenues from audit client and its subsidiaries.</td></tr>
<tr><td>German Commercial Code
Sec. 319 (3) HGB
Sec. 319a HGB</td><td>Independence impaired if auditor's fees represent more than 30% of total firm revenues from client and its affiliates (>20% of total shares).
Source: Sec. 319 (3) of the HGB</td><td>Independence impaired if auditor's fees represent more than 15% of total firm revenues from client and its affiliates (>20% of total shares)
Source: Sec. 319a of the HGB</td></tr>
</table>

90 European Commission (2002), Sec. 5.3 (Public disclosure of fees).

regulations, and IFAC Code of Ethics and German national requirements.[91] The same applies to overdue fees. A self-interest threat exists, when audit or other work become significantly overdue. The sum of all overdue positions can be regarded as a loan given to the client. In this situation an independent auditor should not accept a reappointment as long as the significant overdue positions are unsettled.[92]

Self-Review Threat

Self-review threat is "the threat that a professional accountant will not appropriately evaluate the results of a previous judgment made or service performed by the professional accountant, or by another individual within the professional accountant's firm or employing organization, on which the accountant will rely when forming a judgment as part of providing a current service."[93]

A self-review threat occurs when the auditor reviews any judgment or conclusion reached in a previous audit or non-audit engagement, or when a member of the audit team was previously a director or senior employee of the client. Examples where such a threat comes to play include (1) when an auditor was recently a director or senior officer of the company or (2) when auditors perform services that are themselves subject matters of the audit.[94] Further examples are given in Sec. 200.5 of the Code of Ethics.

Especially, the provision of non audit services increases the threat of self-reviewing. The APB Ethical Standard defines non-audit services as "any engagement in which an audit firm provides professional services to an audited entity other than pursuant to:

a) the audit of financial statements; and

b) those other roles which relevant legislation or regulation specify can be performed by the auditor of the entity."[95]

---

91 IESBA (2012): Code of Ethics, Sec. 290.224, Sec. 291.154, Sec. 240.3; European Commission (2002), p. 32, AICPA ET Sec. 302; SEC (2001), "D. Specific Applications of the Independence Standard", PCAOB Section 3, Professional Standards, Rule 3521 "Contingent Fees"; and Section 55a (1) of the WPO.

92 IESBA (2012): Code of Ethics, Sec. 290.223, 291.153; European Commission (2002), p. 32.

93 IESBA (2012): Code of Ethics, Sec. 112 (b).

94 IESBA (2012): Code of Ethics, Sec. 200.6.

95 FRC (2008b): APB Ethical Standards, Glossary of Terms, "non-audit services", p. 5; "In the case of a group, non-audit services include services provided by the audit firm, to the parent company or to any affiliate" (FRC 2008b), p. 5.

Simplified, non-audit services are any service provided by the external auditor under engagement with the group outside of the external audit.

Generally, the more non-audit services are provided to the audit client, the higher is the risk of self-reviewing. However, not only the extent of non-audit services but also their nature has to be taken into account. Some non-audit services are irrelevant for the audit of financial statements such as certain tax services (preparing of tax returns, transfer pricing documentation as well as tax compliance audits). Some other services, such as valuations, preparation of financial reports, or design and implementation of financial information technology systems, are highly relevant and therefore in conflict with the role of the independent auditor. The "significance of the self-review threat is considered too high" to be accepted in those cases.[96]

Consequently, the Sarbanes-Oxley Act has prohibited explicitly the provision of specific non-audit services for a PCAOB registered audit firm to their SEC listed audit clients. According to Sec. 201 of the Sarbanes-Oxley Act, the following non-audit services are prohibited:

1) "bookkeeping or other services related to the accounting records or financial statements of the audit client;
2) financial information systems design and implementation;
3) appraisal or valuation services, fairness opinions, or contribution-in-kind reports;
4) actuarial services;
5) internal audit outsourcing services;
6) management functions or human resources;
7) broker or dealer, investment adviser, or investment banking services;
8) legal services and expert services unrelated to the audit; and
9) any other service that the Board determines, by regulation, is impermissible."[97]

Other non-audit services not listed above (for instance tax services) are permitted only if the activity is approved by the audit committee.[98]

International and national regulations apart from Sec. 201 of the Sarbanes Oxley act are not that concrete as far as the prohibition of certain non-audit services is concerned.

---

96 European Commission (2002), Sec. 7.2.1 (2).
97 SOX (2002), Sec. 201 (g).
98 SOX (2002), Sec. 201 (h).

The IFAC Code of Ethics does not strictly prohibit non-audit services.[99] However, in terms of accounting, bookkeeping and valuation services, the Code of Ethics refers to the self-review threat.[100] If the auditor ensures appropriate safeguards are in place, the risk from the threat will be mitigated to an acceptable level. Those safeguards can be: (1) "Having a professional who was not involved in providing the valuation service review the audit or valuation work performed"; or (2) "making arrangements so that personnel providing such services do not participate in the audit engagement". [101]

Accounting and bookkeeping services may also be permitted "in emergency or other unusual situations, when it is impractical for the audit client to make other arrangements". [102] The codes lists two cases for that exceptional rule: "when (a) only the firm has the resources and necessary knowledge of the client's systems and procedures to assist the client in the timely preparation of its accounting records and financial statements, and (b) a restriction on the firm's ability to provide the services would result in significant difficulties for the client (for example, as might result from a failure to meet regulatory reporting requirements)".[103]

Similar to Sarbanes Oxley Act, the German Corporate Governance Codex requires the auditor of a public interest entity to communicate significant non-audit services to the audit committee. [104] Further, where a German auditor provides non-audit services to a public interest entity, these services shall be communicated to the audit committee and non-audit fees must be separately disclosed in the financial statements.[105]

According to the German Commercial Law, the total fee income has to be broken down into four broad categories: statutory audit services, further assurance services, tax advisory services, and other non-audit services. The fees for "other non-audit services should be further broken down into subcategories so

---

99 The Code of Ethics uses the term „non-assurance service". Both terms „non-audit service" and „non-assurance services" are used synonymously in this study.

100 IESBA (2012), Code of Ethics, Sec. 290.168 self-review threat for accounting and bookkeeping services and Sec. 290.176 for valuation services.

101 IESBA (2012), Code of Ethics, Sec. 290.176.

102 IESBA (2012), Code of Ethics, Sec. 290.174.

103 IESBA (2012), Code of Ethics, Sec. 290.174.

104 DCGK (2010), Sec. 5.3.2, p. 10.

105 DCGK (2010), Sec. 5.3.2, p. 10; Sec. 285 No. 17 and Sec. 314 (1) No. 9 of the HGB, changes in code triggered by European Directive 2006/43/EC, European Commission (2006b), p. 91.

far as items in them differ substantially from one another".[106] According to the European Commission's recommendation, "this break-down into subcategories should at least provide information on fees for the provision of financial information technology, internal audit, valuation, litigation and recruitment services".[107] In respect of each (sub-)category, the figure relating to the corresponding (sub-)category iteem for the preceding reporting period should be also disclosed, including a percentage breakdown for the (sub-)categories.[108]

The German Balance Sheet Control Law reflects the European Directive fee requirements through slight different wording. Since the effective date of the Balance Sheet Control Act, January 2005, publicly traded firms have to disclose the fees paid to their auditors according to Sec. 285 No. 17 (individual financial statements) and Sec. 314 paragraph 1 No. 9 (consolidated financial statements) of the HGB. The firms have to split the total audit fees into the following four categories:[109]

a) Audit Fees: The sum of fees billed for the fiscal year for professional services rendered by the audit firm or auditor for the audit of the annual financial statements, and for services that are normally provided by the audit firm or auditor in connection with statutory and regulatory filings and engagements for the fiscal year.

b) Audit Related Fees: The sum of fees billed in the fiscal year for assurance and related services by the audit firm or auditor which are reasonably related to the performance of the audit or review of the registrant's financial statements.

c) Fees for Tax Services: The sum of aggregate fees billed in the last fiscal year for professional services rendered by the audit firm or auditor for tax compliance, tax advice and tax planning services.

d) All Other Fees: The sum of fees billed for services rendered by the audit firm or auditor other than those disclosed in the above items a), b), and c) for the fiscal year.

---

106 European Commission (2002), Sec. 5.3 (Public disclosure fees).
107 European Commission (2002), Sec. 5.3 (Public disclosure fees).
108 European Commission (2002), Sec. 5.3 (Public disclosure fees).
109 Sec. 285 No. 17 and Sec. 314 (1) No. 9 of the HGB.

Currently, a draft regulation of the European Commission proposes a complete prohibition of non-audit services in general within the European jurisdiction.[110]

Advocacy Threat

Advocacy threat is "the threat that a professional accountant will promote a client's or employer's position to the point that the professional accountant's objectivity is compromised."[111] It occurs when the auditor promotes, or is perceived to promote, a client's opinion to a point where people may believe that objectivity is compromised, e.g. when an auditor deals with shares or securities of the audited company or becomes the client's advocate in litigation and third party disputes.[112]

Advocacy is a phenomenon that probably occurs often within the auditor-client-relationship. Since the risk is likely to increase with the extent of consultancy services (NAS) provided to the client, it co-appears with the self-review threat. Jenskins and Lowe (1999) researched auditors' attitudes within the auditor-client-relationship and found out that there is a bias towards advocacy. In a survey of 58 auditors, 32.8% of the respondents agreed to the statement that auditor's primary responsibility is to act as an advocate for his/her client.[113] Although auditors' attitude in Jenskins and Lowe's survey is surely not representative for all auditors, it pinpoints the core issue. The threat of advocacy is always around and to a certain extent the auditor helps the client where possible. This is highlighted in the same survey as 65.5% of the respondents agreed to the statement that "auditors generally support their clients' position in accounting matters".[114]

As advocacy is a result of a good relationship between auditor and clients, it probably increases with the duration of the engagement. In so far it goes along with the familiarity threat which grows over the years of audit tenure.

---

110 European Commission (2011), p. 4.

111 IESBA (2012): Code of Ethics, Sec. 112 (c).

112 IESBA (2012): Code of Ethics, Sec. 200.7.

113 Jenskins and Lowe (1999), p. 75.

114 Jenskins and Lowe (1999), p. 75.

Familiarity Threat

Familiarity threat is "the threat that due to a long or close relationship with a client or employer, a professional accountant will be too sympathetic to their interests or too accepting of their work."[115]

It occurs when auditors form relationships with the client where they end up being too sympathetic to the client's interest, which can be given in many ways: (1) close relative of the audit team working in a senior position in the client company, (2) former partner of the audit form being a director or senior employee of the client, (3) long association between specific auditors and their specific client counterparts, and (4) acceptance of significant gifts or hospitality from the client company its directors or employees.[116]

Familiarity threat is also driven by the fact that there is a general cognitive familiarity bias inherent in all of us.[117] The familiarity bias is the tendency to choose the same decision alternative in a new decision-making context that is identical or similar to a decision context faced in the past.[118] Very critical in terms overlooking financial reporting risks is the so called SALY (Same As Last Year) effect where the auditor relies too much on the past and the used environment when drawing certain conclusions. The more the auditor gets used to the client's environment and to the client's decision making process, the more likely he/she accept clients' work and clients' accounting policies neglecting his/her due care obligation according to professional codes.

In the context where familiarity threats are positively affected by a long term auditor-client-relationship, a mandatory auditor rotation requirement would mitigate this risk. Due to a proposal of a new European regulation, the auditor rotation topic is currently a much discussed issue in Europe and Germany.[119] At the same time, the PCAOB has also published a proposal on mandatory auditor rotation.[120]

The current regulations in Europe require only an internal audit partner switch, not a complete switch of the audit firm. Italy, however, has both a man-

115 IESBA (2012): Code of Ethics, Sec. 100.12 (d).

116 IESBA (2012): Code of Ethics, Sec. 200.4.

117 The term "cognitive bias" was coined by the nobel prize winner in psychology Daniel Kahneman in 1972.

118 Knapp and Knapp (2012), p. 42.

119 European Commission (2010), European Commission (2011) and Köhler (2012), Velte (2012).

120 Concept Release on Auditor Independence and Audit Firm Rotation, PCAOB (2011).

Table 2.4: Specific Auditor Rotation Requirements of Selected European Countries (Source: Sipple/Glemser 2012[121])

Country	Source of law code	Enterprises in Scope	Rotation type	Rotation period
Germany	Sec. 319a (1) No. 4 of the HGB	Public Interest Entities	internal	7 years
France	Art. L. 822-14 Code de Commerce	Public Interest Entities	internal	6 years
Italy	Art. 17 Decreto legislative n. 39	Public Interest Entities incl. Insurances, Investment banks, Governmental companies.	internal external	7 years 9 years
Austria	Sec. 271a (1) No. 4 of the UGB	Companies according to Sec. 221 (3) Sentence 2 of the UGB as well as companies which exceed one of the size criteria [€] of Sec. 221 (1) to (3)	internal	5 years
Spain	Art- 19 Real Decreto Legislativo 1/2011	Public Interest Entities and companies which have sales of more than € 50 Mil.	internal	7 years
UK	Sec. 290.151, Code of Ethics	Public Interest Entities	internal	7 years

datory internal audit partner rotation in every 7 years as well as a complete audit firm rotation in a cycle of every 9 years. Sipple and Glemser (2012) summarized the requirements for 7 European jurisdictions (table 2.4).

Intimidation Threat

Intimidation threat is "the threat that a professional accountant will be deterred from acting objectively because of actual or perceived pressures, including attempts to exercise undue influence over the professional accountant." [122]

An intimidation threat occurs when auditors are deterred from acting objectively with an adequate extent of professional skepticism. Basically, this could happen due to the threat of replacement over disagreements with the application

[121] Sipple/Glemser (2012), p. 880.

[122] IESBA (2012): Code of Ethics, Sec. 112 (e).

of accounting principles, or pressure to disproportionately reduce work in response to reduced audit fees.[123] Indirectly this type of threat occurs also with the phenomenon of *opinion shopping*.

According to the SEC, opinion shopping is "the search for an auditor willing to support a proposed accounting treatment designed to help a company to achieve its reporting objectives even thought that treatment might frustrate reliable reporting".[124] As a possible outcome of managers' ability to "shop" for auditors, Chow and Rice (1982) express the concern that "managers can pressure auditors into giving clean opinion by threatening to switch to a new auditor."[125]

Another possible example of an intimidation threat is when an audit firm is being threatened with litigation by its client.[126] In this situation the auditor-client-relationship might slide in tensions. In this situation the auditor should consider a withdrawal from the engagement as independence and objectivity requirements are very difficult to maintain.

2.3.3 Audit Firm Size

The most commonly used indirect measure of audit quality is the Big4[127] / Non-Big4 dichotomy. DeAngelo (1981a) furnished the theoretical foundation for the use of this measure, which is based on the relationship between auditor size and costs related to loss of reputation.[128] According to her, audit firms with "a greater number of clients have 'more to lose' by failing to report a discovered breach; this collateral aspect increases the audit quality supplied by larger audit firms".[129]

Another argumentation is based on independence. Audit firms with larger number of clients do not depend on the revenue generated by one client, whereas an audit firm with only a couple clients has in implicitly higher economic dependency on one single client.[130]

---

123 IESBA (2012): Code of Ethics, Sec. 200.8.

124 SEC (1988), FRR (Financial Reporting Release) No. 31, 1988.

125 Chow and Rice (1982), p. 327.

126 IESBA (2012): Code of Ethics, Sec. 200.8.

127 When DeAngelo developed her research design she considered the comparison Big8 vs. non-Big8. Big4 refers to the biggest four audit firms globally since 2002. After the merger of Coopers & Lybrand with Price Waterhouse in 1998 and the demise of Arthur Anderson in 2002 (due to the Enron scandal) only four large audit firms share the biggest part of the audit market worldwide.

128 DeAngelo (1981a), pp. 183-199.

129 DeAngelo (1981a), p. 183.

130 Compare to chapter 2.2.2 Independence, "self interest threat" and "financial interest".

Further, Bedard et al. (1993) recommend the use of the size dichotomy (big, non-big). According to them, the Big6[131] have higher technical competence and greater resources due to the larger company size and they have the motivation to deliver high quality services in order to protect their brand name reputations.[132] Big audit firms have the critical mass to organize the firms' structure in very specialized subservice divisions, specializing in both in certain industries and certain services. They can also afford to operate a technical accounting and legal department in the back office in form of a shared competence center where all difficult issues can be delegated. Both industry specialization and shared competence functions lead to higher audit quality.

In recent decades, empirical studies delivered a vast amount of evidence supporting DeAngelo's arguments that big auditors provide higher audit quality than smaller auditors.[133] Nevertheless there is also a different point of view on the auditor size matter from other researchers. For instance, Larence, Minutti and Zhang (2007) indeed confirm that statements audited by Big4 auditors in general have higher quality. However, this fact is not necessarily due to the excellent auditor's performance but mainly due to the large client effect.[134] Large companies have in general a better financial statement quality than small ones. Large companies are typically audited by the Big4 auditors. Larence, Minutti and Zhang (2007) furnished evidence that when Big4 auditors have similar smaller clients typical for Non-Big4 auditors, both types of auditors provide the same audit quality.[135]

2.3.4 Audit Fees

Economically, audit fees are agency costs for the principal according to the Agency Theory. The essence of the Agency Theory is that the principal (the shareholders) employs the auditor as an agent for an annual fee to protect his interests. These principal interests trigger the demand for audit services, which

---

131 From 1989 to 1998 six audit firms dominated the audit service market globally: Arthur Andersen, Coopers & Lybrand, Deloitte & Touch,Ernst & Young, e, KPMG and Price Waterhouse.

132 Bedard et al. (1993), pp. 21 et seq.

133 The following selected studies provide such evidence (explicitly or implicitly): Palmrose (1988), DeFond (1992), DeFond and Subramanyam (1998), Raghunandan and Rama (1999), Francis and Krishnan (1999), DeFond, Raghunandan and Subramanyam (2002), Chung and Kallapur (2003), Bauwhede & Willekens (2004), Mansik, Maxwell and Miller (2004), Jeong & Rho (2004), Geiger and Rama (2006), Maijoor & Vanstraelen (2006), and Hoitash et al. (2007).

134 Larence, Minutti, and Zhang (2007), p. 2.

135 Larence, Minutti, and Zhang (2007), p. 2.

explains the demand side for audit service and therefore for determining the pricing of audit fees. Legally, the demand for audit services is ensured as firms has to be audited by independent auditor if they meet specific size criteria and/or have certain legal forms.[136]

A large body of research has examined the supply side for of audit services and the determinants of the audit fees in the last 30 years.[137] A lot of this research work has based its theoretical pillars on the audit fees pricing model of Simunic (1980). According to Simunic's model, audit fees are determined basically on the cost structure, i.e. by the quantity of resources utilized by the auditor in performing the audit and the per-unit factor cost of external audit resources to the auditor, including all opportunity costs.[138] In subsequent research based on Simunic's model, all types of correlations between audit fees and proxies for audit quality such as restatements, discretional accruals, auditor size, litigations and audit risk have been analyzed in many studies.[139]

At a first glance, the theory of audit quality in regard to audit fees seems to be very obvious. Evidently, fees paid to auditors can affect audit quality in different ways. Large fees paid to auditors may allow the auditor to increase the effort, which will increase audit quality. Contrarily, high fees paid to auditors, notably those that are related to non-audit services, make auditors more economically dependent on their clients.[140] High audit fees alone can already lead to an independence issue for the auditors.[141]

When the auditor receives unusually high audit fees from a client, the auditor may allow the client to engage in opportunistic earnings management.[142] Kinney and Libby (2002), assume that "unexpected non-audit and audit fees may more accurately be likened to attempted bribes" and will reduce the quality of

---

136 This generalization is applicable to almost all European jurisdictions.

137 For instance, compare to the meta analysis on audit fees from Hay, Knechel and Wong (2006)

138 Simunic (1980), p. 163.

139 Audit fees and restatements: for example, Agrawal & Chadha (2005) or for non-audit fees and restatements: Raghunandan, Read and Whisenant (2003); discretional accruals and audit fees: for example, Abbott et al. (2006) and Antle et al. (2006); auditor size and audit fees: Palmrose (1986); litigations and audit fees: for example, Venkataraman, Weber and Willenborg (2005) and Huang, Lee and Green (2010).

140 Compare to chapter 2.2.2 threats on independence such as self interests in form of financial interests.

141 Compare to chapter 2.2.2 threats on independence such as self interests in form of financial interests.

142 Krauss et al. (2010), p. 8.

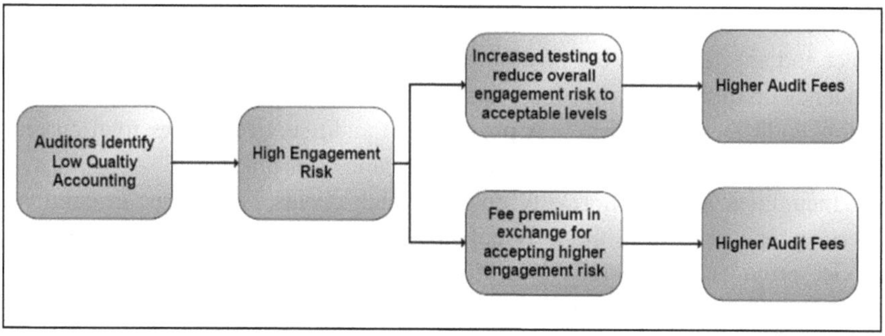

Figure 2.6: Relationship between Low Quality Accounting, High Risk Engagements and Higher Audit Fees (Kraus et al. 2010)

reported earnings through the auditor's reduced willingness to resist client biases to manage earnings.[143] For instance, Enron´s actual audit fee in the year 2000 amounted to more than 250 % of the estimated normal audit fee.[144] In this regard, abnormal fees[145] could be an appropriate measure to estimate the degree of economic interest in and dependence on a specific client. Also Hoitash et al. (2007) hold the view that economic dependency of an auditor on the client increases when the auditor receives higher total fees from the clients.[146]

Apart from complexity in accounting standards and in business models, high audit fees could be also a result of high audit risk and low accounting quality. Auditors will receive a higher risk premium if they agree on a high risk engagement. According to the audit risk model, auditor will have to perform more substantive testing in order to reduce risk. Higher audit effort justifies higher audit fees. This relationship is shown is figure 2.6.

On the other hand, low fees paid to the auditor can lead to a decrease of audit quality, which arises from two aspects. First, the auditor will not put as much effort in the engagement compared to large fees engagement, which directly decreases audit quality. Second, in terms of initial engagement when total fees are set below total costs, the auditor probably is motivated to be further engaged in consecutive years, where he/she will work much more cost efficient (and may reach a profit in the total periods over several years from the specific audit en-

143 Kinney and Libby (2002), p. 109.

144 Kinney and Libby (2002), p. 110.

145 Abnormal fees, are abnormal high or abnormal low fees, compared to the fees that would be expected according to the results of an estimation model.

146 Hoitash et al. (2007), pp. 761 et seq.

gagement) due to experienced made at the client, the general learning curve effect and any fees from the provisions of non-audit services. Therefore, the dependency on quasi-rents over the years from the engagement is particularly given in low audit fees situations.[147] A provision of audit services below total current costs of the audit at the initial engagement is called *low balling*.[148]

Incumbent auditors normally do not switch clients every year; in contrast, once a proposal is won, the duly appointed auditor can expect to be the audit service provider for several consecutive years. This leads to the expectation of client-specific quasi-rents. DeAngelo (1981b) argues that the existence of client-specific quasi-rents to the auditor both impairs auditor independence and leads to "low balling" in the initial period.[149]

According to DeAngelo (1981b) low balling occurs in settings "where

a) incumbent auditors earn quasi-rents, due, e.g., to transactions costs or technological advantages, and

b) the initial market for audit services is competitive."[150]

DeAngelo explains her approach with a multi-period model ($t = 1, 2, \dots, \infty$) in which the market for audit engagement is perfectly competitive at time $t=1$, insofar as all potential auditors provide equivalent audit services at equivalent costs.[151] The market for subsequent audits (in future periods $t = 2, 3, \dots, \infty$) is not perfectly competitive because the incumbent auditors possess experience advantages and therefore cost advantages in performing the audit. Any new auditors will face transaction costs in form of technological start-up costs (which are sunk costs to the incumbent auditors) for taking over a new client. As a consequence, "incumbent auditors expect to earn quasi-rents on subsequent audits and 'low balling' in the initial period is the competitive response required to capture the quasi-rents".[152]

The cost of producing an audit in time period t is represented by A_t. The initial audit cost A_1 can be broken down in two cost parts: A regular cost portion

147 Compare to DeAngelo (1981b) and DeFond et al. (2002).
148 DeAngelo (1981b), p. 113.
149 DeAngelo (1981b), p. 113.
150 DeAngelo (1981b), pp. 118-119.
151 DeAngelo (1981b), p. 119.
152 DeAngelo (1981b), p. 119.

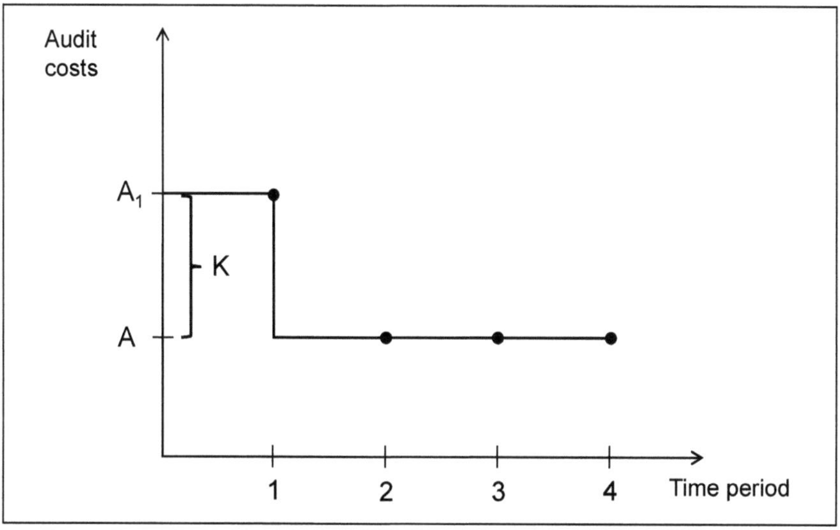

Figure 2.7: Low Balling According to DeAngelo's Audit Cost Model (Source: DeAngelo 1981b[153])

A for normal audit cost and an additional start-up cost K for the initial audit.[154] Thus, the subsequent normal audit costs for all remaining periods starting in $t=2$ are all constant and equal to A.[155] Formally this means that $A_2 = A_3 = A_4 = ... = A_\infty = A$. The audit costs at each period are depicted in figure 2.7.

In each time period t, the client pays an audit fee F_t. For simplicity reasons, we assume that the fee is constant in all periods, i.e. $F = F_1 = F_2 = F_3 = ... = F_\infty$.[156]

The low balling theorem assumes that initial audit fees are lower than the initial audit cost in period 1: $F < A_1 \equiv F < A + K$.[157] Further, it is obvious that fees in subsequent periods must exceed audit costs ($F > A$), otherwise no auditor

153 DeAngelo (1981b), p. 119.

154 DeAngelo (1981b), p. 119.

155 For simplification reasons, DeAngelo did not consider any fee changes due to inflation, client's business risk, etc.

156 DeAngelo (1981b), p. 120.

157 DeAngelo (1981b), p. 120.

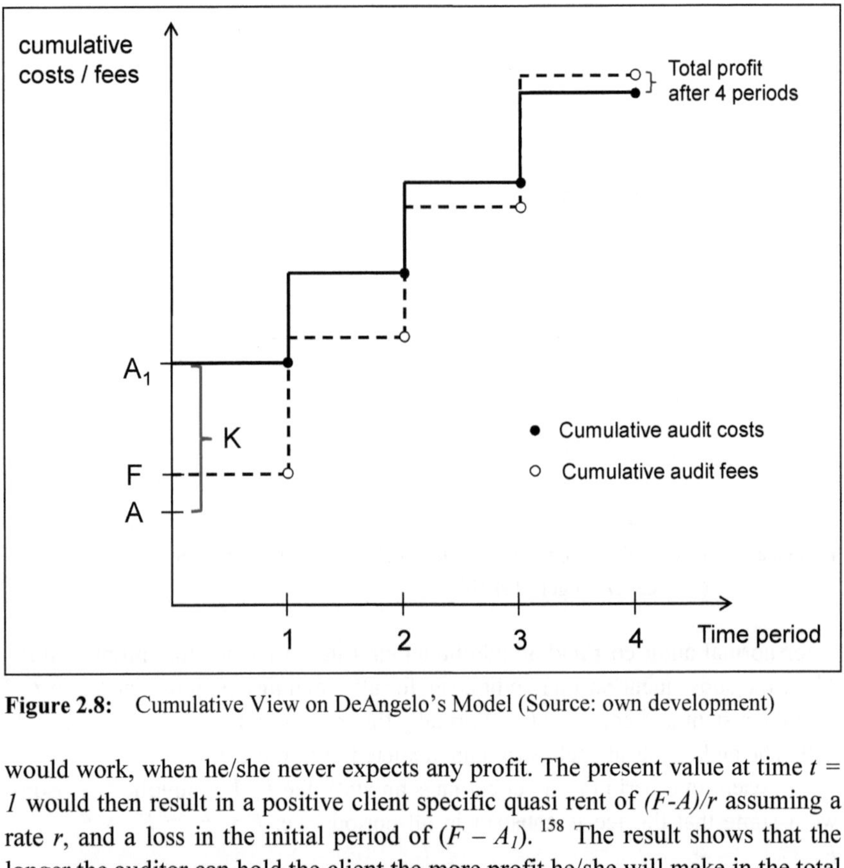

Figure 2.8: Cumulative View on DeAngelo's Model (Source: own development)

would work, when he/she never expects any profit. The present value at time $t = 1$ would then result in a positive client specific quasi rent of $(F\text{-}A)/r$ assuming a rate r, and a loss in the initial period of $(F - A_1)$.[158] The result shows that the longer the auditor can hold the client the more profit he/she will make in the total period. A withdrawal from the engagement in the very first periods would possibly result in no or very little profit (exemplarily compare to figure 2.8).

Consequently, the effect of low balling jeopardizes auditor independence especially in the very first years of the engagement where he/she is motivated to break-even at least.

Another phenomenon which is encountered in the research of audit markets is the phenomenon of *fee cutting*. Fee cutting often occurs after an auditor's switch. It is defined as "lower initial audit fees than continuing engagement fees for a comparable audit".[159] According to Köhler et al. (2010), auditor switches in

158 DeAngelo (1981b), p. 120.
159 Francis (1984), p. 138.

2005 reduced audit fees by 24% and in the two subsequent years 2006 and 2007 by each 15% on average in the German audit market of public interest entities.[160] Wild (2010) provides further evidence for fee cutting in the German audit market in the period from 2005 to 2008. In the mentioned period, Wild (2010) found that fee cutting occurs, when an auditor switch from a non-Big4 to a Big4 audit firm took place.

In this context, the current issue in Germany is the decrease of audit fees in the last couple of years. Decreasing fees are a clear sign of a competitive market, which is good on the one hand. On the other hand, as mentioned in the beginning of this chapter, low fees may lead to lower audit effort and therefore to decreasing audit quality. Peemüller (2012) has analyzed empirical studies on fees paid to auditors and he concluded that audit fees have significantly decreased both absolutely and relatively.[161] The relative indicator “audit fees to total assets” decreased by 27% and the relative indicator “audit fees to client sales” decreased by 5% in the years from 2004 to 2008 on average for all DAX listed companies.[162] Continued price cutting in subsequent years is considered very likely due to cost cutting pressure of enterprises since the beginning of the financial crisis in 2008. Further, according to the latest fees survey of the German Chamber of Public Accountants in December 2011 and January 2012, 59% of the respondents stated that the received audit fees are too low to fulfill all requirements in terms of quality controls and documentation.[163]

This is why the Chamber of Public Accountants in Germany (WPK) suggests a regulation of audit fees with a binding act.[164] In Germany, practitioners in some professions such as physicians, lawyers and tax advisors have to adhere to their specific fee ordinance. This is also to consider for accountants as a fee regulation would result in minimum fees for statutory audits, which would ensure a certain level of audit effort in order to reach a target assurance level. The base for the fee determination could be derived from e.g. client’s sales and/or total assets. In principle, this is how it works for German tax advisors.[165] As a consequence

160 Köhler et al. (2010), p. 5.

161 Peemüller (2012), p. 38.

162 Peemüller (2012), p. 39.

163 WPK (2012a), Fees survey of the German Chamber of Public Accountants, p. 16.

164 WPK (2012b), p. 17.

165 “Gegenstandswert” is the bases multiplied with a complexity factor which varies from 1/10 to 12/10 (Sec. 10 of the StBGebV). Besides that, there is always the option to agree on a time & expense fee (Sec. 13 of the StBGebV) or on a fixed price fee (Sec. 14 of the StBGebV). Appro-

of this reasoning, the German Chamber of Public Accountants has addressed the need of a regulation of audit fees in a letter directed to the German Bundestag as of March 15, 2012.[166] The further development of this issue is followed closely by both practitioners and audit researchers.

2.3.5 *Provision of Non-Audit Services*

The potential effect on independence and on audit quality of an auditor, who provides non-audit services to an audit client has been subject to many studies by a variety of observers:[167] This includes the Securities and Exchange Commission (SEC), the European Union, the Public Company Accounting Oversight Board (PCAOB), academics and the professional institutions such as AICPA, ICAEW, IDW, WPK, etc.

The provision of non-audit services provides ambiguous benefits to the auditor. Some non-audit services may certainly lead to more assurance as gained knowledge and experience from non-audit engagement can be shared to better understand clients' industry, clients' business, clients' control system and clients' business risks.[168] Every additional hour spent on client premises and in clients' discussions enriches the experience and accumulates knowledge about the client and its environment.

The two problems are the extent and the nature of non-audit services.[169] Some types of non-audit services such as appraisal or valuation services, book keeping, legal services, etc. are prohibited when auditors are registered at PCAOB and perform audits for SEC listed companies.[170] Obviously, a very comprehensive provision of non audit services will increase the threat of self-review for the auditor. This threat increases the closer the non-audit services impact accounting decisions, internal control, and accounting systems. Independence is

priateness of the fees considering permitted minimum and maximum fees according the StBGebV has always to take into account.

166 http://www.wpk.de/pdf/WPK_Schreiben_Gebuehrenordnung_gesetzliche_Abschluss pruefungen.pdf.

167 Panel on Audit Effectiveness, Report and Recommendation, Chapter 5, Sec. 5.7; http:// www.pobauditpanel.org/download/chapter5.pdf.

168 This effect is called "spillover effect", because knowledge and experience can be spilt over from non-audit services to audit services.

169 For a detailed discussion refer to chapter 2.2.2.

170 Refer to chapter 2.2.2.

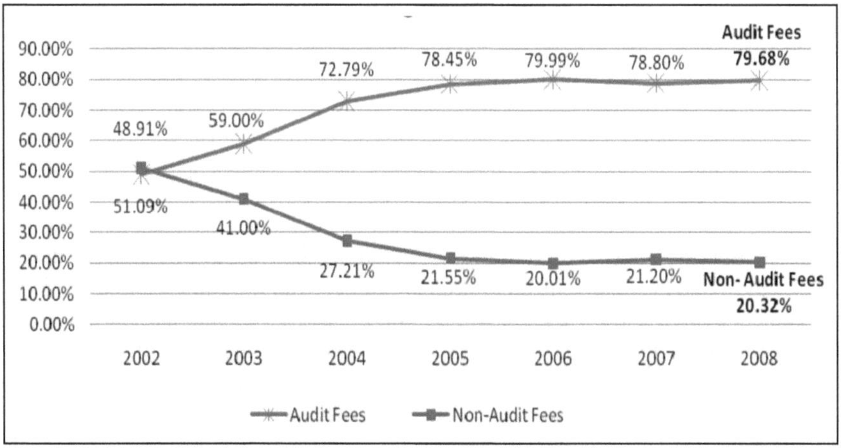

Figure 2.9: Audit Analytics, Audit Fees and Non-Audit Fees – A Seven Year Trend (Source: Audit Analytics 2010)

particularly compromised when significant fees are generated from the provision of non-audit services to one audit client or its affiliates.

Evidence that the ratio of non-audit service fees to total auditors' fees (proxy for the economic dependence of the auditor) is positively associated with the extent of discretionary accruals (proxy for earnings management) is furnished by Frankel et al. (2002).[171] Niehus (2003) and others found evidence that audit quality decreases when non-audit service fees generate more than 50% of the total fees.[172] One potential regulation to prevent such an extent of non-audit services would be an implementation of a percentage threshold e.g. a maximum of 30% of non-audit services in relation to total audit fees.

Audit Analytics (2010) has analyzed the audit fees and non-audit fees from 2002 to 2008 for SEC registrants. Since SOX was enacted in 2002, the extent of non-audit services has steadily decreased in following years from 2003 to 2006. The relationship between audit fees and non-audit fees settled around 80%-to-20%-relation in the last four years of the study (figure 2.9).[173]

In Germany, the non-audit services fees (including audit related services fees, tax services fees and other services fees) portion of total fees on average in

[171] Lin and Hwang (2010) p. 60, Frankel et al. (2002), p. 71.
[172] Niehaus (2003), p. 616.
[173] Audit Analytics (2010), p. 1.

years from 2004 to 2008 amounts to 43%; the pure audit fees instead amounts to 57% on average in the same period.[174]

2.3.6 *Audit Tenure*

Audit tenure is the "audit firm's total duration to hold their client, or number of consecutive years that the audit firm has audited the client."[175] The relationship between audit tenure (client duration) and audit quality has been discussed intensively and controversially in literature. The longer the duration to hold a client, the more client-specific experience and client-specific knowledge can be accumulated. Contrarily, with a lengthy client-auditor relationship familiarity threats can impair independence.[176] It is not unlikely that sympathy between the auditor and the client increases in the long-tenured relationship. This phenomenon may lead to a lower audit quality since the auditor becomes more prone to the danger of 'turning a blind eye' on inappropriate managerial actions.[177] An auditor rotation, in contrast, brings "fresh eyes" at company's financial statement and strengthens skepticism, which possibly increases the likelihood that the auditor will detect misstatements and/or challenge questionable accounting practices. A mandatory rotation is also considered as a means to prevent "opinion shopping".[178] Therefore, a mandatory auditor rotation has frequently been suggested as an instrument of reinforcing independence and reducing the incidence of audit failure.[179]

Opponents of the mandatory auditor rotation think that a short-tenured relationship between auditor and client would lead to a decline in audit quality because the auditors do not acquire sufficient client-specific knowledge.[180] The opponents also assert that mandatory auditor switch increases audit costs and increases audit failure risk; especially in the initial years, where they must rely heavily on management estimates.[181] With the course of the engagement over years, auditors learn the client and its business processes resulting in a more

---

174 Peemöller (2012), p. 39.
175 Johnson et al. (2002), p. 640.
176 Refer to chapter 2.2.2, familiarity threat.
177 Fairchild (2008), p. 23.
178 Crabtree et al. (2006), p. 97; Lu and Sivaramakrishnan (2009), p. 72.
179 Catanach/Walker (1999), p. 43; and chapter 2.2.2, intimidation threat, p. 34.
180 Meyer et al. (2007), p. 66; Shockley (1981), p. 785.
181 Siregar/Amarullah/Wibowo/Anggraita (2012), p. 56 ; Myers et al. (2003), p. 779.

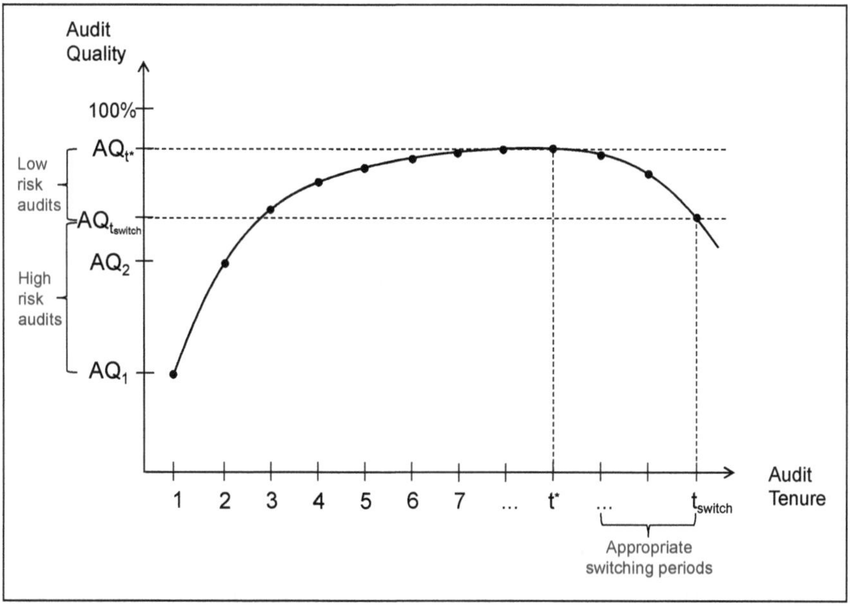

Figure 2.10: Audit Quality and Audit Tenure Relation (Source: own development)

effective audit and better assessment of management estimates.[182] In other terms, opponents believe that a long-tenured auditor-client relationship actually increases audit quality due to the fact that the clients' operations and reporting issues become more familiar and known to the auditor.[183] Further, due to the fact that a new auditor will not have the benefit of client-specific knowledge and experience of the previous auditor, audit quality likely to decrease in the year of the auditor switch.[184]

As a synthesis of proponents and opponents arguments, the relationship between audit quality and audit tenure is likely to have the graphic in figure 2.10.

In the early years, audit failure risk and therefore audit quality is lower than in the following years. Audit quality increases with the course of time since client-specific knowledge and client-specific experience is gathered.

After a certain period of years, advocacy and familiarity threats may gain ground such that there is a year in period t^* where audit quality declines. A simi-

182 Siregar (2012), p. 56.

183 Carcello/Nagy (2004), p. 55; Mansi, Maxwell & Miller (2004), p. 755.

184 GAO (2003), refer to the section "What GAO found", before page i.

lar assumption of the audit-quality-to-audit-tenure relation is found in the study of Siregar et al. (2012).[185]

However, despite of these theoretical considerations, empirical studies do not deliver consistent results. Based on the audit quality proxy, variables and data selection, some confirm the proponents' hypothesis of mandatory rotation; some others furnish evidence to the opponents' argumentations. In this context, Velte and Stiglbauer (2012), for instance, summarize a couple of diverse research studies, resulting in contradictory empirical evidence.[186] GAO (2003), 9 years earlier, drew the same conclusions.[187]

Currently, a mandatory auditor rotation regulation is again in discussion both in Europe and in the U.S. PCAOB released a discussion paper about mandatory auditor rotation in August 2011.[188] According to this discussion paper, the board is particularly focused on weighing the pros and cons of audit terms of 10 years or greater.[189] The European Commission started its action with a green paper in October 2010 followed by a regulation proposal in November 2011 where a 6 year mandatory auditor rotation cycle for public interest entities is proposed.[190]

The European Commission regulation proposal is questionable. A six years rotation cycle would mean, that we will have an uniform distributed duration time within the PIE market after the first cycle has passed: one sixth of all audits performed will be in the first year, one sixth of all audits will be in the second year, one sixth of all audits will be in the third year and so on. Taking into account that audit failure risk is highest in the very first two years means that one third of all audit engagements would be high audit failure risk engagements.

Because of the latter reasoning, it is doubtful whether such the European Commission's regulation improves the overall audit quality and financial reporting assurance for the capital markets. Derived from the theoretical considerations above, PCAOB proposal about a 10 years' rotation cycle or greater would be more reasonable.

---

185 Siregar et al. (2012), p. 64.

186 Velte/Stiglbauer (2012), pp. 5-6.

187 GAO (2003), p. 13.

188 PCAOB (2011), PCAOB Release No. 2011-006.

189 PCAOB (2011), PCAOB Release No. 2011-006.

190 European Commission (2010) "green paper", European Commission (2011) "regulation proposal".

2.3.7 Legal Liability

The core auditors' liability is derived from the contractual relationship with the client. If the auditor does not perform the audit service according to contract terms, the client can sue the breach of contract. Besides adherence to contract terms, it is presumed that the auditor shall perform the work with the care and diligence expected of a member of the profession.[191]

Beyond liability to the client, there is also a liability to non-contractual third parties, such as creditors and investors. Creditors and investors must heavily rely on the auditors' opinion when they provide credit or are willing to invest in the company, since financial reporting is the only attested information. The auditor can be held liable for the financial losses of third parties resulting from an inappropriate client audit opinion, unless he can prove that he worked with due care and diligence in accordance with all relevant accounting and auditing standards.[192]

Liability has two functions: Prevention and restitution.[193] Due to the fact that liability norms exist, damage should be prevented through compliance with laws and regulations as well as professional codes and accounting and auditing standards. The stricter the liability rules are in a jurisdiction, the higher the incentive for the auditor to work more carefully. Therefore, audit quality is positively affected with strict liability norms. When damage is not prevented by the auditor, the auditor may need to provide restitution to the damaged parties.

In Germany, the auditors' liability is capped to a maximum of € 4 million for public interest engagements and for non public interest engagements, the cap is € 1 million.[194] Further, liability is restricted to third parties. However, German auditors may have legal liability to non-contractual third parties in certain circumstances. Apart from tort law, the typical instrument of liability to third parties is called "Vertrag mit Schutzwirkung zugunsten Dritter". According to the "Vertrag mit Schutzwirkung zugunsten Dritter", both contractors could have accepted in behalf of third parties some of the implications of the agreement. "Occasionally, the mutual consent to imply the agreement to third parties is contracted tacitly by means of a 'stillschweigenden Vereinbarung'. Thus, the contract between the audited company and the auditor could embrace a protective

---

191 Compare to Sec. 43 (1) of the WPO (Public Accountants Act).

192 Scherl (1994), p. 257.

193 Rüchardt (1995), pp. 32-35.

194 Sec. 323 (2) of the HGB.

function towards third parties (Schutzwirkung zugunsten Dritter)."[195] The legal foundation of this approach is not explicitly found in the German civil code. It is an interpretation of the principle of "Treu und Glauben", meaning that the protective function is fair and reasonable.[196] A concretization of these principles follows the requirements of the Bundesgerichtshof in 1985.[197]

On a European level, liability regulations vary between the different jurisdictions. This is why the European Commission initiated a harmonization of auditors' liability in pursuance of article 31 of the Statutory Audit Directive 2006/43/EC.[198] Up to now this initiative has not yet brought results.

The following three subchapters from 2.3.8 to 2.3.10 cover human resources and audit team personnel. On the one hand it about human resources' quality in terms of technical abilities (chapter 2.3.8) and working experience (chapter 2.3.9), on the other hand it is about quantity in terms of audit effort (audit time in hours) and the resource mix in audit engagement teams (chapter 2.3.10).

2.3.8 Accounting and Audit Knowledge

The basic prerequisite of delivering appropriate audit quality is that audit professionals possess the required capabilities to perform statutory financial audits. In this context, IFAC defines capabilities as the "professional knowledge; professional skills; and professional values, ethics, and attitudes required to demonstrate competence".[199] Competence is the attribute of "being able to perform a work role to a defined standard, with reference to real working environments."[200] In its explanation, the term competence refers to "the demonstrated ability to perform relevant roles or tasks to the required standard. Whereas capability refers to the attributes held by individuals that give them the potential to perform, competence refers to the actual demonstration of performance. Competence may

195 De Poorter, I. (2008), p. 73.

196 Sec. 242 of the German Civil Code "Treu und Glauben".

197 These requirements are: (1) Leistungsnähe – third party indirectly connected to the service performed, (2) Gläubigernähe – third party have a special interest in the contract, (3) Erkennbarkeit für den Schuldner – the auditor must be aware that third parties are also concerned (4) Schutzbedüftigkeit des Dritten – third parties need to be protected (compare to Quick, R. 1996, p. 514 and De Poorter, I. 2008, p. 73).

198 European Commission (2006b), Art. 31 of the directive 2006/43/EC.

199 IESBA (2010), glossary of terms "capabilities".

200 IESBA (2010), glossary of terms "competence".

be assessed by a variety of means, including workplace performance, workplace simulations, written and oral tests of various types, and self assessment."[201]

The core elements of the required professional knowledge for audit professionals are: advanced knowledge about *audit of historical financial information*, advanced knowledge about *financial accounting and reporting*, and (basic) knowledge about *information technology*.[202]

The knowledge about *audit* of historical financial information shall contain best practices in the audits, including relevant current issues and development, International Standards on Auditing (ISAs) and International Auditing Practice Statements (IAPSs) and any other applicable standards and law.[203]

The knowledge about financial accounting and reporting is subject to financial accounting and reporting processes and practices, including relevant current issues and developments, International Financial Reporting Standards (IFRSs); and any other applicable standards or laws.[204]

The knowledge content of the *information technology* addresses information technology systems for financial accounting and reporting, including relevant current issues and developments as well as frameworks for evaluating controls and assessing risks in accounting and reporting systems as appropriate for the audit of historical financial information.[205]

Apart from professional knowledge, a professional accountant should have professional skills such as problem solving, team working, presentation and discussion skills.[206] He further has to adhere to professional values, ethics, and attitudes.[207]

In order to acquire the required skills, the IESBA developed an education framework for professional accountant. Since entry and licensing requirements vary in different jurisdiction, the framework is a recommendation to all members of the IFAC. Figure 2.11 depicts the IESBA framework on professional accountants' education in accordance to the International Education Standards (IES) 1 to 8:[208]

---

201 IESBA (2010), glossary of terms "explanation for capabilities".
202 IESBA (2010), IES 8.36, IES 8.38, IES 8.40.
203 IESBA (2010), IES 8.36.
204 IESBA (2010), IES 8.38.
205 IESBA (2010), IES 8.40.
206 IESBA (2010), IES 8.42.
207 IESBA (2010), IES 1.7.
208 IESBA (2010), Framework for International Education Standards for Professional Accountants, Framework Sec. 1 to Sec. 42, pp. 9-19.

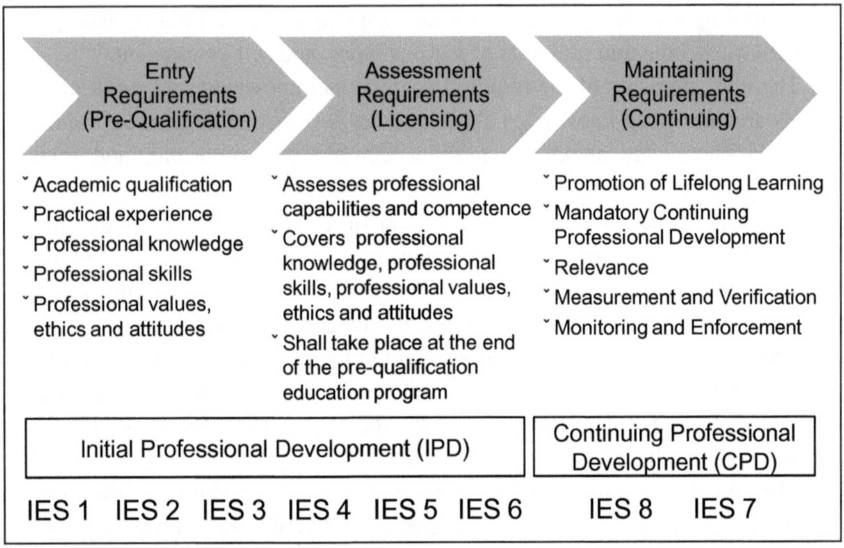

Figure 2.11: Professional Accountants Education Framework according to IESBA 2010 (source: own development)

The pre-qualification phase takes several years. For instance, in Germany, after completing an academic degree such as a master degree, the accounting professional has to acquire at least 3 years of practical experience in audit engagements before he/she can register for the certification program.[209]
However, the most audit work in an audit engagement is not performed by licensed and experienced auditors, but by audit professionals in the pre-qualification phase. Due to extensive workload and close reporting timelines, audits of public interest entities are regularly not audited by a single person but in audit engagement teams.[210] Such audit engagement teams consist at least of

---

209 Refer to the prerequisites of the certification program and the admission of certified public accountants in Germany, Sec. 1 (1) of the WiPrPrüfV in connection with Sec. 9 (1) and (2) of the WPO.

210 Especially capital market oriented companies do report financial figures as early as possible. Fast close processes are very common. Some DAX companies (MAN, Henkel) receive a clean audit opinion within 20 working days of year-end.

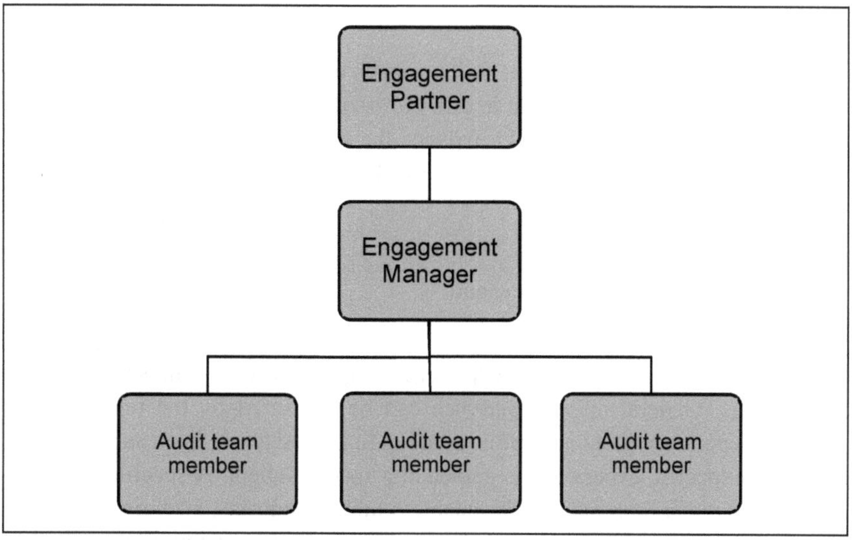

Figure 2.12: A standard "Audit Engagement Team Structure" (source: own development)

one to several staff audit professionals, the audit engagement manager and the audit engagement partner (figure 2.12).

The audit staff members are fulltime present at the client. They have on average a practical experience of less than 3 years and are not certified.[211] In contrast, the engagement manager, who normally is certified and well experienced, may have also other audit assignments at the same time; the same applies to the audit engagement partner. Nevertheless, these are assumptions that cannot be generalized. The frequency of the presence of engagement managers and engagement partners in the audit teams is likely to depend on the importance of the client, the extent of the audit and business complexity as well on occurring difficulties in performing the audit.

211 The average experience years can be indirectly determined by the attrition rate (refer to chapter 4). According to a report of the Center for Audit Quality 2008 (CAQ 2008, P.57), the attrition rate on audit staff level on average is 16.8%. This attrition rate results in a practical working experience of about 2.5 years on average per audit staff member. In Germany, PwC, for instance, has an overall attrition rate for all its employees of 19% in 2009, resulting in an average practical experience of 2.1 years per employee (PwC Annual Report 2009 und PwC Annual Report 2010).

2.3.9 Client, Industry and Audit Experience

Besides professional knowledge, skills, values, ethics and attitudes, practical experience is a further requirement in order to become a professional accountant.[212] Practical experience significantly expands the base professional knowledge and is a key to delivering high audit quality. Practical experience can be broken down as follows:

- Client-specific experience,
- Industry-specific experience, and
- General audit experience.

At an individual view, practical experience is gathered with time spent on audit assignments. General audit experience can be measured by the total years of working experience of an auditor or of all audit professionals in an audit firm.

Client-specific experience is gained at a specific client. A specific client has specific characteristics such as its business model, industry, size, organizational structure, legal form, culture, and others. Client-specific experience goes along with the audit tenure and is reflected by the duration of the client-auditor relationship.[213]

Industry experience is often referred to industry expertise. Industry expertise is the combination of industry-specific experience an industry-specific knowledge. An audit firm gains industry expertise on both levels: on an individual and on the audit firm level. Auditor industry expertise is the focus of many studies. Since the emergence of industry expertise, researchers have made extensive research about the definition of the concept, industry expertise measure, industry expertise and audit quality, industry expertise and audit fees, industry expertise and the audit market.[214]

A very often used proxy for industry expertise is the auditor market share in a specific industry.[215] The higher the industry market share for an auditor in a specific industry, the higher the degree in industry specialization. Lys and Watts (1994) investigated the relationship between the industry market share and legal proceedings and found that audit firms with higher market share are subject to proportionally fewer legal proceedings and therefore provide better audit quali-

212 IESBA (2010), Sec. 10 to Sec. 17 of the IES 5 "Practical Experience Requirements".
213 Refer to chapter 2.2.6 and the positive effect of audit tenure.
214 Yang (2011), p. 156.
215 For examples: Gramling and Stone (1999); Krishnan, (1997), Krishnan (2003), Schauer (2002).

ty.[216] Krishnan (2003) found that auditors industry expertise (measured by industry market share) moderates accruals-based earnings management. According to Krishnan (2003) "specialist auditors have the expertise resources, and the incentive to constrain opportunistic reporting of accruals and thereby enhance quality of earnings."[217] Also Schauer (2002), Gramling et al. (2000), Balsam et al. (2003) and Kwon et al. (2007) furnish evidence that audit quality improves as the industry market share of the auditor increases.[218]

Another approach to measure industry specialization is the auditor portfolio share approach. This approach calculates auditor industry specialization as the percentage of overall revenues that an auditor derives from a particular industry. Results from the study of DeFond et al. (2000) also indicate a higher audit quality (earnings quality) with a higher degree of industry specialization.[219]

2.3.10 *Audit Effort and Resource Mix*

Audit effort is the actual hours worked for an audit engagement. Higher audit quality is "greater assurance, which requires more audit work."[220] The challenge is to estimate audit effort since audit hours per engagement are not reported publicly by the audit firms; only fees have been disclosed.[221] Leventis and Caramanis (2005) examined auditor- and auditee-related factors that determine audit time as a proxy for audit quality in Greece. They found that audit hours positively correlate both with auditee size and auditor size. Since the Hellenic Institute of Certified Auditors prescribe minimum audit hours for listed companies, an audit effort indicator could be developed as the ratio of actual audit hours to minimum prescribed audit hours. Based on a research of 9738 audits in Greece between 1994 and 2002, Caramanis and Lennox (2008) conclude that low audit effort increases the extent to which managers are able to report aggressively high earnings.[222] Zhang (2012) provides evidence that audit effort is reduced by account-

216 Lys and Watts (1994), p. 65.

217 Krishnan (2003), p. 15.

218 Gramling et al. (2000), Balsam et al. (2000) and Kwon (2007) used earnings quality and abnormal accruals as proxy for audit quality. Schauer (2002), instead, used "bid-ask spread" as a proxy for quality; bid-ask spread arises from difference in information asymmetry among stock market participants.

219 DeFond et al. (2000), p. 1.

220 Carcello et al. (2002), p. 368.

221 Refer to chapter 2.2.2 and chapter 2.2.4.

222 Caramanis and Lennox (2008), p. 122.

ing comparability. A higher degree of accounting comparability entails less audit risk and thus less audit effort.[223]

When O'Keefe et al. (1994) developed the audit production model, they used data from one audit firm and documented that both audit hours and the mix of labor are sensitive to client size, complexity, leverage, and inherent risk.[224] It is apparent that not only the audit hours are relevant for audit quality but also the respective resource (labor) mix. It obviously makes a difference whether a junior audit professional works 200 hours for an audit engagement or a senior audit professional works 200 hours for the engagement. Increasing the seniority results in a better output, meaning a higher assurance level, but also higher cost rates. The audit firms bear higher labor costs when audit fees are correspondingly higher. This view on audit quality and audit effort leads back to Simunic's audit pricing model, where audit fees are directly linked to resource cost rate multiplied with quantity (hours).[225] The resource mix topic will be further discussed as part of the audit production theory of O'Keefe et al. (1994) and Francis in chapter 4.

2.3.11 Audit Methodology and Tools

In general, methodology in academia is the study of research methods. In particular, related to a discipline, a methodology is a body of practices, procedures, and rules used by those who work in a discipline.[226] It is a set of working methods, which has to be followed.

Applied to the discipline of financial auditing, an audit methodology defines standards and practices to be adhered in performing the audit. It is an inherent aspect of what the audit team does, how it does it and why it does and provides the structure within which the audit team exercises professional judgment in order to provide a final audit opinion. Audit methodology is best described with the elements audit approach, audit process, audit planning, audit team organization, and audit team communication.

Audit firms deploy audit support systems to achieve efficient and effective audits.[227] These systems ensure that the firm's audit methodology is applied

223 Zhang (2012), p. 45.
224 O'Keefe et al. (1994).
225 Refer to chapter 2.2.4.
226 Kamitz (1980), p. 429.
227 Dowling and Leech (2007), p. 92.

globally.[228] Large audit firms invest significantly in developing proprietary audit support systems for global deployment across their global network.[229] Ideally, the audit support system covers the elements:

- Audit software & information technology deployed,
- Supporting tools for testing/sampling,
- Documentation templates, and
- Communication tools.

The better the audit approach is supported by software tools, the more efficient and consistent the audit can be performed. Audit support software may also ensure completeness of audit steps by automated documentation controls. Sophisticated software helps in communication with audit team members as well as information sharing within the whole audit team. An effective audit software package ensures retraceable documentation of the complete audit process from engagement planning and audit execution to engagement completion and archiving.

2.4 Criticism on Selected on Audit Quality Measures

2.4.1 Earnings Management

Earnings management is defined in different ways. Healy & Wahlen (1999) state that "earnings management occurs when managers use judgment in financial reporting and in structuring transactions to alter financial reports to either mislead some stakeholders about the underlying economic performance of the company or to influence contractual outcomes that depend on reported accounting numbers."[230] In the same sense, Schipper (1989) understands earnings management as the "purposeful intervention in the external financial reporting process with the intent of obtaining private gain".[231] Notwithstanding the definition applied, earnings management is inherently unobservable. Most prior studies use different measures of discretionary or abnormal accruals as proxies for earnings management. Typically, a regression model (e.g. OLS) is used to investigate the impact of various independent variables on earnings management.

---

228 Manson et al. (2001), p. 109; Dowling and Leech (2007), p. 96.

229 Manson et al. (2001), p. 109.

230 Healy & Wahlen (1999), p. 85.

231 Schipper (1989), p. 1.

According to this earnings management approach, total accruals, which can be calculated from net profit minus net cash flow, can be decomposed into a discretionary and a non-discretionary portion.

$$TA_t = NP_t - NCF_t = NDA_t + DA_t \ (1)$$

Where:
NP_t = Net Profit in year *t*
NCF_t = Net Cash Flow in year *t*
TA_t = Total accruals in year *t*
NDA_t = Non-discretionary accruals in year *t*
DA_t = Discretionary accruals in year *t*

The underlying assumption is that the discretionary or abnormal portion of accruals is triggered by management in order to control earnings in the way they want. In fact, Managements' bias tends towards an aggressive or even creative accounting[232], since their variable compensation normally depends on an earnings measure.[233] Auditors, in contrast, should be independent and objective, but may tend towards conservative accounting, since audit comfort is highest when the audit risk is lowest. The more the auditor agrees with aggressive accounting, the higher the audit risk. Hence, there is a conflict of interests between the auditor and management in terms of accounting practices. The interest conflict is exhibited in figure 2.13.

Audit quality in this point of view is the question of how effectively the auditor prevents arbitrary earnings management in terms of discretionary accruals.

---

232 Aggressive accounting policies tend to inflate earnings and raise asset values; reserves and allowances are low, which keeps profits high (Ittelson 2009, chapter 14). Aggressive accounting policies may be still compliant with accounting standards, if not exaggerated. Creative accounting policies are accounting practices, which may not or may be considered as illegal, but are considered to be somewhat out of the ordinary.

233 For instance, variable compensations often depend on EBIT, or other key performance indicator such as EVA (economic value added), which itself depends on the net operating profit (after taxes).

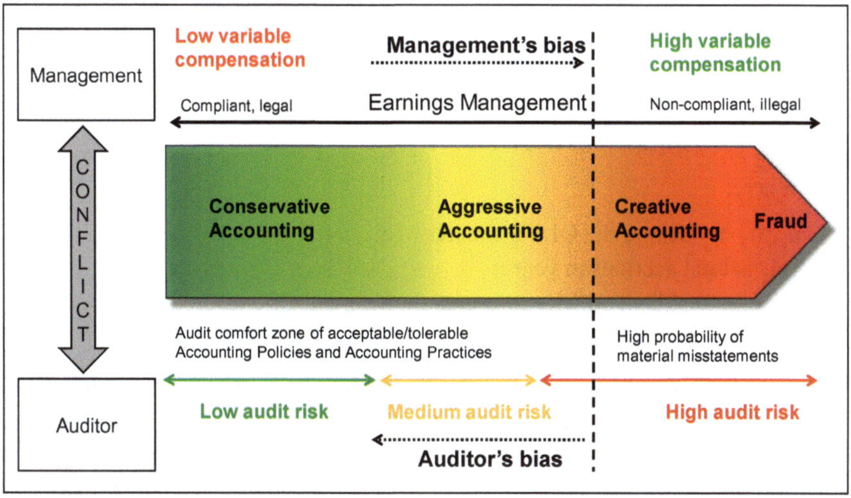

Figure 2.13: Management's and Auditor's Accounting Biases (source: own development)

The most popular four regression models for estimating the non-discretionary part of accruals stem from DeAngelo (1986), Healy (1985), Jones (1991), and Dechow et al. (1995).[234] Jones (1991) for instance, estimates the non-discretionary portion in the year *t* as follows:

$$NDA_t = \alpha_1 \frac{1}{A_{t-1}} + \alpha_2 \frac{\Delta REV_t}{A_{t-1}} + \alpha_3 \frac{PPE_t}{A_{t-1}} \quad (2)$$

Where:

NDA_t is nondiscretionary accruals in year t scaled by lagged total assets;
ΔREV_t is revenues in year t less revenues in year *t-1*;
PPE_t is gross property plant and equipment at the end of year *t*;
A_{t-1} is total assets at the end of year *t-1*; and
α_1, α_2, α_3 are estimated firm-specific parameters.

234 In literature, the model of Dechow et al. (1995) is often referred to the modified Jones' model.

The firm-specific parameters α_1, α_2, α_3 are estimated by using the following regression model:

$$\frac{TA_t}{A_{t-1}} = a_1 \frac{1}{A_{t-1}} + a_2 \frac{\Delta REV_t}{A_{t-1}} + a_3 \frac{PPE_t}{A_{t-1}} + \varepsilon_t \text{ (3)}$$

Where:

a_1, a_1, a_3 denote the OLS estimates of α_1, α_2, α_3
TA_t is total accruals in year *t*;
ε_t is the residual, which represents the firm-specific discretionary portion of total accruals

The meta-analysis of Lin and Hwang (2010) gives an overview of dozens of empirical studies about discretionary accruals, earnings quality and earnings management in relation to audit quality. Depending on which estimation model is used, the studies deliver different results on the portion of discretionary accruals, which hamper the comparability of the results. [235]

In a critical view, the question arises whether the ability to prevent earnings management is the appropriate measure to evaluate audit quality. What is the auditor's responsibility? What is his main task? The overall objective of an audit is to obtain "reasonable assurance about whether the financial statements as a whole are free from material misstatement, whether due to fraud or error, thereby enabling the auditor to express an opinion on whether the financial statements are prepared, in all material respects, in accordance with an applicable financial reporting framework".[236] In short terms, the auditor has to ensure financial reporting quality. Obviously, financial reporting quality is affected by discretionary accruals; above all in cases, when discretionary accruals have material effects. However, financial reporting quality depends on much more items than solely accruals. For instance, shifts within the income statement between operating profit and non-operating profit, presentation and classification of assets and liabilities, accounting of business combinations, as well as certain notes are as important as accruals. Moreover, in terms of audit quality, issuing a going concern opinion or a qualified opinion (instead of an unqualified opinion) is even more important and represents true audit quality in some situations.

---

235 Lin and Hwang (2010), pp. 57-77.

236 ISA 200.11, refer to also upcoming discussion in chapter 3.1 "Overall audit objectives and audit failures".

Second, not all abnormal changes in accruals are discretionary. Movements may arise from improved accounting policies or more accurate accounting estimates and fair value practices. Furthermore, the auditor will probably not mind, if management returns from an aggressive accounting policy to a more conservative one. This can also result in significant changes in accruals, which might be interpreted as discretionary accruals, according to earnings management estimation models.

In sum, earnings management may be appropriate to evaluate the financial reporting quality to a limited extent (accruals and earnings quality); however, it is questionable – because of the arguments mentioned above – that earnings management estimation models are also appropriate to evaluate the auditor's performance, that is, the quality of his audit service.

2.4.2 Restatements

Empirical studies show that there is an implicit relationship between financial statement restatements and low audit quality. For instance, Raghunandan et al. (2003) assert that their examination of the relationship between non-audit fees and subsequent restatements "constitutes a direct test of the association between non-audit fees and audit quality."[237] Palmrose and Scholz (2000) studied auditor litigation resulting from restatements. They state that accounting issues, which lead to restatements, are "at the intersection of financial reporting quality and audit quality".[238] Accoding to them, misstatements arise from not adequately identifying of high risk accounts and transactions by the auditors. Restatements in their sample identified accounting issues such as revenue recognition which could have been identified by the auditors as high risk in their audit planning and performance. Analyzing the relationship between audit committee characteristics and financial statement misstatements, Abbott et al. (2002) indirectly support the connection between certain restatements and low audit quality in this context.[239]

The fact that financial statements are restated in some cases is not necessarily due to preparer's failure or implicitly due to an auditor's failure. At a first glance, it only states, that financial statements of prior periods have changed. Changes in financial statements can result from material misstatements and

237 Raghunandan et al. (2003), p. 223.

238 Palmrose and Scholz (2000), p. 4.

239 Abbott et al (2002), p. 1, Woodland and Reynolds (2003), p. 4.

changes in accounting policies.[240] In order to provide accounting and reporting comparability across multiple years, financial statements have to be changed to reflect the impact of changes in accounting policies, which could result from changes in accounting principles. Thus, not all restatements are related to poor accounting and/or auditing quality.

A further discussion whether the use of restatements is an appropriate quality indicator can be found in chapter 3.1.3.2.2.[241]

2.4.3 Going-Concern Reporting

Another binary audit quality metric is based on the relation between a going-concern audit report and client business failure. An audit failure could be deemed to occur when client business failure is not preceded by a going-concern audit report (Francis 2011).[242] Lennox (1999) uses the going concern/client failure framework in a different way to measure auditor reporting accuracy.[243] Auditors report accurately if client failures are preceded by a going-concern opinion, and if clients that do not fail receive a clean opinion (Francis 2011).[244] Hence, according to Francis (2011), auditors can make two types of errors in such opinions "(1) issuing a modified opinion for a company that remains viable and (2) failing to issue a going concern opinion for a company that becomes bankrupt before the next audit".[245]

Incorrect going concern opinions definitively are an appropriate indicator for low audit quality. However, the going concern assessment is very challenging, as much more facts than negative trends in operating results, delay in payments, or denial of trade credit from suppliers have to be considered. It is more about business forecasting and assumption making than reviewing facts derived from historical financial reporting. Moreover, impacts of global shocks such as the financial crises cannot be foreseen by anyone.

Next to that, auditors are very cautious in issuing audit opinions, since a negative one can accelerate or even cause client's ruin when banks and suppliers deny credits to a company because of the auditor's going concern opinion.

---

240 IAS 8.7, 8.14 (retrospective application of accounting policy), 8.42 (retrospective restatement).

241 Chapter 3.1.3.2.2.

242 Francis (2011), p. 127.

243 Lennox (1999), p. 217.

244 Francis (2011), p. 128.

245 Francis (2011), p. 128.

Furthermore, inappropriate going concern opinions are only a small portion of all occurrences of low audit quality. The auditor's failure in general is not detecting material misstatements. A missing or a wrong going concern opinion is definitely material. However numerous different types of material misstatements may occur, which are not connected to a going concern opinion, such as over- or undervaluation of assets and debts in a good financial situation.

Hence, audit quality indicators derived from going concern opinions are delicate. The situations where an incorrect going concern opinion is an appropriate measure of audit quality can only be assessed on an individual case-by-case basis.

2.5 Conclusion and Knowledge Gap

Audit quality has been in focus of theoretical and empirical audit quality research for the last 30 years. Worldwide, the concepts of earnings management and earnings quality are dominating audit quality considerations on audit engagement level. Audit quality surrogates such as auditor size, audit fees, provision of non-audit services, audit tenure and auditors' industry expertise have been researched intensively. Only some research has been performed on the basis of audit inputs and audit firm characteristics.

In Germany, empirical audit research focused mainly on audit fees (especially since 2006 when audit fee disclosures were enacted), audit market concentration and auditor rotation, as well as earnings management. Empirical research on audit inputs and audit production related theories have been considered only to a minor extent. The relationship between accounting errors and audit firm characteristics based on audit input measures has not been empirically researched for the German audit market.

3 Audit Quality Measure Based on Reporting Errors

3.1 Overall Audit Objectives and Audit Failures

3.1.1 Overall Objectives of the Auditor

According to ISA 200.11 the overall objectives of the auditor in conducting an audit of financial statements are twofold[246]:

a) Obtaining "reasonable assurance about whether the financial statements as a whole are free from material misstatement, whether due to fraud or error, thereby enabling the auditor to express an opinion on whether the financial statements are prepared, in all material respects, in accordance with an applicable financial reporting framework" and

b) To report and communicate auditor's findings in accordance with ISAs.

If the auditor cannot obtain reasonable assurance about the financial statements the auditor's report should not contain an unqualified opinion. Moreover, ISAs require that the auditor disclaim an opinion or withdraw (or resign) from the engagement, where withdrawal is possible under applicable law or regulation.

The auditor is not expected to obtain absolute assurance that the financial statements are free from material misstatement due to fraud or error (ISA 200.A45). There are inherent limitations of an audit based on the nature of audit evidence and the characteristics of fraud (ISA 200.A45, AU Sec. 110.02). Furthermore, audits that require absolute assurance would not be economically reasonable as costs would be immense.

The overall objective of an audit based on the concept of reasonable assurance is not only required according to auditing standards (international and local ones), but also – and this is much more important for this study – codified in the German Commercial Code (HGB). According to Sec. 317(1)2 of the HGB, an audit has to be conducted in the way that reasonable assurance has to be obtained, which means that misstatements, which would materially impact the

246 ISA 200.11, IAASB (2012b).

correct presentation of net assets, financial positions and results of operations, have to be detected by the independent auditor.[247]

3.1.2 Material Misstatements

3.1.2.1 Misstatements in Financial Statements

In this study, the term "misstatement" comprises all terms such as error, omission, or infringement, which are sometimes used synonymously. Misstatements can "arise in respect of the recognition, measurement, presentation or disclosure of elements of financial statements".[248]

IAASB defines a misstatement very generally as a difference between the amount, classification, presentation, or disclosure of a reported financial statement item and the amounts, classification, presentation, or disclosure that is required for the item to be in accordance with the applicable financial reporting framework.[249]

In all cases, it is appropriate to distinguish whether a misstatement is the result of error (unintentional) or fraud (intentional).[250] An error is defined as "an unintentional misstatement in financial statements, including the omission of an amount or a disclosure", whereas fraud is defined as "an intentional act by one or more individuals among management, those charged with governance, employees, or third parties, involving the use of deception to obtain an unjust or illegal advantage".[251] Figure 3.1 summarizes the definition and causes of misstatement.

---

247 The original wording of Sec. 317(1)2 of the German Commercial Code: "Die Prüfung ist so anzulegen, daß Unrichtigkeiten und Verstöße gegen die in Satz 2 aufgeführten Bestimmungen, die sich auf die Darstellung des sich nach § 264 Abs. 2 ergebenden Bildes der Vermögens-, Finanz- und Ertragslage des Unternehmens wesentlich auswirken, bei gewissenhafter Berufsausübung erkannt werden."

248 IAS 8.41 "Errors can arise in respect of the recognition measurement, presentation or disclosure of elements of financial statements."

249 IAASB (2012b), Glossary of Terms p. 23.

250 ISA 240.2 "Characteristics of Fraud", IAASB (2012b).

251 IAASB (2012b), Glossary of Terms p. 21 and p. 22.

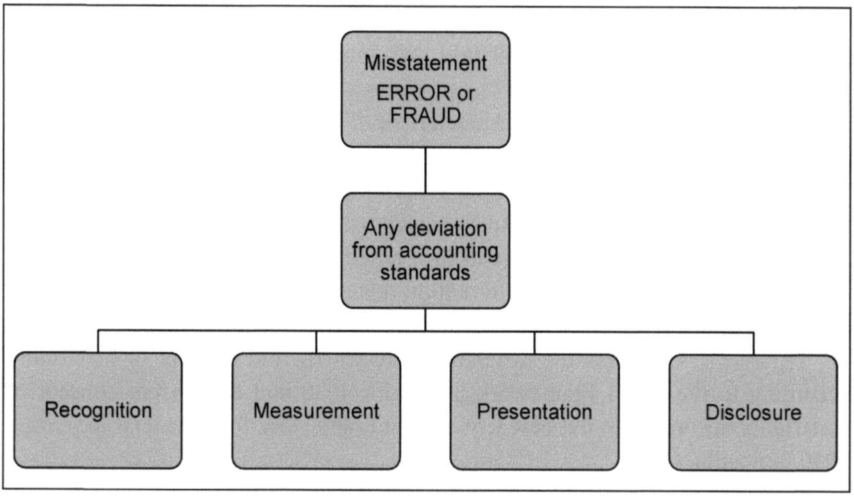

Figure 3.1: Misstatements in Financial Statements
(own development based on IAS 8.41 and ISA 240.2)

3.1.2.2 Materiality

3.1.2.2.1 Concepts of Materiality

What all concepts of materiality descriptions have in common is that a misstatement is material if it influences the user's decision.[252] What that means concretely and how it could be further defined, is a recurring theme of discussions led by rules makers, academia, and professionals in accounting and financial reporting.[253] Since there is no objective, quantitative rule for the determination of materiality, the concept of materiality remains subject to professional judgment.[254] At the present, referring to international standards, there are definitions and explanations of the concept of materiality both in accounting standards and in auditing standards. With the revision of IAS 1 and the release of the new Conceptual Framework, both in 2010, the perspectives on materiality have changed.

---

252 Sec. QC11 of the IASB Conceptual Framework for Financial Reporting 2010, IAS 1.7, ISA 320.2, Sec. QC of the SFAC No. 8, PCAOB AU Sec. 312.04 (SAS 107).

253 ESMA (2011): Consultation Paper, Considerations of materiality in financial reporting; and Baldauf/Steckel/Steller (2012).

254 For instance refer to ISA 320.4, IAASB (2012b) and PCAOB AU Sec. 312.04 (SAS 107): "the auditor's determination of materiality is a matter of professional judgment, and is affected by the auditor's perception of the financial information needs of users of the financial statements".

Formerly, the concept of materiality was dominated by its quantitative characteristic. The IASB Framework 1989 says that "materiality depends on the size of the item or error judged ..." and "... provides a threshold or cut-off point rather than being a primary qualitative characteristic...".[255]

In the new conceptual framework, IASB refrains from its original concept of materiality. Moreover, it stresses both aspects equally: nature (qualitative characteristic) and magnitude (quantitative characteristic) of materiality: "... materiality is an entity-specific aspect of relevance based on the nature and magnitude, or both of the items to which the information relates in the context of an individual entity's financial report".[256]

Figure 3.2 visualizes the difference between the old concept of materiality according to the IASB Framework in Section F.30 and the current concept of materiality according to the new Conceptual Framework for Financial Reporting 2010 in Section QC11.

Consistent to the new framework, IAS 1.7 has different wording but the same meaning as both aspects are also considered: "Materiality depends on the size and nature of the omission or misstatement judged in the surrounding circumstances". The revision of the framework and IAS 1 was performed in the context of the convergence project, where IASB and FASB agreed on a common development on accounting standards. FASB itself has reworked its former framework, especially "Statement of Financial Accounting Concepts No. 2"[257] and had set up the new framework paper "Statement of Financial Account Concepts No. 8" (SFAC No. 8) in 2010. SFAC No. 8 now contains equivalent definitions as the new IASB Conceptual Framework for Financial Reporting.

---

255 Sec. 30 of the IASB Framework 1989 (F.30).

256 Sec. QC11 of the IASB Conceptual Framework for Financial Reporting 2010.

257 The revision also took into consideration the SEC Staff Accounting Bulletin (SAB) No. 99. SAB 99 explicitly makes it clear, that arbitrary materiality (e.g. 5 % of income) is not acceptable. Assessing materiality, the standard requires to take three elements into account: (1) the context, (2) the surrounding circumstances and (3) qualitative factors: "Under the governing principles, an assessment of materiality requires that one views the facts in the context of the 'surrounding circumstances', as the accounting literature puts it, or the "total mix" of information, in the words of the Supreme Court. In the context of a misstatement of a financial statement item, while the 'total mix' includes the size in numerical or percentage terms of the misstatement, it also includes the factual context in which the user of financial statements would view the financial statement item. The shorthand in the accounting and auditing literature for this analysis is that financial management and the auditor must consider both 'quantitative' and 'qualitative' factors in assessing an item's materiality. Court decisions, Commission rules and enforcement actions, and accounting and auditing literature have all considered 'qualitative' factors in various contexts." (SEC 1999).

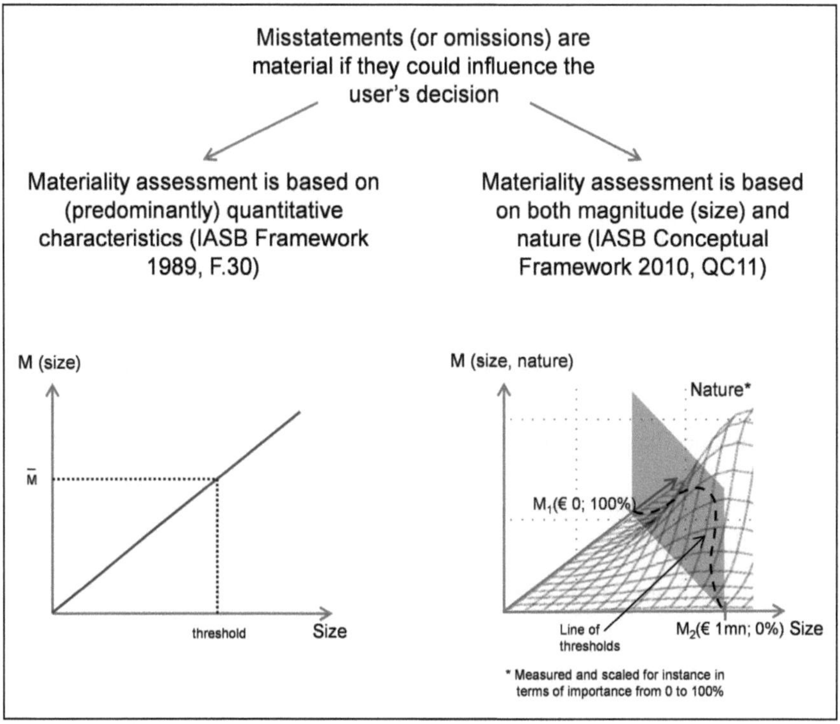

Figure 3.2: Concepts of Materiality: Framework 1989 and Conceptual Framework 2010 (source: own development)

Correspondingly, IAASB in the revised ISA 320[258] defines materiality exactly the way it is defined in IAS 1.7.: "materiality depends on the size and nature of the omission or misstatement judged in the surrounding circumstances." However, ISA 320 gives more guidance on what that means, especially for the qualitative aspect[259]. There are three characteristics of materiality to be considered by the auditor in ISA 320.2:

- A misstatement is considered to be material if they, individually or in the aggregate, could reasonably be expected to influence the economic deci-

258 IAAASB (2012b), ISA 320.2.

259 A catalogue of qualitative materiality factors can be found in ISA 450.A16 (refer also to chapter 3.1.2.2.3 Qualitative Considerations of Materiality").

sions of users taken on the basis of the financial statements (ISA 320.2, item 1).[260]

- Consider not only size but also the nature of the misstatement and the surrounding circumstances (ISA 320.2, item 2).
- For general purpose financial statements, what is considered depends on the common information needs of a wide variety of users (ISA 320.2, item 3).

Consequently, the auditor who performs his/her audit work in line with ISA 320.2 has to review and possibly adjust the preparers' materiality determination as he/she has to take into account the wide range of qualitative materiality factors listed in ISA 450.A16 (refer to chapter 2.2.2.3); for instance, an omission of information not specifically required by the applicable financial reporting framework but which, in the judgment of the auditor, is important to the users' understanding of the financial position, financial performance or cash flows of the entity.[261]

In the course of an audit, the concept of materiality has to be applied in all stages of the audit process:

- Audit Planning (ISA 320 – Materiality in Planning and Performing an Audit),
- Audit Performing (ISA 450 – Evaluation of Misstatements identified during the Audit),
- Audit Reporting (ISA 700 – Forming an Opinion and Reporting on Financial Statements).[262]

Hence a planning materiality which is based on expected financial statement has to be updated during the audit with actual figures in order to appropriately evaluate and aggregate uncorrected misstatements, if any, on the financial statements.[263]

Referring back to figure 3.2 and to new concept of materiality, theoretically, determining a single materiality threshold on magnitude (e.g. size of a financial position) is not appropriate anymore (it probably never was). However, the dimension "nature" could be translated in a scale of importance from 0% to 100%. Materiality can then be calculated, combining both together, an importance percentage and a size value, a line of materiality thresholds could be determined.

---

260 IAASB (2012b), ISA 320.2.
261 IAASB (2012b), ISA 450.A16.
262 IAASB (2012b), ISA 200.6.
263 IAASB (2012b), ISA 320.5.

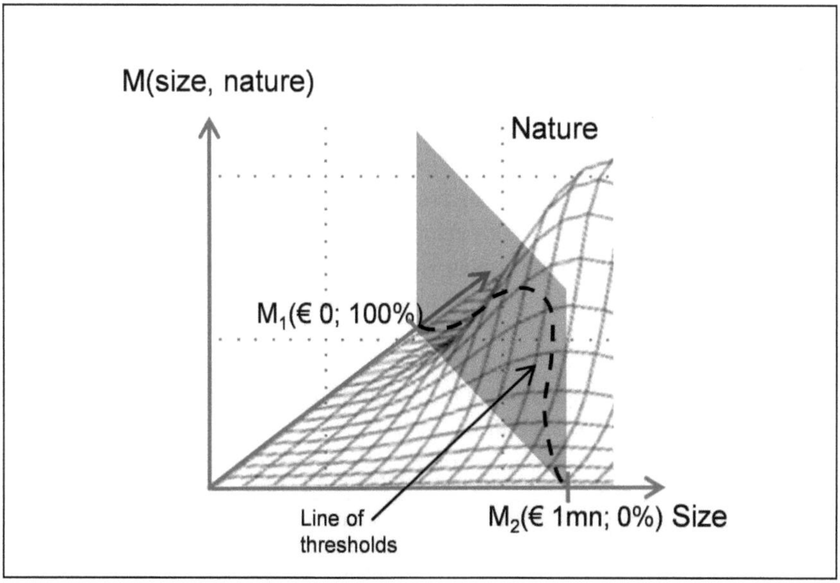

Figure 3.3: Line of Materiality Thresholds (source: own delopment)

At the one end of the line lies the point pair M_1(€ 0; 100%), at the other end, for instance, the point pair M_2(€ 1 million; 0%). M_1 is a threshold point, where the qualitative aspect is that important such the size can be totally ignored. In contrast, M_2 is a threshold point, where the situation is completely inversed: The misstatement is not considered as qualitative important, but has reached a quantitative magnitude, which is material. For instance, this could be the case where several small errors are detected, all with a nature of low importance, but in sum resulting in a material magnitude. Depending on the materiality function, a curve can be developed within the point pairs M_1 and M_2. Figure 3.3 (which is also contained in figure 3.3 in a small version) visualizes an example line of thresholds.

For examples of mathematical threshold functions based solely on size, refer to the next chapter.

3.1.2.2.2 Quantitative Considerations of Materiality

ISA 320.A3 provides some benchmarks examples for the use in determining a materiality threshold such as profit, total assets, net assets or equity.[264] However, concrete factors for those benchmarks are not indicated.

McKee and Eilifsen (2000) classified the quantitative materiality approaches in four categories. Table 3.1 summarizes their results.[265]

The once calculated materiality on a benchmark basis is often referred as the overall materiality, which is broken down into component materiality levels based on single financial statement, items, accounts, group of accounts or classes of transactions.[266]

Table 3.1: Quantitative Approaches of Materiality Thresholds (source: McKee and Eilifsen 2000)

Method	Description	Examples
Single rules	Are rules of thumb that use a single financial variable for computing materiality	5% of pre-tax income 0.5% of total assets 1% of equity 0.5% of total revenues
Variable or size rules	Are similar to single rules but differ in that they provide a range of possible different materiality levels for companies of different size	2 to 5% of gross profit, if less than $20,000 1 to 2% of gross profit, if between $20,000 and $1 million 0.5 to 1% of gross profit, if between $1 and $100 million 0.5% of gross profit, if more than $100 million
Average or blending methods	Typically average rules of thumb or weight each according to a particular formula	½*(1% total assets + 0.5% of total revenues)
Formula methods	Are often estimated by a statistical analysis of a sample of companies; e.g. compare to the KPMG formula used in 1998	$\beta \cdot (\max(\sum_{i=1}^{N} Assets_i, \sum_{i=1}^{N} Revenues_i))^{\alpha}$ where β: 1.84 and α: 2/3 (KPMG)

264 IAASB (2012b), ISA 320.A3.

265 McKee, T. E. and Eilifsen, A. (2000), pp. 54-57.

266 IAASB (2012b), ISA 320.13 and Marten, Quick, Ruhnke (2007) in „Wirtschaftsprüfung".

3.1.2.2.3 Qualitative Considerations of Materiality

According to ISA 320.2[267], not only the size of an item but also the nature of the misstatement and the surrounding circumstances has to take into account when evaluating materiality. In addition to that, the revised ISA 450 includes in paragraph A16 an explicit list of 11 qualitative materiality factors (QMF), refer to table 3.2.

Montoya del Corte, Garcia, and Laviada (2010) provide evidence concerning the effective use of qualitative materiality factors (exactly the way they are defined in ISA 450.A16[268]) from Spanish independent auditors and preparers of financial statements.[269] According to their research where a sample of 352 auditors and 121 preparers participated on filling the respective questionnaire, the most important quantitative quality factors were QM-6 (ranking position 1), QM-11 (Ranking position 2) and QM-3 (Ranking position 3).

Three years ago in 2009, a German trial (OLG Frankfurt) decided that the omission of the "Prognosebericht"[270] as part of the "Konzernlagebericht"[271] is a material misstatement.[272] This shows how important it is to consider the qualitative aspects of materiality.

---

[267] IAASB (2012b), ISA 320.2 is in this context equivalent to QC11 of IASB Conceptual Framework 2010.

[268] IAASB (2012b), ISA 450.A16.

[269] Montoya del Corte, Garcia and Laviada (2010), pp. 458 et seq.

[270] A qualitative forecast or outlook report as part of the "Lagebericht".

[271] A „Konzernlagebericht" is required by Sec. 315 of the HGB additional to the IAS/IFRS reporting requirements. It is similar to the Management Discussion and Analysis (MDA) including a business risks and business rewards assessment. Further on in this study "Konzernlagebericht" is translated into "Management Report".

[272] OLG Frankfurt a.M., Decision of November24, 2009 (Der Betrieb vom December 11, 2009, Issue 50, pp. 14-16); Gödel, RD. (2010): "Unverzichtbarkeit der Prognoseberichterstattung im (Konzern-) Lagebericht". Der Betrieb (DB), Issue 6, p. 435; and Zülch, H & S Hoffmann. (2010). "Fehlen eines Prognoseberichts als wesentlicher Fehler der Rechnungslegung". Steuer- und Bilanzpraxis (StuB), Issue 3, p. 87.

Table 3.2: QMF According to ISA 450.A16

No.	Qualitative Materiality Factor Description
QMF-1	Affects compliance with regulatory requirements
QMF-2	Affects compliance with debt covenants or other contractual requirements
QMF-3	Relates to the incorrect selection or application of an accounting policy that has an immaterial effect on the current period's financial statements but is likely to have a material effect on future periods' financial statements
QMF-4	Masks a change in earnings or other trends, especially in the context of general economic and industry conditions
QMF-5	Affects ratios used to evaluate the entity's financial position, results of operations or cash flows
QMF-6	Affects segment information presented in the financial statements (for example, the significance of the matter to a segment or other portion of the entity's business that has been identified as playing a significant role in the entity's operations or profitability)
QMF-7	Has the effect of increasing management compensation, for example, by ensuring that the requirements for the award of bonuses or other incentives are satisfied
QMF-8	Is significant having regard to the auditor's understanding of known previous communications to users, for example, in relation to forecast earnings
QMF-9	Relates to items involving particular parties (for example, whether external parties to the transaction are related to members of the entity's management)
QMF-10	Is an omission of information not specifically required by the applicable financial reporting framework but which, in the judgment of the auditor, is important to the users' understanding of the financial position, financial performance or cash flows of the entity
QMF-11	Affects other information that will be communicated in documents containing the audited financial statements (for example, information to be included in a "Management Discussion and Analysis" or an "Operating and Financial Review") that may reasonably be expected to influence the economic decisions of the users of the financial statements

3.1.2.3 Audit Risk and Materiality

According to ISA 200.13c, the audit risk is "the risk that the auditor expresses an inappropriate audit opinion when the financial statements are materially misstated. Audit risk is a function of the risk of material misstatement and detection risk".[273]

$$AR = RMM * DR \quad (4)$$

The risk of material misstatement (RMM) can be further broken down into two components: inherent risk (IR) and control risk (CR).[274]

$$AR = IR * CR * DR \quad (5)$$

The inherent risk (IR) is the susceptibility of a relevant assertion to misstatements that could be material, either individually or when aggregated with other misstatements, assuming there are no related controls. In other words, IR is the likelihood that a material misstatement exists in the financial statements without the consideration of internal control.[275] The control risk (CR) is the risk relates to the internal control system. It is the risk that a material misstatement that could occur in a relevant assertion (for example: completeness or accuracy of an financial statement item) will not be prevented, or detected and corrected on a timely basis by the entity's internal control system.[276] Hence, the control risk depends on the appropriateness of the design of the internal control system and its effectiveness in achieving the entity's objectives relevant to preparation of the entity's financial statements.

Since the auditor has little or no control over these risks, auditing standards refer to the combination of IR and CR as entities' risks[277] (client's risks) because it depends on decisions made by the client (e.g., decisions over the riskiness of business transactions and how much to spend on internal controls). In order to assess and evaluate the control risk, the auditor must understand the client's

273 IAASB (2012b), ISA 230.13c.

274 The audit risk model was first codified in US GAAS, primarily in SAS No. 47, which was issued by the ASB in 1983 and amended in 1997 by SAS No. 82. Today SAS No. 47 is superseded by SAS No. 107, codified in AU Sec. 312.

275 PCAOB AU Sec. 312.21.

276 PCAOB AU Sec. 312.21.

277 PCAOB AU Sec. 312.22 „Inherent risk and control risk are the entity's risks, that is, they exist independently of the audit of financial statements".

internal control system and must perform audit and tests to determine if the controls are well designed and operating effectively.[278]

The only parameter the auditor can adjust in the context of the "client's risk" is the materiality threshold as it is his/her professional judgment to define it.[279] There is an inverse relationship between audit risk and materiality. In a situation where an appropriate audit risk level is given, raising the materiality threshold would allow the auditor to take more detection risk. An increased detection risk means that the auditor can put less effort in the audit.

3.1.2.4 Consequences

Ideally, material misstatements (if any) will be detected by the auditor and corrected by the preparer before the financial statements are published.

In case a material misstatement is detected only after financial statements have been published, it depends on two main factors what will happen. The factors are:

1) Who (auditor, preparer, oversight inspectors, enforcement examiners, shareholder, creditors) detects the material misstatement?
2) Does the material misstatement stem from error or fraud?

The consequences vary from error correction in the current period, to restatements and accounting enforcements, as well as penalties and litigations for preparers and auditors, which could lead to the demise of the company and the auditor (e.g. Enron).

3.1.3 Audit Failures

3.1.3.1 Definitions

What is an audit failure? Does an auditor fail when he/she does not comply with auditing standards (ISA) in terms of risk based approach, audit planning, analytical procedures, substantive and controls testing procedures, engagement documentation etc.? Is he/she responsible for any kind of accounting errors that has not been detected during his/her audit?

According to ISA 200.6 "the auditor's opinion deals with the financial statements as a whole and therefore the auditor is not responsible for the detection of

---

278 IAASB (2012b), ISA 320.2.

279 IAASB (2012b), ISA 320.2.

misstatements that are not material to the financial statements as a whole".[280] Consequently, any undetected material misstatement is the result of an audit failure. However, ISA 200.24 defines "failure to achieve an audit objective" more general:

> "If an objective in a relevant ISA cannot be achieved, the auditor shall evaluate whether this prevents the auditor from achieving the overall objectives of the auditor and thereby requires the auditor, in accordance with the ISAs, to modify the auditor's opinion or withdraw from the engagement (where withdrawal is possible under applicable law or regulation). Failure to achieve an objective represents a significant matter requiring documentation in accordance with ISA 230."

Obviously, the auditor has to take all responsibility if audit work is not compliant with ISA, but which situation is more preferable:

a) an auditor completely complies with ISA in terms of all formalities (procedures in planning, performance, documentation) but misses the overall objective in detecting material misstatements or

b) an auditor documents his/her audit steps very poorly but overlooks not a single accounting issue which could lead to a material misstatement?

Assuming that the material misstatement in situation a) will be revealed only at the date of an auditor's switch or after a PCAOB inspection had been performed, the oversight board inspectors will probably reward him/her with excellent inspection results, without any deficiencies in the inspection report, since they focus on audit methodology, compliance with auditing standards, and audit documentation. In contrast, inspectors will state that auditor's performance in situation b) is significant deficient[281] since the auditor has not documented his/her audit planning, procedures and conclusions in accordance with auditing standards. Hence, to bypass this dilemma, this study defines audit failures as following:

---

280 IAASB (2012b), ISA 200.6.

281 PCAOB Auditing Standard No. 7 "Engagement Quality Review" provides a description of a significant audit engagement deficiency as "exists when (1) the engagement team failed to obtain sufficient appropriate evidence in accordance with the standards of the PCAOB, (2) the engagement team reached an inappropriate overall conclusion on the subject matter of the engagement, (3) the engagement report is not appropriate in the circumstances, or (4) the firm is not independent of its client.

An audit failure is given if the auditor does not meet the overall audit objectives according to ISA 200.11.[282]

In other terms, an audit failure occurs if the auditor cannot obtain reasonable assurance and does not detect material misstatements in the client's financial statements during an audit engagement.

The chart in figure 3.4 summarizes all definitions mentioned in this chapter. These definitions are subject to subsequent discussions in this research work. They also build the fundament for the underlying assumption A1 "Material misstatements remaining in audited financial statements are audit failures and therefore an indicator of low audit quality".

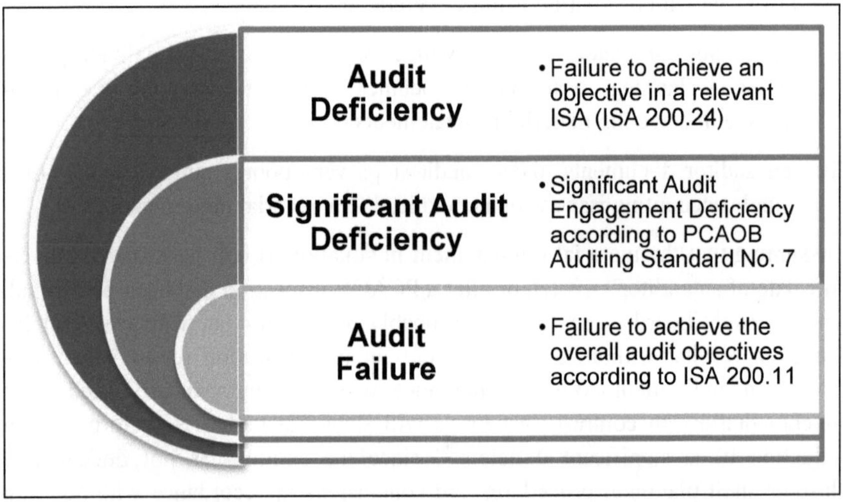

Figure 3.4: Definitions of Audit Deficiency, Significant Audit Deficiency and Audit Failure
(source: own development)

282 Palmrose (1988), p. 58, defines the term „audit failure" in a footnote very similar to this definition: "Here, audit failures include financial statements with material omissions/misstatement whether or not auditors have obtained adequate audit evidence."

3.1.3.2 Indicators of Audit Failures

3.1.3.2.1 Significant Audit Engagement Deficiencies

With the enactment of the Sarbanes-Oxley Act in 2002, the Public Company Accounting Oversight Board (PCAOB) was established. The PCAOB mission is "to oversee the audits of public companies in order to protect the interests of investors and further the public interest in the preparation of informative, accurate and independent audit reports".[283]

To satisfy the regulation of Sec. 104 of the Sarbanes-Oxley Act, PCAOB conducts inspections of registered audit firms and its associated persons in order to assess the degree of their compliance with the Act, the rules of the PCAOB and the SEC, the professional standards and related matters involving public companies.[284]

The result of an inspection is published in a so-called inspection report. All inspection reports which have been released until today are accessible on PCAOB's web site.[285]

An analysis of the Big4 audit firms indicates a negative trend in engagement quality. From 2009 to 2010, the portion of audit engagements with deficiencies has more than doubled (figure 3.5).

In 2010, PCAOB found deficiencies in 79 issuers (31.6% of audits reviewed), whereas in 2009, the inspection reports for the same four firms revealed deficiencies in only 36 issuers (13.5% of audits reviewed).[286]

On basis of gathered experiences during the inspections performed from 2004[287] to 2009, PCAOB released the Auditing Standard No. 7 in 2009, where it

283 "Our Mission" on http://pcaobus.org/About/History/Pages/default.aspx (August 21, 2012, 15:00 CET).

284 Section 104 of the Sarbanes-Oxley Act of 2002.

285 http://pcaobus.org/inspections/reports/pages/default.aspx (August 22, 2012, 18:45 CET).

286 Acuitas, inc.'s survey of fair value audit deficiencies, April 2012.

287 The first inspections reports of PCAOB date as of Aug. 25, 2004 and cover all Big4 audit firms.

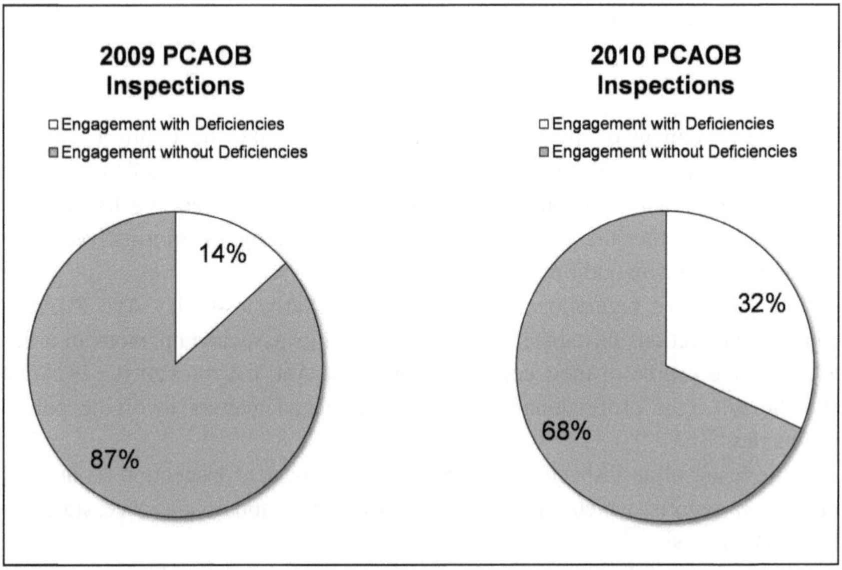

Figure 3.5: Trends in Audit Deficiencies
(Source: Acuitas 2012)

defines "significant audit engagement deficiencies": A significant (audit) engagement deficiency exists "when

1) the engagement team failed to obtain sufficient appropriate evidence in accordance with the standards of the PCAOB,
2) the engagement team reached an inappropriate overall conclusion on the subject matter of the engagement,
3) the engagement report is not appropriate in the circumstances, or
4) the firm is not independent of its client".[288]

Especially the second characteristic "the engagement team reached an inappropriate overall conclusion on the subject matter of the engagement" could indicate an audit failure as defined in chapter 3.1.3.1. In the context of a financial statement audit, the release of an unqualified audit opinion on financial statements containing material misstatements reflects an inappropriate overall conclusion. In this case, the significant audit engagement deficiency would be equivalent to the definition of audit failure in this study. Hence, focusing on characteristic no. 2

288 PCAOB Auditing Standard No. 7 Engagement Quality Review.

and assuming the equivalence of significant audit engagement deficiency and audit failure in this case, the PCAOB inspection reports could be an appropriate basis for studying audit failures.

However, only some German PIE[289] auditors are subject to PCAOB inspections. Auditors who are engaged "only" in pure German PIE's audit engagements (not affiliated or associated to an U.S. company, which is listed on the U.S. stock exchange) will not be in the scope of PCAOB inspections as they are not obligated to register with PCAOB.[290]

Auditors or audit firms which perform statutory audits of public interest entities (PIEs) based in Germany are subject to inspections of the Auditor Oversight Commission (AOC or APAK[291]) according to the Sec. 61a Sentence 2 No. 2 and Sec. 62b (1) of the Public Accountant Act.[292] According to the AOC guidelines, AOC conducts independent inspections "on a random basis and without the need of a prior indication of misconduct".[293]

The inspection cycle for each audit firm depends on the number of audit engagements of PIEs in the previous calendar year: An audit firm is inspected annually if it performs more than 25 relevant audit engagements; audit firms with fewer relevant audit engagements are inspected at least every three years.[294]

Additionally to the random selection, "audit firms are also selected on a risk basis (i.e. by taking into account the particular industry sectors or exchange segments of audit engagements or specific technical themes)".[295]

Although purpose and scope of inspections of the AOC are similar to the inspections performed by PCAOB, inspection reports of the reviewed audit firms

289 Public interest entities as stipulated by Sec. 319a (1) in connection with Sec. 264d of the HGB. PIEs are by definition all companies listed on a regulated market. PIEs are sometimes also referred to "capital market oriented companies".

290 SOX Sec. 102(a) requires a mandatory registration of public accounting firms if they prepare or issue or participate in the preparation or issuance of, any audit report with respect to any (U.S. stock exchange) issuer.

291 APAK = Abschlussprüferaufsichtskommission (Auditor Oversight Commission).

292 Public Accountant Act = Wirtschaftsprüferordnung, short: WPO.

293 APAK (2012): Headline "Background" http://www.apak-aoc.de/english/inspections/inspections.asp (August 22, 2012, 18:45 CET).

294 APAK (2012): Headline "Inspection Cycle and Selection of auditors/audit firms" http://www.apak-aoc.de/english/inspections/inspections.asp (August 22, 2012, 18:45 CET).

295 APAK 2012, Headline "Inspection Cycle and Selection of auditors/audit firms" http://www.apak-aoc.de/english/inspections/inspections.asp (Aug 22, 2012, 18:45 CET).

are not published.[296] Instead, inspection reports are forwarded to the Chamber of Public Accountants (WPK), where the results in the report are assessed to conclude whether "any breaches of professional duties have taken place".[297]

The only published report from the AOC is a summary report of inspection results for the years 2007 to 2010[298]. Unlike PCOAB inspection reports, auditors are not named and the failures are not explicitly classified in AOC summary reports. Since the inspection reports of the AOC are not being published per each audit firm and audit deficiencies or failures are not classified, they cannot be used for empirical research on audit failures.

3.1.3.2.2 Restatements

The dramatic number of restatements filed over the past years with its peak in 2006 (figure 3.6) has attracted scholars, professional institutions and the U.S. government to research the causes for restatements.[299]

The fact that a financial statement has to be restated indicates that something must have been wrong in the previously issued financial statement. The evident question that arises from that fact is what went wrong. Can any error be corrected by releasing a restated financial statement or only material ones? Do detected material misstatements always result in restatements? Is there a legal basis for restatements and what are the causes and the effects of a restatement? If it is all about material misstatements, restatements can also be used as an audit quality indicator based on assumption A1 (chapter 1.4. basis assumptions and hypothesis). Before addressing this issue, it is helpful to understand what restatements are and when financial statements are required to be restated.

---

296 APAK 2012, Headline "Purpose and scope of Inspections" http://www.apak-aoc.de/english/inspections/inspections.asp (Aug 22, 2012, 18:45 CET).

297 On basis of its judgment the WPK decides whether the responsible auditor has to take any kind of instruction, reprimand or penalty. APAK (2012) "Inspection Reporting" http://www.apak-aoc.de/english/inspections/inspections.asp (Aug 22, 2012, 18:45 CET).

298 APAK 2011, Report of the Auditor Oversight Commission on the results of the inspections according to § 62b WPO for the years2007-2010 http://www.apak-aoc.de/english/pdf/APAK-AOC--News_Report_Inspections_2007-2010.pdf.

299 For instance Plumlee and Yohn (2009) "An Analysis of the Underlying Causes Attributed to Restatements", IMA (2008) "Accounting Control Assessment Standards: The missing piece of the restatement puzzle, or Scholz (2009) "The Changing Nature and Consequences of Public Company Financial Restatements", U.S. Department of Treasury (2008), or GAO (2002): Financial Statement Restatements – Trends, Market, Impacts, Regulatory Responses, and Remaining Challenges.

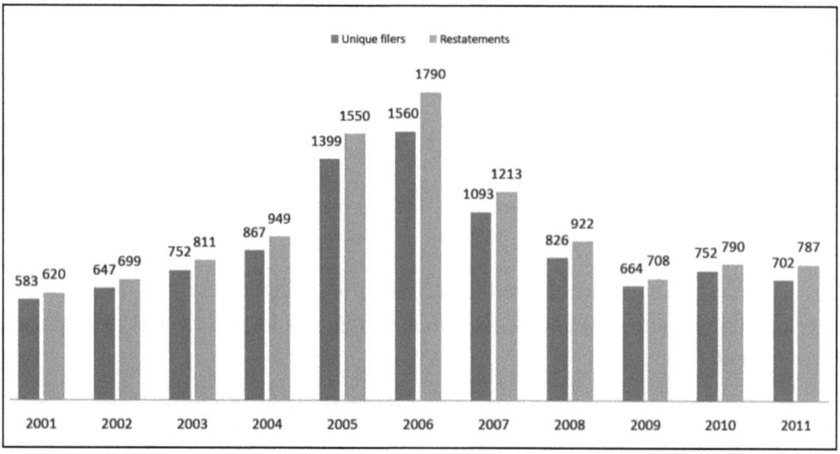

Figure 3.6: Total Number of Restatements of U.S. Stock Exchange Listed firms (Source: Audit Analytics 2012)

In the definitions section of IAS 8[300], retrospective restatements are "correcting the recognition, measurement and disclosure of amounts of elements of financial statements as if a prior period error had never occurred".[301]

In addition, *prior period errors* are defined as "arising from a failure to use, or misuse of, reliable information that:

a) was available when financial statements for those periods were authorized for issue; and

b) could reasonably be expected to have been obtained and taken into account in the preparation and presentation of those financial statements.

Such errors include the effects of mathematical mistakes, mistakes in applying accounting policies, oversights or misinterpretations of facts, and fraud."[302] It is

[300] U.S. GAAP is quite similar both in definition and requirements of restatements. Accounting Standard Codification (ASC) Topic 250, Statement of Financial Accounting Standards (FAS) 154 "Accounting Changes and Error Corrections", Sec. 2(j) defines a restatement quite similar to the IAS 8 definition: "The process of revising previously issued financial statements to reflect the correction of an error in those financial statements." Also the error definition is almost identical FAS 154 Sec. 2(h) "An error in recognition, measurement, presentation, or disclosure in financial statements resulting from mathematical mistakes, mistakes in the application of GAAP, or oversight or misuse of facts that existed at the time the financial statements were prepared."

[301] IAS 8.5, definition of „retrospective restatement".

[302] IAS 8.5, definition of „prior period errors".

important to mention that IAS 8 clarifies changes in accounting estimates are not considered as errors in this context.[303]

According to IAS 8.42[304] "an entity shall correct *material prior period errors* retrospectively in the first set of financial statements authorized for issue after their discovery by:

a) restating the comparative amounts for the prior period(s) presented in which the error occurred; or

b) if the error occurred before the earliest prior period presented, restating the opening balances of assets, liabilities and equity for the earliest prior period presented."

Implicitly, IAS 8.42, in connection to the definition of retrospective restatements, allows corrections of immaterial corrections. It is consequent to conclude that if material errors shall be corrected immaterial errors can be restated as the definition of retrospective refers only to prior period errors.

In IAS 8.43-48 (headlined with "limitations on retrospective restatement"), exceptions can be found for retrospective restatements. In general, prior period errors shall be corrected by retrospective restatement "except of the extent that it is impracticable to determine either the period-specific effects or the cumulative effect of the error".[305]

In cases that it is impracticable[306] to determine "the cumulative effect, at the beginning of the current period, of an error on all prior periods, the entity shall

303 IAS 8.5, definition of „change in accounting estimate".

304 Compare to FAS 154 Sec. 25: "In the event that an error is identified, a restatement is required if the error is considered material". FAS 154 Sec. 25 requires that errors in previously issued financial statements be reported as a prior period adjustment by restating those financial statements and requires that: "a) The cumulative effect of the error on periods prior to those presented shall be reflected in the carrying amounts of assets and liabilities as of the beginning of the first period presented. b) An offsetting adjustment, if any, shall be made to the opening balance of retained earnings (or other appropriate components of equity or net assets in the statement of financial position) for that period. c) Financial statements for each individual prior period presented shall be adjusted to reflect correction of the period-specific effects of the error. An important aspect of the process of establishing whether an error should be restated or not, is the determination that the error is material."

305 IAS 8.43.

306 "Applying a requirement is impracticable when the entity cannot apply it after making every reasonable effort to do so. For a particular prior period, it is impracticable to apply a change in an accounting policy retrospectively or to make a retrospective restatement to correct an error if: (a) the effects of the retrospective application or retrospective restatement are not determinable; (b) the retrospective application or retrospective restatement requires assumptions about what management's intent would have been in that period; or (c) the retrospective application or retro-

restate the comparative information to correct the error prospectively from the earliest date practicable".[307]

Hence, the question of whether all detected material misstatement result in restatements has to be negated because some material misstatements are being corrected prospectively due to impracticability to determine the cumulative effect of an error.

Therefore, focusing on restatements we will not cover all detected material misstatements in published financial statements as 1) some misstatements are being corrected prospectively and 2) some restatements theoretically can be based on the correction of immaterial prior period errors.

Nevertheless, a selective and differentiating analysis of restatement can provide insights to auditor's malperformance.[308]

3.1.3.2.3 Litigations

An important aspect of financial statement audits is the auditor's liability allows financial statement users such as investors to sue auditors in an effort to recover damages. Francis (2004) states that "audit quality is inversely related to audit failures: the higher the failure rate, the lower the quality of auditing ... the most convincing evidence of an outright audit failure occurs when there is litigation against auditors..."[309].

When audit failures occur in conjunction with investor losses, lawsuits against independent auditors are very likely[310]. However, lawsuits become much less likely when audit failures do not affect income of the audited financial statements or have positive effects for investors.

Kinney and McDaniels (1989) model the probability of lawsuits against auditors as follows:[311]

---

spective restatement requires significant estimates of amounts and it is impossible to distinguish objectively information about those estimates that: (i) provides evidence of circumstances that existed on the date(s) as at which those amounts are to be recognized, measured or disclosed; and (ii) would have been available when the financial statements for that prior period were authorized for issue from other information." (IAS 8.5 "impracticable")

307 IAS 8.45.

308 For instance, refer to empirical studies of Plumlee and Yohn (2009), Woodland and Reynolds (2003); Hennes, Leone, Miller (2010); and Audit Analytics (2012).

309 Francis, J. R. (2004), p. 352.

310 Palmrose, Z.-V. (1989). pp. 55-73 and Van Dijk, M. (1998), p. 4.

311 Kinney, W. and L. McDaniel (1989), pp. 71 et seq.

P(lawsuit) = f(actual user losses, amount of misstatement in audited financial statements, reputation of auditor for audit quality, auditor legal posture, and user's and client's costs to sue)

The fact that auditors typically face lawsuits only in cases of investor losses, litigations as a measure of audit failures tell only a portion of the story. Many audit failures are not revealed by lawsuits against auditors, since there is no motivation to do so either from the client's or user's side. Hence, this study will not focus on litigations and lawsuits against auditors as proxy for audit failures.

3.1.3.2.4 Accounting Enforcement Releases

What had been practiced for years by the SEC – namely issuing and publishing Accounting and Auditing Enforcement Releases (AAERs) when companies violate securities laws – was adopted in Germany in 2005 with the foundation of the FREP.

Unlike the AAER by SEC, the accounting enforcement releases by FREP are solely addressed to the company, not to the involved audit firms. According to Rollings and Bremser (1997), in approximately one-third of the cases, the SEC also takes enforcement actions against the auditor.[312]

In Germany instead, a FREP accounting enforcement release triggers often an AOC inspection of the involved auditor, which could lead to lawsuits against the auditor.[313]

According to the assumptions A2 (refer to chapter 1.4 "Basis assumptions"; all financial reporting failures detected by FREP are material) and A3, we conclude that published reporting errors (PRE) can be used as Audit Quality indicator as long as the enforcement selection process and the examination procedure are fair and somehow equally applied to all public interest entities.

In order to assess the enforcement regime in Germany, chapters 3.2.1 to 3.2.3 describe the legal basis, the enforcement process itself and the way errors are published in Germany. Chapter 3.2.4 gives an overview on the results of the examinations performed from 2005 to 2012. Finally, chapter 3.2.5 assesses the enforcement procedure on the basis of predefined evaluation criteria.

312 Theresa P. Rollins, Wayne G. Bremser, (1997), p. 191.

313 "Any indications for breaches of the auditor's duties found by the accounting enforcement authorities have to be reported to the auditor oversight for further investigations." APAK (2012), http://www.apak-aoc.de/english/apak/auditor_oversight_germany.asp (September 5, 2012, 10:00 CET).

3.2 Accounting Enforcement in Germany

3.2.1 Legal Basis

The Balance Sheet Control Law, enacted on December 15, 2004, is the legal basis of the accounting enforcement regime in Germany. It established a two stages enforcement process in order to enforce German public interest entities to comply with endorsed international accounting standards (IFRS/IAS) and German Commercial Code (HGB) relating its (consolidated) financial statements and management reports. For a simplified sketch of the process, refer to figure 3.7.

The responsible institution at the first stage is the Financial Reporting Enforcement Panel (FREP). FREP is organized under private law and recognized by the German Ministry of Justice together with the German Ministry of Finance (Sec. 342b to 342e of the HGB).[314] FREP performs examinations with cause, by request, or by random sample selection for public interest entities i.e. companies, whose securities (shares, bonds, etc.) are traded at regulated markets on German stock exchanges.

In the second stage, the Federal Financial Supervisory Authority (BaFin) mediates interactions between companies and the FREP (Sec. 37n to 37s of the WpHG (Securities Trading Act). When the company's opinion differs from that of the FREP, BaFin determines whether an error has occurred and it orders the error publication in the German Federal Gazette. In case that the company does not cooperate voluntarily with FREP, BaFin can order an FREP examination with sovereign means.

The enforcement institutions (FREP and BaFin) have to examine whether the most recently adopted individual financial statement and the related management report (Lagebericht) or the most recently adopted consolidated financial statements and the related management report (Konzernlagebericht) comply with the applicable principles and regulations, including the accounting standards permitted by law.[315]

---

314 http://www.frep.org.

315 FREP (2009b): Information relating to the Examination Process of the Financial Reporting Enforcement, available at: http://www.frep.info/docs/pruefverfahren/.

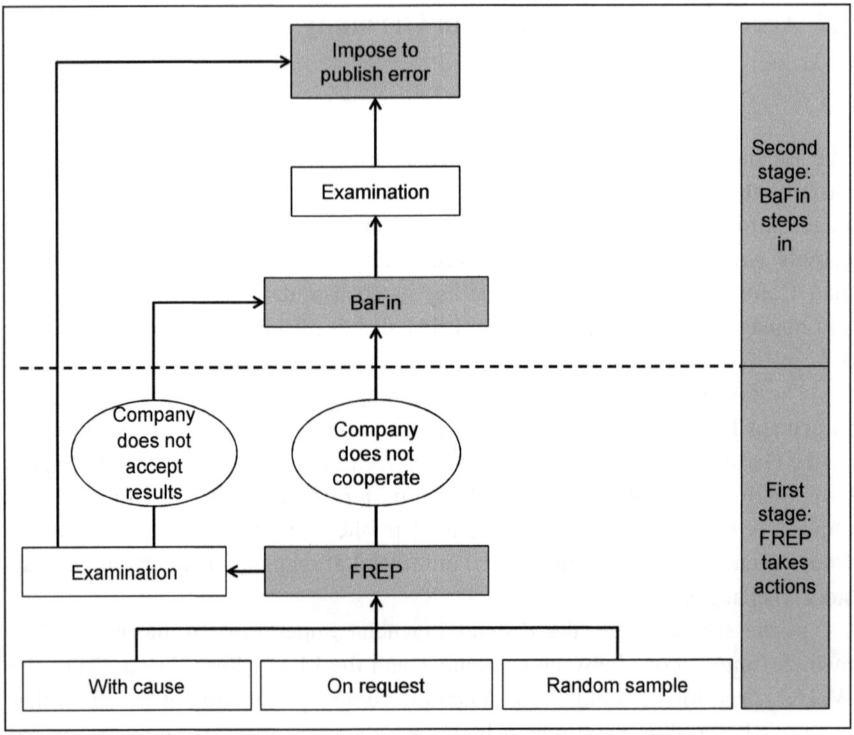

Figure 3.7: Accounting Enforcement in Germany
(source: own chart based on Paulitscheck 2009 , Zülch 2010)

The Balance Sheet Control Law was one of the reactions of the EC Transparency Directive from 2004, where it was codified that "each competent authority shall have all the powers necessary for the performance of its functions. It shall at least be empowered to: ... examine that information referred to in this Directive is drawn up in accordance with the relevant reporting framework and take appropriate measures in case of discovered infringements."[316]

In the previous year, in March 2003, the Committee of European Securities Regulators (CESR)[317] had developed a common enforcement approach to be applied by all members of the EU. The Committee released several standards, on

316 European Commission (2004), EC Transparency Directive 2004/109/EC, p. 54.

317 The CESR was established under the terms of the European Commission's Decision of June 6, 2001 in the context of the IAS regulation (European Directive 1606/2002).

top the CESR Standard No. 1[318] and CESR Standard No. 2[319], which both aim to harmonize the oversight enforcement systems in the EU.

In January 2011, the Committee of European Securities Regulators (CESR) was replaced by the European Securities and Markets Authority (ESMA). It came into force as part of a reworked regulatory framework adopted by the EU in the aftermath of the financial crisis.[320] This framework consists of three new European Supervisory Authorities (ESAs), ESMA, EBA and EIOPA, which have the function to settle disputes between national financial supervisors as well as impose temporary prohibitions on risky financial products and activities and, "if national supervisors fail to act, then the authorities may also impose decisions directly on financial institutions, such as banks, so as to remedy breaches of EU law".[321]

3.2.2 *Examination Triggers*

The FREP will initiate an examination in 3 triggering cases. Cases 1 and 2 are reactive measures, whereas case 3 is a proactive one:

1) if there are concrete indications of an infringement of financial reporting requirements (examination with cause)[322]
2) at the request of BaFin, when certain indications exist[323], or
3) without any concrete indications based on random sampling (random sampling examination).[324]

All three examination triggers are explained in the next subchapters.

---

318 ESMA (2003): CESR Standard No. 1.

319 ESMA (2004): CESR Standard No. 2.

320 REGULATION (EU) No. 1095/2010 OF THE EUROPEAN PARLIAMENT AND OF THE COUNCIL of 24 November 2010 establishing a European Supervisory Authority (European Securities and Markets Authority), amending Decision No 716/2009/EC and repealing Commission Decision 2009/77/EC.

321 EU press release as of September 2, 2010, EP adds bite to EU financial watchdog rules, available at: http://www.europarl.europa.eu/committees/en/econ/press-releases.html.

322 Sec. 342b(2)(1) of the HGB.

323 Sec. 342b(2)(2) of the HGB.

324 Sec. 342b(2)(3) of the HGB.

3.2.2.1 Examination with Cause (Concrete Indicators)

FREP initiates an examination if any cause is given. A cause as such is a concrete indicator of accounting infringement which can be communicated from shareholders, creditors or employees, for instance by whistle blowing.[325] Even press articles, breaking news, public discussions and interviews are sufficient to start an examination; however, blank hypotheses, guesses or speculations are insufficient.[326]

According to Sec. 342b (2) sentence 4 of the HGB, an examination with cause (trigger 1) shall not be conducted if it is evident that the conduct of the examination is not in the public interest.[327] However, law maker can insist on his right to initiate an examination if a material breach of accounting principles, which may impact investors' decision in the capital market, is possible.[328]

3.2.2.2 Examination on Request by BaFin (Certain Indicators)

According to Sec. 37p (2) of the WpHG, BaFin can request an examination by FREP under the conditions of Sec. 37o (1) of the WpHG, where concrete indicators of accounting infringements are given. In this regard, the wording of the law of Sec. 37o(1) of the WpHG is identical to Sec. 342 (2)(1) of the HGB.[329] Effectively, BaFin's right to request examinations is only a right to highlight concrete indicators of accounting infringement to FREP, or an formalized extension of trigger 1. In all other cases except of "concrete indicators of accounting infringement" BaFin can only trigger examinations, where double audits are required by law, such as Sec. 44(1)(2) of the KWG (German Banking Act) or Sec. 83 (1)(2) of the VAG; these are so-called special assignments to the Federal Financial Supervisory Authority.[330]

---

[325] Bundesministerium der Justiz (2004), Press release as of October 29, 2004: „Bundestag verabschiedet Bilanzrechtsreformgesetz und Bilanzkontrollgesetz".

[326] Bundestag (2004), p. 14.

[327] Compare to Bundestag (2004), p. 14; and Hennrichs (2004), p. 523.

[328] Bundestag 2004, p. 14.

[329] Sec 37o (1) of the WpHG: „Die Bundesanstalt (BaFin) ordnet eine Prüfung der Rechnungslegung an, soweit konkrete Anhaltspunkte für einen Verstoß gegen Rechnungslegungsvorschriften vorliegen"; Sec. 342b(2)(1) of the HGB: „...soweit konkrete Anhaltspunkte für einen Verstoß gegen Rechnungslegungsvorschriften vorliegen".

[330] Ellrott and Aicher (2006), p. 2302 and p. 2303.

3.2.2.3 Examination by Random Sampling (no Indicators)

The random sample selection is the proactive and preventive element of the enforcement procedure in Germany.

FREP describes its principles of random sample selection in the paper "Grundsätze für die stichprobenartige Prüfung gemäß § 342b Abs. 2 Satz 3 Nr. 3 HGB"[331] which had been agreed with both the Ministry of Finance and the Ministry of Justice in Germany. In its introduction, it refers to two standards of the ESMA (former: CESR), which build the basic principles of the random sample selection process. The first mentioned standard from ESMA "CESR Standard No. 1 on Financial Information – Enforcement of Standards on Financial Information in Europe"[332] contains 21 principles divided in six categories: definition of enforcement, enforcers, issuers and documents, methods of enforcement, coordination in enforcement and reporting (refer to table 3.3).

The second mentioned standard "CESR Guidelines on Application of Selection Methods" concretizes the principles 13 and 16 as well as the concept of risk of the CESR Standard No. 1. Principle 13 recommends a risk based approach which is combined with a rotation and/or a sampling approach. Additionally, principle 16 requires appropriate actions where a material misstatement is detected, it states that "where a material misstatement in the financial information is detected enforcers should take appropriate actions to achieve an appropriate disclosure and where relevant, public correction of misstatement...".[333]

Principles 16 and 13 (refer to table 3.3) synthesized result in a concept of risk that considers on the one hand the likelihood of a material misstatement in the financial statements and on the other hand the potential impact that such a material misstatement would have on market confidence and investors protection.[334]

The combination of the probability of an existence of a material misstatements and the potential impact on market confidence and investors' protections

331 FREP (2009a).

332 ESMA (2003): CESR Standard No. 1.

333 ESMA (2003): CESR Standard No. 1.

334 ESMA (2005), p. 3.

Table 3.3: Principles of Enforcement According to CESR Standard No. 1 (source: ESMA 2003[335])

Sub-ject	#	Principle
Definition	1	The purpose of enforcement of standards on financial information provided by the issuers mentioned by principle 9 is to protect investors and promote market confidence by contributing to the transparency of financial information relevant to the investors' decision making process. With regard to financial statements, the above implies that enforcement contributes to a consistent application of the IFRSs in the EU financial regulated markets.
	2	For the purpose of this standard enforcement may be defined as: – monitoring compliance of the financial information with the applicable reporting framework; – taking appropriate measures in case of infringements discovered in the course of enforcement. The reporting framework includes the accounting and disclosure standards adopted by the EU.
Enforcers	3	Competent independent administrative authorities set up by member States should have the ultimate responsibility for enforcement of compliance of the financial information provided by the issuers identified by Principle 9 with the reporting framework.
	4	Other bodies might carry out enforcement on behalf of the competent administrative authorities, provided that these bodies are supervised by and responsible to the relevant competent administrative authority.
	5	Irrespective of who carries out enforcement any standard on enforcement established by CESR should be complied with.
	6	Competent administrative authorities shall have adequate independence from government, and market participants, possessing the necessary powers and having sufficient resources.
	7	The necessary powers – which may be delegated to those acting on behalf of the competent independent administrative authority – should at least include power to monitor financial information, require supplementary information from issuers and auditors, and take measures consistent with the purposes of enforcement.
	8	The competent administrative authorities should be responsible for: – the setting up of an appropriate due process of enforcement consistent with the application of the principles hereby stated – the implementation of that due process.

335 ESMA (2003), pp. 2-5.

Subject	#	Principle
	9	The principles for enforcement here identified should apply to financial information provided by issuers: a) whose securities are admitted to trading on a regulated market; b) that applied for admission to trading of their securities on a regulated market.
	10	The principles for enforcement here identified should apply to financial information provided by all harmonized documents, including annual and interim financial statements and reports, prepared on individual and consolidated basis as well as prospectuses and equivalent documents.
Methods	11	For financial information other than prospectuses ex-post enforcement is the normal procedure, even if pre-clearance is not precluded.
	12	For prospectuses ex-ante approval is the normal procedure as specified by the EU directives, which also identify the nature of the approval. Ex-post enforcement of financial information provided by prospectuses is possible as a supplementary measure.
	13	Enforcement of all financial information is normally based on selection of issuers and documents to be examined. The preferred models for selecting financial information for enforcement purposes are mixed models whereby a risk based approach is combined with a rotation and/or a sampling approach. However, an approach based solely on risk may be an acceptable selection method. A pure rotation approach as well as a pure reactive approach is not acceptable. However, indications of misstatements provided by auditors or other regulatory bodies as well as well grounded complaints should be considered for enforcement investigations.
	14	In order to allow enforcers to adopt gradually the selection methods provided for by Principle 13, a mixed selection technique based on a combination of a random selection and rotation is considered a workable transitional step. However, such a methodology should be designed to give an adequate level of detection risk.
	15	Methods of enforcement on selected information cover a wide spectrum of possible checking procedures, ranging from pure formal checks to in-depth substantive in-nature checking. The level of risk should normally determine the intensity of the review to be performed by the enforcers. The type of document to be examined and the level of information available on the issuer is also to be taken into consideration.

Subject	#	Principle
Actions	16	Where a material misstatement in the financial information is detected enforcers should take appropriate actions to achieve an appropriate disclosure and where relevant, public correction of misstatement (in line with the requirements of the reporting framework). Non-material departures from the reporting framework will not normally trigger public correction even though they normally deserve an action as well. Materiality should be assessed according to the relevant reporting framework.
	17	Actions taken by the enforcers should be distinguished from sanctions imposed by the national legislation. Actions are measures generally aimed at improving market integrity and confidence.
	18	Actions should be effective, timely enacted and proportional to the impact of the detected infringement.
	19	A consistent policy of actions should be developed, whereby similar actions are adopted where similar infringements are detected
Co-ordination	20	In order to promote harmonization of enforcement practices and to ensure a consistent approach of the enforcers to the application of the IFRSs, coordination on ex-ante and ex-post decisions taken by the authorities and /or delegated entities will take place. Material controversial accounting issues will be conveyed to the bodies responsible for standard setting or interpretation. No general application guidance on IFRSs will be issued by the enforcers.
Reporting	21	Enforcers should periodically report to the public on their activities providing at least information on the enforcement policies adopted and decisions taken in individual cases including accounting and disclosure matters.

gives a measure of the overall risk to the objectives detailed in principle 1 (refer to table 3.3) of the CESR Standard No 1. ESMA therefore concludes that the concept of risk can be described with the following function:[336]

$$R = f(Prob; Impact) \tag{6}$$

Where:

R is the risk in the context of CESR Standard No. 1

Prob is the probability of material misstatement in the financial statements

Impact is the potential impact of such a misstatement on market confidence and investors protection

[336] ESMA (2005), p. 3.

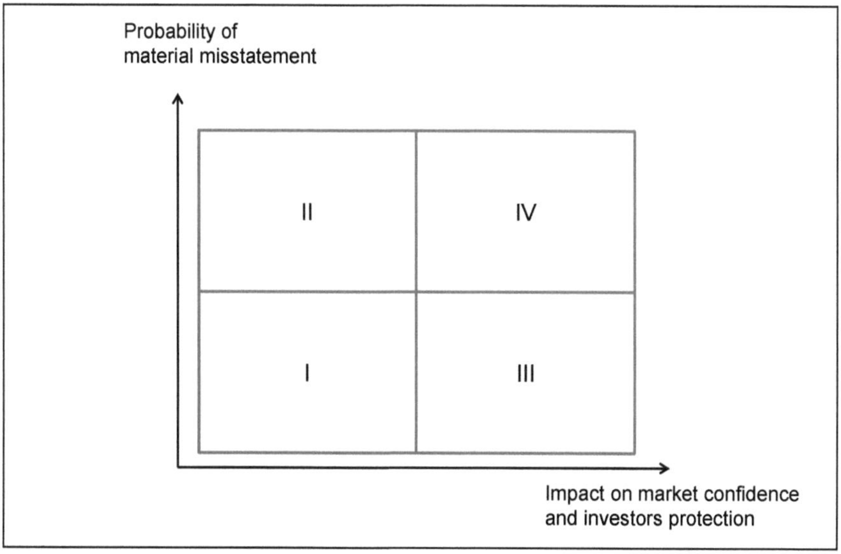

Figure 3.8: Applied Risk Function on Financial Statements Examinations (source: ESMA 2005[337])

Applying this risk function, all public interest entities could be distributed in one of the four boxes in the chart in figure 3.8.

Evidently, box IV contains the most risky issues on both dimensions. Thus, according to ESMA, enforcers should concentrate most of their effort on box IV. Nevertheless companies in boxes II and III should be selected for examination purposes as well.

Furthermore, ESMA adds that it is up to each EU enforcer to draw its selection line at the level appropriate to the characteristics and circumstances on its local jurisdiction. Based on figure 3.7 ESMA provides visually guidance on what is an appropriate selection and what is not appropriate (figure 3.9).

337 ESMA (2005), p. 4.

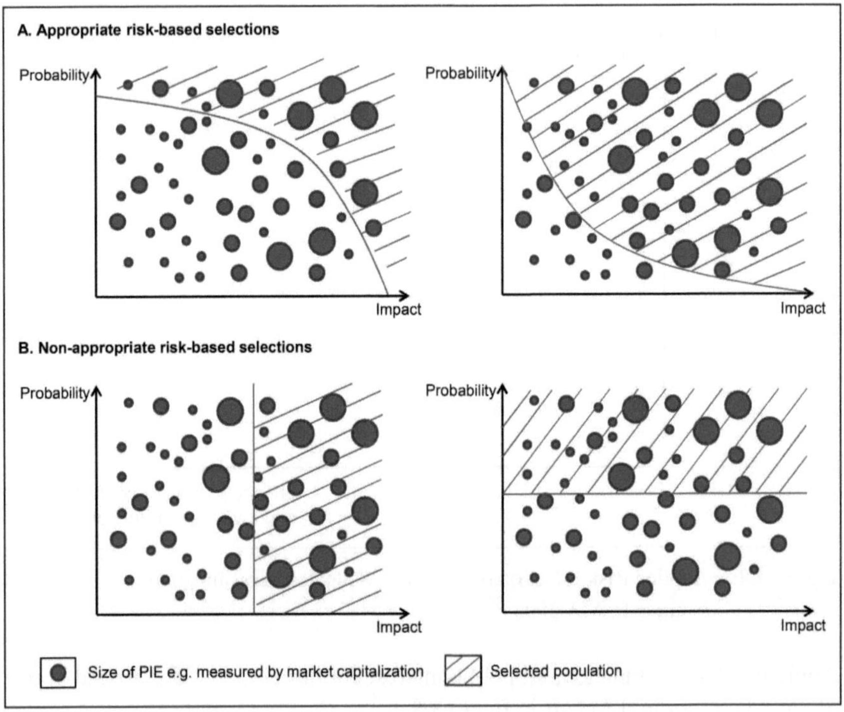

Figure 3.9: Guidance on Appropriate and Non-Appropriate Selection (source: own chart based on ESMA 2005[338])

As required, FREP has implemented this ESMA risk-based approach in a two components selection process:[339]

Component 1: pure risk-based selection
On the basis of any publications in news papers, television, journals or other public media, as well as of any hints that signal risk-carrying circumstances (e.g. first listing after IPO, extraordinary transactions such as acquisitions, mergers, corporate sales an transactions with related parties), economic situation and presentations on facts, FREP includes 30% of such cases in a sample.[340]

338 ESMA(2005), p. 4 and p. 5.

339 The two described components refer to FREP (2009a): p. 3 and p. 4.

340 FREP (2009a), p. 3.

Component 2: Stratifying risk-based selection
The other 70% of the examined cases shall be based on a stratified risk approach. The stratification is performed in two layers:

All entities of layer one are examined at least once within a cycle of 4 to 5 years. Layer one contains public interest companies listed in DAX, MDAX, SDAX and TechDAX. Entities of layer two are examined only within a cycle of 8 to 10 years. It contains all other public interest entities which are not covered by layer one.[341]

In order to ensure the objective of full coverage in the given cyclic periods of public interest entities in Germany, FREP takes 20% more companies than necessary. This makes sense since some companies will be put back to the population due to following facts: [342]

- Companies that are being dissolved
- Companies with headquarters abroad, which are in scope of another enforcer
- Companies with headquarters abroad, whose stock market turnover are negligible and therefore cost of the examination would exceed the benefit of it (cost-benefit-trade-off).

The samples are drawn annually and planned in line with the work force capacity planning. If FREP does not succeed in finishing all examinations according its planning the remaining examinations are forwarded to the subsequent year.[343]

3.2.3 *Enforcement Process*

3.2.3.1 Examination Commencement

As soon as one public interest entity is selected by one of three cases (with cause, by request of BaFin or random sampling) FREP clarifies the preconditions by reporting its examination intention to BaFin[344] and by contacting the selected company where it considers any potential reasons for examination exemption.[345]

---

[341] FREP (2009a), p. 3.

[342] FREP (2009a), p. 3.

[343] FREP (2009a), p. 4.

[344] The intention of an examination has to be reported to BaFin according to Sec. 342b (6) (1) of the HGB.

[345] Compare to chapter 2.2.2.3.

FREP only examines financial statements when the selected company accepts the cooperation with the enforcement panel. If the selected company declares officially its willingness to cooperate, the legal representatives of the company and the other assisting persons involved in the examination are obligated to provide accurate and complete information and to submit accurate and complete documents".[346]

If the selected company refuses its cooperation on the first stage of the enforcement process, FREP has to notify BaFin about the situation.[347] Subsequently, BaFin steps in and imposes an examination on the selected company at the second stage of the enforcement process.[348]

In the case of willingness to cooperate, FREP contacts the legal representatives of the company and requests responsible persons and other persons who can provide information about the company in terms of its financial reporting.[349] The independent auditor may also be involved in the examination process as he/she is competent in this matter and therefore can facilitate an efficient and appropriate examination process.[350] Note the independent auditor may only assist in the examination if released from his/her confidentiality obligation.[351] As it is preferred by FREP that the examination at the first stage should have access to the same sources of information as the second stage, it is appropriate to involve the independent auditor because he/she is required to provide information to BaFin at the second enforcement stage without any additional conditions.[352] Before the examination can start, FREP assigns internally a responsible chamber, a responsible panel member and a quality review panel member to the examination.[353] The complete commencement activities are summarized in figure 3.10.

346 Sec. 342b (4) sentence 1 of the HGB.

347 Sec. 342b (6) (2) of the HGB.

348 The rights of BaFin in this situation are codified in Sec. 37p (1) and 37o (1) of the WpHG.

349 FREP (2009b), p. 3.

350 FREP (2009b), p. 3.

351 Zülch, H. (2005), p. 5: "Voraussetzung für eine Auskunft durch den Abschlussprüfer ist allerdings, dass dieser durch das zu prüfende Unternehmen zuvor von seiner Verschwiegenheitspflicht entbunden wurde (vgl. Regierungsbegründung zum BilKoG, Abschnitt B, zu Art. 1, zu Nr. 2 zu § 342b, zu Abs. 4)".

352 FREP (2009b), p. 3.

353 FREP (2009b), p. 4.

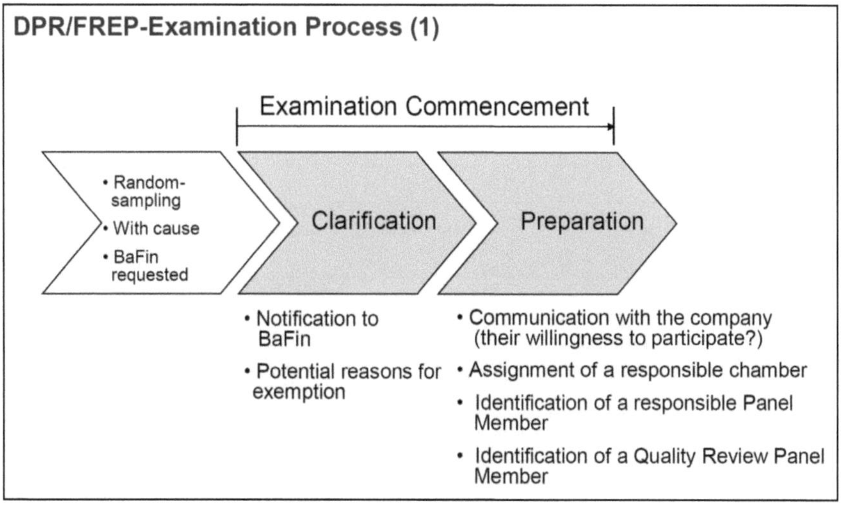

Figure 3.10: Commencement Process (source: FREP 2009c[354])

3.2.3.2 Examination Process

The assigned panel member contacts the company and requests the audit reports in addition to the individual or consolidated financial statements and the related management reports as well as the list of unadjusted audit differences; based on these first documents, he communicates the scope of the examination.[355]

The scope of both an examination with cause and an examination by request of BaFin are not congruent with a complete financial statements audit and should not function like a replacement of it; instead, the FREP initially focuses solely on key financial reporting areas.[356] Nevertheless, FREP is not impeded extending the scope in the course of the examination if other deviations from accounting standards are observed.[357]

Regarding a random-sample examination, FREP determines also based on the first documents (audit reports, financial statements, list of unadjusted audit differences) critical accounting areas for which questions exist concerning the

354 FREP (2009c): Examination Process (Graphic Chart).

355 FREP (2009b), p. 3 and p. 4.

356 Berger and Zemper (2012), comment on Sec. 342b of the HGB, recital 53, p. 2618; and Mareva, Milla (2010), p. 15.

357 FREP (2009b), p. 4.

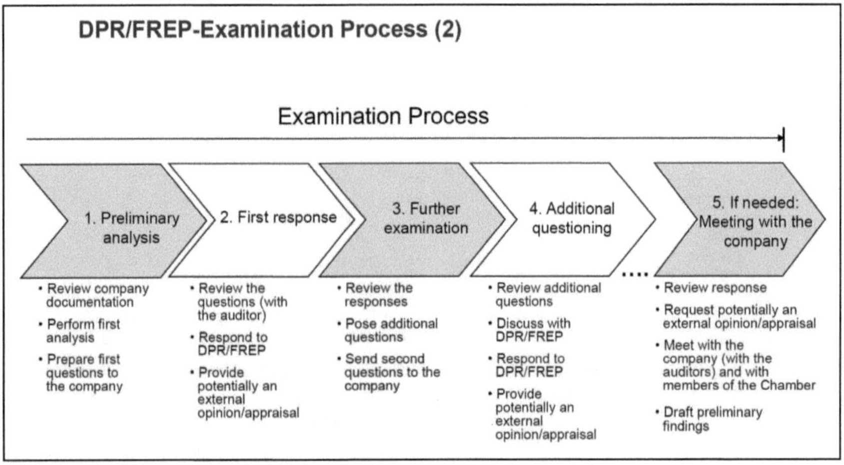

Figure 3.11: Examination Process (source: FREP 2009c[358])

appropriateness of the financial statements.[359] Hence, also in this case FREP starts its examinations based on a limited scope.

Normally, FREP corresponds with the company in a written form either via mail (not e-mail) or fax back and forth by reviewing documents and posing additional questions; however, in certain cases it can be appropriate to discuss complex accounting issues directly in a meeting, to which the financial statement auditors are also included, or to review detailed documents at the company's location; ideally, the responsible auditor will coordinate this with the company.[360]

The complete examination process is depicted in the exhibit (refer to figure 3.11).

3.2.3.3 Process for Publication

At the end of the examination, the chamber of the panel assesses the examination results and determines whether the company's accounting complies with the required standards or whether erroneous accounting exists.[361] If the chamber deter-

358 FREP (2009c): Examination Process (Graphic Chart).

359 FREP (2009b), p. 4.

360 FREP (2009b), p. 4.

361 FREP (2009b), p. 4.

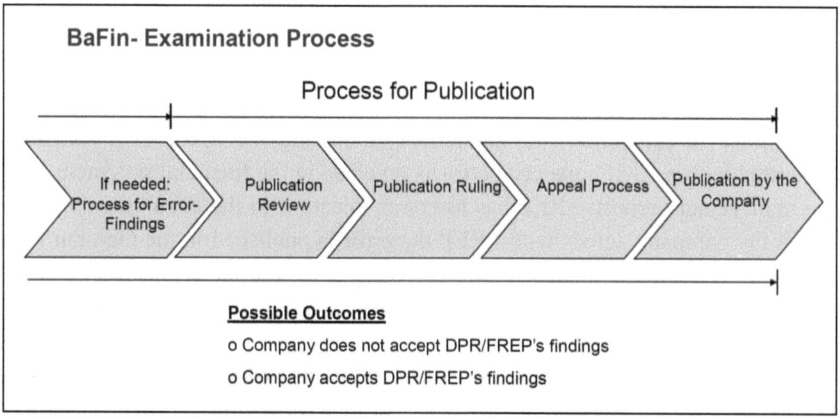

Figure 3.12: Process for Publication (source: FREP 2009c[362])

mines that the accounting is not erroneous, the FREP reports the results to both the examined company and to the BaFin.[363] In case the company agrees with FREP's finding of an accounting error, BaFin is informed again and orders the publication of the error (unless no public interest for such a publication exists); in case the company completely or partially does not accept the error assertion, BaFin will initiate an enforcement examination at the second stage and subsequently confirm or refuse FREP's results.[364] Afterwards, BaFin will order a publication of the error, if appropriate.

At the second stage of the enforcement procedure the company has the option to initiate a "Widerspruchsverfahren" (internal administrative appeal) against the order of publication of the error if it has serious concerns.[365] After this remedy has been exhausted, it can run for an appeal to court.[366] Once all appeals are unsuccessfully exhausted, the error is published" in the German Federal Gazette (for the complete process, refer to figure 3.12).

[362] FREP (2009c): Examination Process (Graphic Chart).

[363] The panel is obliged to do so according to Sec. 342b (5) of the HGB and Sec. 342b (6) (3) of the HGB.

[364] Sec. 37o (1) 19 of the WpHG „Anordnung einer Prüfung der Rechnungslegung…".

[365] Sec. 37t (1) of the WpHG; compare to Schmidt, Sutherland, van Schalkwyk, Low, Bockmann 2011.

[366] Sec. 37u (1) "Beschwerde" of the WpHG.

3.2.3.4 Materiality in the Enforcement Process

In the enforcement procedure in Germany, it is examined whether the financial statements and the management report of a selected company is compliant with the applicable principles and regulations, including the accounting standards permitted by law.[367] If a material error is revealed in the financial statement or in the management report, FREP has to communicate it to the examined company and if the company agrees with FREP the error is published in the German Federal Gazette by the company. If the company does not agree, but BaFin at the second stage confirms the error, the company is ordered to publish the error in the German Federal Gazette.[368]

At a first glance, this procedure seems to be quite easy. However, after a second reflection the question arises: what is an error for the enforcer? Is it any error or only materiality ones? And does the enforcer uses the concept of materiality the same way as the preparer and/or the auditor do?

In order to answer this question we need to go back to the ESMA enforcement framework, documented in its standards CESR Standard No. 1 and CESR Standard No. 2. According to principle 16 in CESR Standard No. 1 first it is mentioned that "where a material misstatement is detected … enforcer should take appropriate actions" and second "materiality should be assessed according to the relevant reporting framework".[369]

This means two things: first, by definition, only in case of material misstatements actions have to be taken, i.e. companies are enforced to publish their errors and second, applied to the German setting, FREP and BaFin have to assess materiality according to concept of materiality codified in the IFRS/IAS for all PIEs which are based in Germany. For all other PIE not based in Germany but trading their equity or bonds title at a regulated market at the Germany Stock exchange in Germany, FREP and BaFin have to assess materiality according to relevant accounting standards applied by the selected company.

Nevertheless, according to ESMA, enforcers in the European Enforcers Coordination Sessions (EECS) have recurring discussions about the "apparent dif-

---

367 Sec. 342b (2) of the HGB, Sec. 37n of the WpHG.

368 Sec. 37n (1) and 37n (2) of the WpHG.

369 Principle 16 of CESR Standard No. 1: "Where a material misstatement in the financial information is detected enforcers should take appropriate actions to achieve an appropriate disclosure and where relevant, public correction of misstatement (in line with the requirements of the reporting framework). Non-material departures from the reporting framework will not normally trigger public correction even though they normally deserve an action as well. Materiality should be assessed according to the relevant reporting framework." (ESMA 2003)

fering views regarding the practical application of the concept of materially amongst preparers, auditors, possibly users of the financial reports and, in some instances, accounting enforcers".[370]

This is why ESMA published a consultation paper containing 12 questions about the concept of materiality. The first question (Q1) opens the discussion again, whether the concept of materiality is clearly and consistently understood and applied in practice by preparers, auditors, users and accounting enforcers or is more clarification required.[371] Based on the first question, the second question (Q2) asked the audience whether more guidance in this regard should issued by ESMA.[372] The question catalogue goes on in asking deeper details about the concept of materiality.

Basically, the outcome of the discussion in the most of the responses by auditors, public interest entities, professional institutions and academics is that ESMA should not give further guidance on the concept of materiality, as it could lead to another version of the concept of materiality, which then is applied by the enforcers and not by the auditors and the preparers of the public interest entities.[373] The German Institute of Auditors (IDW) states in its response, that "by definition, materiality for the presentation of financial statements by prepares, and for auditors, financial reporting enforcement authorities and regulators, cannot be different than the materiality for users".[374]

In Germany, after having detected a potential misstatement the enforcer has to perform a so-called "Vertretbarkeitskontrolle".[375] When the FREP and/or BaFin identify a potential misstatement, they need to take into account the complete range of all possible accounting treatments to determine whether there is an actual misstatement.[376] Only if the stated deviation is outside of the range of all possible accounting treatments, an misstatement has been identified and should

370 ESMA (2011), Consultation Paper, Chapter "I. Introduction, item 2", p. 4.

371 ESMA (2011), Consultation Paper, Chapter "I. Introduction, Q1", p. 5.

372 ESMA (2011), Consultation Paper, Chapter "I. Introduction, Q2", p. 5.

373 The only one who has the legitimization to enhance the concept of materiality is the user (compare to IDW 2012: Response to "ESMA Consultation Paper: Considerations of Materiality in Financial Reporting", March 9, 2012, p. 2).

374 IDW 2012: Response to "ESMA Consultation Paper: Considerations of Materiality in Financial Reporting", March 9, 2012, p. 2.

375 Hennrichs (2009), p. 1452; and Sec. 342b of the HGB, Sec. 37q of the WPG; "Vertretbarkeitskontrolle" could be translated as "tenability test" or "check whether it is rationally defensible or justifiable".

376 Hennrichs (2009): Fehlerbegriff und Fehlerbeurteilung, DStR 2009, p. 1452.

then be evaluated as material or immaterial, depending whether it could influence users' decision or not.

3.2.4 *Summary of Enforcement Results*

3.2.4.1 Error Rate Trend

In the period from July 2005 to December 2012, FREP completed in total 848 examinations including 747 sampling examination, 77 examinations that were indication-based, and 24 on request by BaFin (figure 3.13).[377]

Fortunately, in terms of examination effort, the total number of companies subject to enforcement in Germany (population of the examination) has decreased in the last couple of years. In the period from July 1, 2005, where FREP started operations, to July 1, 2011, the number of PIEs in Germany decreased by more than 30% (from 1.249 to 873 entities).[378]

Hence, the yearly number of examinations[379] can be reduced and FREP will still meet its policy for sampling examinations, which requires an examination every 4 to 5 years of all companies included in a stock index, and every 8 to 10 years for all other companies.

The overall error rate for the years 2005 to 2012 is 22.6%, while the normalized[380] error rate in the same period is 21.6% on average. Based on FREP's activity reports from 2008 to 2011, the indication based examinations and the examinations on request by BaFin result in an error rate of 74.6% on average, whereby the examination by sampling result in an average error rate of 18.5.[381]

Each error in figure 3.13 reflects a set of erroneous financial statements. For instance, there were 27 financial statements found to be erroneous in 2011; only 18 in 2012. Each set of erroneous financial statements contains on average two to three infringements per company.[382]

---

377 Own analysis based on FREP's annual activity reports 2005 to 2011.

378 These figures include all PIEs examined by FREP both domestic and foreign based PIEs (FREP 2012, Annual Activity Report 2011, January 18, 2012, p. 3).

379 FREP's target corridor went down from 120-140 examinations in 2007 to 105-130 examinations in subsequent years

380 The normalized error rate reflects adjustments for duplicate errors as well as for examinations confirming known errors (FREP 2012, Annual Activity Report 2011, Berlin, January 18, 2012)..

381 Own analysis based on the FREP's activity reports 2008-2011 (FREP 2006, FREP 2007, FREP 2008, FREP 2009d, FREP 2010, FREP 2011, FREP 2012).

382 FREP (2012), Annual Activity Report 2011, Berlin, January 18, 2012, p. 7.

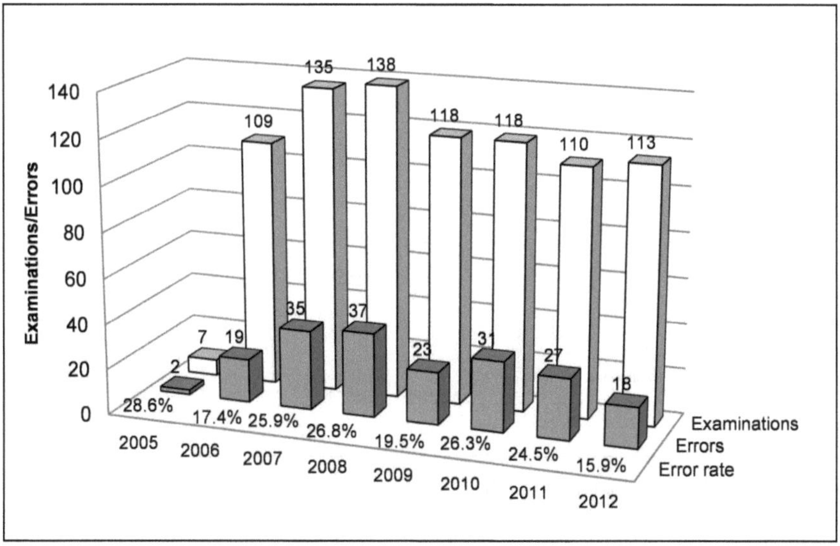

Figure 3.13: Completed Examinations, Error Rate Trend (source: FREP activity reports 2006-2012; www.frep.info)

3.2.4.2 Error Categories

FREP categorizes 15 major error types in its 7 activity reports from 2005 to 2012. The most frequent 8 errors types are ranked as follows:

1) Business combinations and disposals
2) Management report, certain note disclosures
3) Deferred taxes
4) Note disclosures (general)
5) Statement of cash flows
6) Financial Instruments
7) Revenue Recognition
8) Goodwill impairment

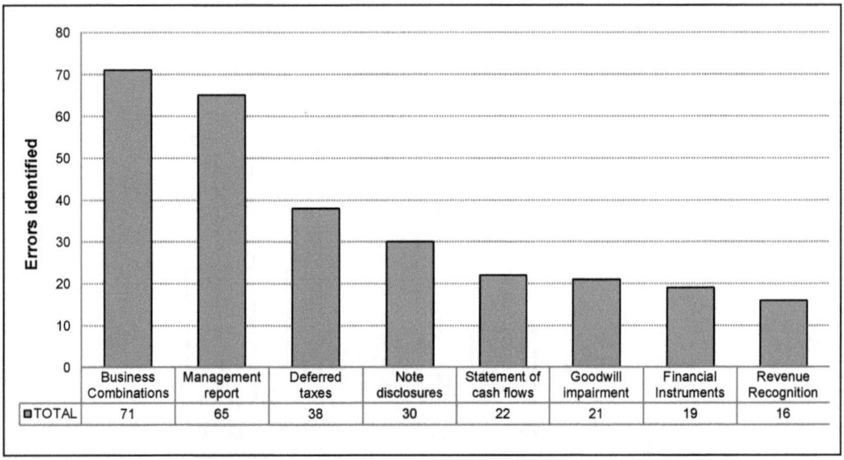

Figure 3.14: Most Frequently Identified Errors
(source: own analysis based on FREP's activity reports 2005-2012)

Figure 3.14 shows the frequencies of each error type. At a rate of about 80% the companies and their auditors accept FREP's findings without any hesitation.[383] In other terms, only in 1 out of 5 cases FREP needs to escalate to BaFin or to revise its findings by further investigations.

After all, the question remains about the root cause of this high error rate. Is the error frequency equally distributed through all stock market indices and what are the overall causes?

An analysis of the last three activity reports show that smaller companies listed in the SDAX, MDAX and TechDAX have higher error rate than the bigger companies listed in DAX; companies not listed have the highest error rate (figure 3.15).[384]

383 FREP (2012), Annual Activity Report 2011, Berlin, January 18, 2012, p. 6.

384 Own analysis on FREP's annual activity reports 2005-2011 (FREP 2006, FREP 2007, FREP 2008, FREP 2009d, FREP 2010, FREP 2011, FREP 2012, FREP 2013).

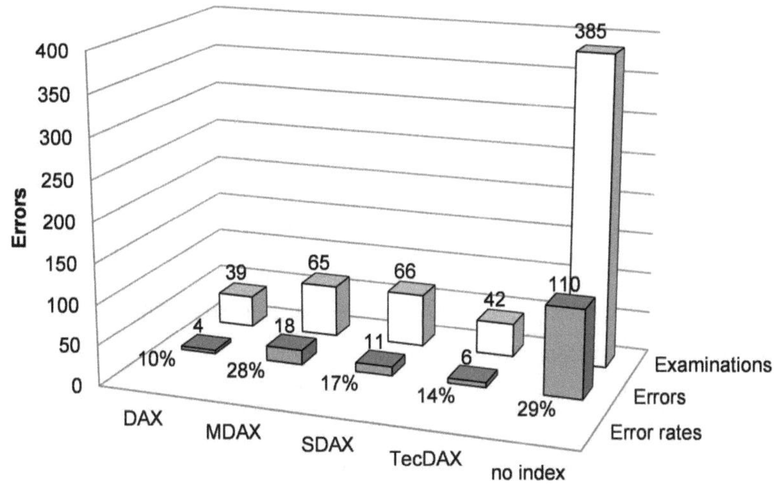

	DAX	MDAX	SDAX	TecDAX	no index
Error rates	10%	28%	17%	14%	29%
■ Errors	4	18	11	6	110
□ Examinations	39	65	66	42	385

Figure 3.15: Error Frequencies per Index
(source: own analysis based on FREP's activity reports 2005-2012)

3.2.4.3 Causes of High Error Rates

In its yearly activity reports, FREP lists the following main causes for the high error rates in its examinations (table 3.4):[385]

- Insufficient reporting in the management report and in the notes,
- Difficult application and interpretation of IAS/IFRS due to complexity
- Lack of knowledge of accounting standards
- Impact of the financial and economic crisis
- Excessive demands on small and medium-sized companies

Table 3.4 shows all main causes mentioned in the FREP's annual activity reports from 2007 to 2012.

---

[385] FREP's annual activity reports 2005-2011 (FREP 2006, FREP 2007, FREP 2008, FREP 2009d, FREP 2010, FREP 2011, FREP 2012, FREP 2013).

Table 3.4: Main Causes for Errors
(source: FREP annual activity reports 2007–2012[386], www.frep.info)

Activity Report	Main Causes of Errors
2012	■ Insufficient reporting in the management report and in the notes ■ Range and challenging application of certain International Financial Reporting Standards (IFRS)
2011	■ Insufficient reporting in the management report and in the notes, primarily on the potential impact of the financial and economic crisis on the situation of the company ■ Range and challenging application of certain IFRS
2010	■ Complexity of IFRS ■ Impact of the financial and economic crisis
2009	■ Scope and complex nature of IFRSs ■ Economic situation of the companies ■ Occasional lack of knowledge of standards ■ A small number of "black sheep"
2008	■ Scope and complex nature of IFRSs ■ Small and medium-sized companies and their auditors are often overwhelmed ■ A small number of "black sheep"
2007	■ Scope and complexity of the IFRS standards ■ Often excessive demands on small and medium-sized companies and their accountants ■ Occasional lack of knowledge of the standards ■ A few "black sheep"

3.2.5 *Evaluation of the Enforcement Methodology*

3.2.5.1 Evaluation Criteria

Before using the errors published in the German Federal Gazette as data basis for an audit quality measurement, it has to be ensured that the process which generates this data has itself a certain level of quality. The process is the enforcement process, which uses a set of methods applied in the sub-processes company se-

386 FREP's annual activity reports 2005-2011 (FREP 2006, FREP 2007, FREP 2008, FREP 2009d, FREP 2010, FREP 2011, FREP 2012, FREP 2013).

lection, examination and error publishing. Therefore, it is necessary to assess FREP's and/or BaFin's applied methodology: whether it is reliable, valid, consistent and objective.

The criteria used are same criteria referenced when assessing the quality of research studies and applied methods for both qualitative and quantitative analysis.[387] These criteria are:[388]

- Objectivity
- Reliability
- Validity
- Transparency
- Indication / adequacy
- Reflexivity
- Discussion of limitation
- Triangulation

Objectivity

The idea of objectivity (or intersubjectivity) in its purest sense assumes that the researcher uncovers a phenomena without affecting it.[389] The result of a study should be independent from the personal biases, values, and emotional involvement of the researcher.[390]

There are three areas to distinguish in terms of objectivity applied to a scientific method: (1) objectivity in (research) processing (Durchführungsobjektivität), (2) objectivity in evaluation (Auswertungsobjektivität) and (3) objectivity in interpretation (Interpretationsobjektivität).[391]

---

387 In this regard the examiner/enforcer is seen as the researcher and the examination is seen as research study.

388 "Gütekriterien" according to Hug/Proscheschnik 2010, p. 93 et seq.

389 Compare to Gabler Verlag (Herausgeber), Gabler Wirtschaftslexikon, Stichwort: Objektivität, online im Internet: http://wirtschaftslexikon.gabler.de/Archiv/8649/objektivitaet-v6.html.

390 Compare to Schurz, Gehard 2005: Einführung in die Wissenschaftstheorie, p. 27.

391 Compare to Gabler Verlag (Herausgeber), Gabler Wirtschaftslexikon, Stichwort: Objektivität, online im Internet: http://wirtschaftslexikon.gabler.de/Archiv/8649/objektivitaet-v6.html.

Reliability

A method is considered to be reliable if the research result can be reproduced under the same conditions such as the same method and the same surrounding circumstances.[392]

In the purpose of quantitative research, Kirk and Miller (1986) identify three types of reliability which relate to: (1) the degree to which a measurement, given repeatedly, remains the same (2) the stability of a measurement over time; and (3) the similarity of measurements within a given time period.[393]

Validity

The criterion of validity refers to how well a scientific method or an instrument truly measures what it is conceived and intended to measure.[394]

In social research, there are several types of validity as there are (1) content validity (refers to the extent to which a measure represents the entire range of possible items being measured), (2) criterion validity (examines the ability of the method to predict a variable that is designated as a criterion – further distinction between predictive and concurrent), (3) construct validity (refers to the degree to which a method measures the theoretical construct it intends to measure, further distinguished between convergent validity and discriminant validity), (4) internal validity (causal relationships can be determined) and (5) external validity (conclusions can be generalized).

Transparency

The requirement of transparency refers to how well the complete research process including all settings, methods, data, results, is documented and comprehensible for another researcher.[395]

---

392 Gabler Verlag (Herausgeber), Gabler Wirtschaftslexikon, Stichwort: Reliabilität, online im Internet: http://wirtschaftslexikon.gabler.de/Archiv/57492/reliabilitaet-v5.html.

393 Kirk and Miller (1986): Reliability and validity in qualitative research, pp. 41-42.

394 Gabler Verlag (Herausgeber), Gabler Wirtschaftslexikon, Stichwort: Validität, online im Internet: http://wirtschaftslexikon.gabler.de/Archiv/978/validitaet-v6.html.

395 "Gütekriterien" according to Hug/Proscheschnik (2010), p. 93 et seq.

Indication / Adequacy

The criterion of indication / adequacy requires that the research method should match best to the research question, i.e. qualitative methods should be used for subjective inquiries, quantitative methods for quantitative characteristics. [396]

Reflexivity

Research methods in social science are reflexive when they take into consideration the effect of the personality or presence of the researcher on the investigation.[397] Reflexivity in this sense is the capacity of the researcher to reflect upon his actions during the research.[398]

Widely interpreted, any kind of reflection even when triggered by outside feedback and/or reviews, serves as a mirror for the researcher and can therefore improve the quality of the research work.

Discussion of Limitation

As all research work unavoidably has some limitations. A good research study names and discusses its limitations. The discussion of limitations is essential for understanding a research finding, translating its importance, and placing the current work in the context within a discipline.[399]

Triangulation

Triangulation refers to the use of more than one approach for answering the research question in order to enhance confidence in the researcher's findings.

Denzin (1989) identified four basic types of triangulation (1) data triangulation (a variety of data sources are used), (2) investigator triangulation (more than one researcher is involved in an investigation), (3) theory triangulation (more than one theoretical scheme is applied in the interpretation of the phenomenon) and (4) methodological triangulation (more than one method is used to gather data, such as interviews, observations, questionnaires, and documents).[400]

---

396 "Gütekriterien" according to Hug/Proscheschnik (2010), p. 93 et seq.

397 Holland (1999), p. 464.

398 www.encyclo.co.uk/define/reflexity, item 4: Researching Society and Culture.

399 Ioannidis (2007), p. 324.

400 Denzin (1989), p. 239 et seq.

3.2.5.2 Evaluation by Criteria

3.2.5.2.1 Objectivity

Selection Methods

The applied selection methods are a combination of direct selections by indicators (concrete indicators or on request by BaFin) and a selection by risk based random sampling.[401] The selection by concrete indicators has a subjective element of judgment about the concreteness of the indicator and the indicators itself. As long as the indicators are publicly known and drawn from public sources such as newspapers, television, internet, they would be considered as least intersubjective, if not objective. However, when concrete indicators are communicated through anonymous letters, insider tips and other non-public ways, it is not possible to evaluate the objectivity in these cases. Instead, the selection is probably subjective. The same applies to the selection on request by BaFin as it follows the same pattern. The only difference is that BaFin triggers the examination by its research of concrete indicators.[402]

On the contrary, the selection performed through risk based random sampling follows always the same algorithm seemingly free from any biases.[403] The only issue here is the determination of the risk.[404] According to FREP's sampling guidelines[405] and CESR Guidelines on Application of Selection Methods[406], the risk is a function of the probability of material misstatement and its impact on market confidence and investor protection.[407] As we have learned from chapter two, the materiality assessment is subject to professional judgment. Therefore, the risk assessment is the subjective component of this approach.[408]

---

401 Sec. 342b(2) of the HGB and refer also to explanations in chapter 3.2.2 "examination triggers".

402 Sec. 37o(1) of the WpHG in conjunction with Sec. 37p(2) of the WpHG, compare also to explanations in chapter 3.2.2.2 "Examination on request by BaFin (certain indicators)".

403 Refer to chapter 3.2.2.3 "Examination by random sampling".

404 Refer to figures 3.7 and 3.8 in chapter 3.2.2.3.

405 FREP (2009a), p. 3.

406 ESMA (2005): Enforcement of Standards on Financial Information – CESR Guidelines on Application of Selection Methods, October 2005.

407 For explanations refer to chapter 3.2.2.3.

408 If risk was defined by business risk considerations according to the CAPM the β-factor of the equity would be an objective measure, which may be also appropriate. Arguments that support this approach in this regard refer to the way the auditor determines his audit risk. Starting from an assessment of the client's business risks, the auditor derives his audit risks (including the risk of material misstatement as there is AR=RMM*DR) and organizes his audit (efficiently) according to a top down risk approach (compare to ISA 300, ISA 315, ISA 320, and ISA 330).

However, the risk based random sampling approach is further combined with a rotation approach.[409] The rotation based selection shall ensure that FREP meets its policy goals. FREP's policy says that index-listed companies have to be examined every 4 to 5 years, non index-listed companies have to be examined every 8 to 10 years. [410] Hence, the more years are considered as data base the more objective the selection process becomes as the subjective components lose weight over the course of time. For instance, in a 10-year period all non-listed PIEs will have been examined at least once and index-listed companies will have been examined at least twice. Additionally, since FREP plans it resources and the number of examination annually, FREP aims to hit its policy goals as close as possible.[411]

Examination Methods

In the examination process, two parties are involved at least: the examined company and FREP (at the first stage).[412] These two parties consist of different individuals: the responsible person of the examined companies (for instance CEO, CFO, finance directors, accountants) and the responsible panel member of FREP.[413] It is very likely that the financial statement auditor is also involved, as FREP recommends its support during the examination. [414]

Both parties have different interests. The examined company (including its independent auditor) is biased to pass the examination without findings (since an error reporting can cause reputational and therefore financial damage). FREP instead follows the interests of the capital markets according to its mission[415] and

---

409 Refer to chapter 3.2.2.3 Component 2: stratifying risk based selection, p.31 and FREP 2009a: Grundsätze für die stichprobenartige Prüfung gemäß § 342b Abs. 2 Satz 3 Nr. 3 HGB, April 20, 2009, Chapter „Auswahlverfahren für die Stichprobenprüfung gemäß § 342b Abs. 2 Satz 3 Nr. 3 HGB".

410 FREP (2009a), p. 4.

411 Compare to the FREP's annual activity reports 2005-2011; for instance, refer to extract from the activity report published in 2010: "In 2009, the FREP completed a total of 118 examinations (previous year: 138; Figure 1) of which 103 were sampling examinations (prior year: 118). We are thus within our target corridor of approximately 110 – 140 examinations per year, which is based on the FREP's code of procedures; this provides that all companies listed in a stock market index are examined every 4 to 5 years and all other publicly traded companies are examined every 8 to 10 years." (FREP 2010)

412 Overview of the enforcement procedure refer to figure 3.7.

413 Refer to chapter 3.2.3.2 and FREP (2009b), p. 3 and p. 4.

414 FREP (2009b), p. 3.

415 "In the interest of the capital market, we wish to contribute to truthful and transparent accounting of capital market oriented companies. Our actions are based on the purpose of accounting and

operates independently, but may have some kind of performance pressure in terms of justifying its existence ("right to exist"). If it does not find any single problem, sooner or later, the questions will be raised why is there an enforcer in Germany and is the enforcer doing his job well enough. So, what we probably encounter at the first stage of the enforcement procedure are two parties with opposing interests. In this constellation, a common point of view about the detected material misstatement would be a good reason for grading the finding to a certain extent as true and therefore objective. Surprisingly, this occurs at around 80% of all cases.[416]

If the company does not agree, BaFin steps into the process.[417] At this point, a third party gets involved. The question here is whether BaFin is free from any biases or not. BaFin may tend to agree with FREP's opinion as BaFin does not want to doubt the credibility of FREPs judgment skills. However, BaFin is not a private institution but a federal authority, which aims not to show any biases. Further, it does not have any pressure to justify its existence in terms of detecting reporting breaches, because enforcement work is only a small portion of BaFin's normal responsibilities. Thus from this perspective BaFin is more neutral in its judgment.

Furthermore, at the second stage BaFin has the right to perform inquiries of the auditor without the requirement to release him first from his confidentiality obligation by his client.[418] At this point the financial statement auditor gets involved (if not already involved at the first stage), which results in having four parties (if every party has one representative, there are four individuals) debating the findings (the company, FREP, the auditor and BaFin). The more individuals in form of experts are involved in the assessment of error findings the more this approach resembles a heuristic method.[419] Nonetheless, at the second stage the errors are not published voluntarily. The publication of the error is ordered by BaFin's subsequent to its final decision on the examinations' finding.[420]

---

the related accounting standards, high professional quality, personal integrity and independence, excellence in our work and a reasonable sense of proportion." (Source: www.frep.info)

416 FREP (2011), p. 6.

417 Refer to chapter 3.6.

418 FREP (2009b), p. 3.

419 For instance compare to Groner, Groner and Bischof (1983): "Methods of Heuristics" p. 89 et seq.; and Kleining and Witt (2000): The Qualitative Heuristic Approach: A Methodology for Discovery in Psychology and Social Science.

420 FREP (2009b), p. 5.

However, if the company including its financial statements auditor does not agree at all, there are legal means to review BaFin's judgment in a lawsuit at a higher regional court.[421] If the higher regional court confirms the error, the examination findings probably are objective since it is reviewed by a court.

In sum, at around 80% percent of the cases – this is the companies' acceptance rate at the first stage – FREP's findings is the result of a possible opinion-trade-off between FREP and the involved public interest entity, which signals a certain level of intersubjectivity.

However, the involuntarily published errors may have a stronger objective note than the voluntary ones at the first stage of the enforcement procedure as more parties and experts get involved at the second stage.

3.2.5.2.2 Reliability

Selection Methods

The reproducibility of the results of the selection methods in terms of the selection by concrete indicators and the selection on request by BaFin (which is also based on concrete indicators see Sec. 37o of the WpHG) depends on how the collection and the evaluation of those concrete indicators work. If FREP gathers the indicators and assesses concreteness always in the same way, the re-performance of the selection method would deliver the same results, i.e. the same companies would be selected. However, evaluating the concreteness of an indicator requires some judgment and may depend on the individual who evaluates the indicators. So, the reproducibility of the selection results cannot be ensured in this regard.

The other element of the selection process is the risk based random sampling method. It delivers a random sample of a preselected population of PIEs minus the ones which are already drawn by direct selection. This method repeated would always deliver a random sample of the preselected population and is therefore reliable. The problem here is the pre-selection of the population. Applying a risk assessment, the population is segmented into more risky PIEs and less risky PIEs.[422] The random sampling is only applied on the riskier PIEs. If the segmentation in more risky and less risky PIEs would always follow the same procedure, the same part of the population would be preselected and the random

---

421 Refer to chapter 3.2.3.3 "Process for Publication", legal means such as "Wiederspruchsverfahren" (Sec. 37t(1) of the WpHG) and "Beschwerde" (Sec. 37u(1) of the WphG).

422 Refer to chapter 3.2.3 as well as the figures 3.7 und 3.8.

sampling would be reliable as such. However, as we have learned in chapter 3.2.3, the risk assessment of both the material misstatement and the estimation of the impact on market confidence have a subjective component.[423] From year to year, the PIEs selection can depend much on subjective parameterization in terms of the collecting and evaluating indicators as well as in risk assessment.

Considering the error reporting in the long run (every 10 years), a total population examination is ensured, as all PIEs are examined at least once (index-listed PIEs at least twice). Focusing on data that has been produced during a 10-year term, we can completely ignore FREP's judgment about indicators and risk assessment.

Examination Methods

According FREP's description of the enforcement procedure, the examination process follows always the same pattern. FREP first assigns internally a responsible chamber, a responsible panel member and a quality review panel member to the examination.[424] The assigned panel member contacts the selected company, clarifies the preconditions and requests the audit reports, financial statements and the management reports as well as the summary of unadjusted audit differences.[425]

FREP initially focuses solely on key financial reporting areas and on issues for which indications are provided for. The indicators based examinations (both concrete indicators or on request by BaFin) result in an error detection rate of 74.6%.[426] The high detection rate implies concrete indicators provide strong evidence of erroneous financial statements. This fact leads to the assumption, that there are good reasons for the reliability of the results, as the results are likely to be reproduced based on examinations of those concrete indicators.

Regarding the random sampling based examination, the assumption that the results can be reproduced is less certain. Although there is a lot of guidance to detect deviations between what is reported and what should be reported, the assessment of a material misstatement is (still) subject to professional judgment.

---

423 Compare to chapter 3.2.5.1 "Objectivity".

424 Refer to chapter 3.2.3.1 "examination commencement", pp. 99-100 and FREP (2009b): Information relating to the Examination Process of the Financial Reporting Enforcement Panel, October 2009, p. 3.

425 Refer to chapter 3.2.3.2 "examination process" and FREP 2009b: Information relating to the Examination Process of the Financial Reporting Enforcement Panel, October 2009, p. 4.

426 Refer to own analysis in chapter 3.2.4.1, p. 105.

However, in the cases where the examined company agreed on the results, the materiality assessment was likely easy to judge. This fact could lead to the assumption that in those cases, the FREP's findings can be reproduced as well. In all other cases where the company does not agree on FREP's findings, either the deviation from accounting standard is more difficult to state or the materiality assessment of the deviation is likely to be challenging. In these cases, the reproducibility of the findings cannot be guaranteed at all.

3.2.5.2.3 Validity

Selection Methods

The enforcement procedure is designed to examine all PIEs in cyclic periods: a 4 to 5 year cycle for index-listed PIEs and an 8 to 10 year cycle for non-listed PIEs.[427] On the other hand the numeric order of which PIE is examined first, second, etc. is determined in a context of a risk assessment. Concrete indicators of infringements, requests by BaFin and a random sample of a risky preselected population are considered first.[428] The remaining companies are selected without any prioritization and examined at least once in 8 to 10 years, with index-listed once at least once in 4 to 5 years.[429]

According to FREP's activity reports from 2005 to 2011 the selection methods work as intended. According to a study by PwC in the four years period from 2005 to 2008, FREP had already examined 89% of all index-listed German PIEs.[430] Thus, the selection methods which are intended to cover the complete PIE population can be rated as valid.

Examination Methods

FREP's examination is aimed to review whether PIE's financial statements and management reports comply with relevant accounting standards and law. The result is either positive or negative. The examination leads to an error reporting if the error is material and the company agrees. Further, the examination is not designed to perform and to replace a complete financial statements audit. In

427 FREP (2009a), p. 3.

428 FREP (2009a), pp. 3-4.

429 It is not clear why FREP overweight's the selection frequency of index-listed companies compared to non-listed companies by the factor of 2. Behind the regulations there is probably the assumption that index-listed have a higher importance for the capital markets.

430 PwC (2009), p. 10.

contrast, FREP normally focuses its examination on the given indicators and on the main areas of emphasis (which are pre-announced on a yearly basis on its homepage under press releases)[431] and has therefore a limited scope. FREP may extend the scope of the examination if there are sufficient reasons.[432] Hence, the examination methods work the way they are intended to work and can therefore be rated as valid.

3.2.5.2.4 Transparency

Selection Methods

The selection process is completely and thoroughly documented in FREP's policies and ESMA standards.[433] In its annual activity report, FREP documents the number of selected companies by selection method and index affiliations.

Examination Methods

The examinations procedure is documented roughly in the Germany Commercial Code (HGB), in the Securities Trading Act (WpHG) and in details in FREPs policy papers.[434] FREP describes the complete enforcement procedure in the sub-processes commencement, examination and publication both verbally and in flow chart diagrams. In its annual activity reports, FREP documents summary results of the work performed in the prior year.[435]

3.2.5.2.5 Adequacy

Selection Methods

The selection methods are a mix of a quantitative method as far as the random sampling is concerned and a set of qualitative and quantitative combined considerations in terms of risk for the capital markets.[436] For the pure quantitative part of the selection, a quantitative method is used. For the risk assessment and indicator evaluation, a rather qualitative approach is applied, since indicators have to

431 http://www.frep.info/presse/pressemitteilungen_en.php.

432 FREP (2009b), p. 4.

433 FREP (2009a): pp. 2-4.

434 FREP (2005): Code of Procedure, FREP (2009a): Grundsätze für die stichprobenartige Prüfung, FREP (2009b): Information Relating to the Examination Process.

435 FREP (2006), FREP (2007), FREP (2008), FREP (2009d), FREP (2010), FREP (2011), FREP (2012).

436 FREP (2009a), pp. 1-2.

be gathered and their concreteness has to be judged with a risk assessment performed.

Examination Methods

In order to detect misstatement, financial figures and contents are compared between what is required by accounting standards and what actually is reported in financial statements and in management reports.[437] This comparison has a mainly quantitative character as figures such as depreciations, amortizations, impairments, valuations, etc. have to be recalculated, with a basic review of recognition, classification, and mandatory disclosures. Underlying assumptions of management especially for impairments and valuations have also a qualitative character. In every case, when potential material misstatements are identified, qualitative factors have to be considered.[438]

All the core concepts and core methods which are used by an auditor are specified in the International Standards on Auditing. If the core concepts and core methods according to ISA are also applied by FREP, the FREP methodology should be considered inherently adequate, as the adequacy of ISAs is permanently reviewed and further developed.

3.2.5.2.6 Reflexivity

Selection Methods

The population, the random sampling and the numbers of examination that has to be performed in the following year is reviewed and adjusted annually in order to meet the overall goal to cover the complete PIE market in a certain period. The overall approach of the sampling selection had been updated in 2009 and reviewed and approved by the Germany Ministry of Finance and Ministry of Justice.[439] Thus, certain reflexivity in terms of selection methods is given.

Examination Methods

FREP's examination methods itself are not explicitly reviewed. However, FREP's examination results are reviewed on different levels. First, within FREP

---

437 Refer to chapter 3.1.2.1 “Misstatements in Financial Statements” as well as definitions in IAS 8.41 and ISA 240.2.

438 Compare to IASB Conceptual Framework 3010 (QC11), ISA 320.2 and ISA 450.A16.

439 FREP (2009a), p. 1: „Beschlossen von der Prüfstelle und Erteilung des Einvernehmens durch das Bundesministerium der Justiz und das Bundesministerium der Finanzen am 20. April 2009”.

there is a quality review (quality control panel) and final approval of the responsible chamber[440]. Second the examined company including its financial auditor is allowed to criticize and disagree with the results. Subsequently, at the second stage of the enforcement procedure BaFin steps in and reviews the results independently.[441] Last but not least, if there is still no agreement reached the enforcers' result can be reviewed in a lawsuit by a higher regional court.[442] So, there is inherently permanent feedback and control over the enforcers' examination results, which can be interpreted as a certain way of reflexivity to the examination process.

3.2.5.2.7 Discussion of Limitations

Selection Methods

The criterion "discussion of limitations" needs a wide interpretation in context of FREP's activities as FREP is neither a scientific researcher who publishes scientific research nor an academic institution producing research results. However, the selection methods are discussed with naming some limitations in the CESR guidelines.[443] In the guidelines there are examples both appropriate and inappropriate selection approaches. FREP continues this discussion in its sampling guidelines policy where is provides further details on how FREP parameterizes the ESMA approach documented in the CESR guidelines.[444]

Examination Methods

FREP discusses limitations in terms of the scope of the examination. The examination is not designed to re-perform or to replace a complete financial statements audit. Usually, the examinations are very focused on indicators and high risk topics derived from the summary of unadjusted audit differences and the examination areas of emphasis ("Prüfungsschwerpunkte") in the relevant examination year.[445]

---

440 FREP (2009b), p. 5.

441 Refer to chapter 3.2.3.2.

442 Refer to chapter 3.2.4.

443 ESMA (2005), pp. 2-4.

444 FREP (2009a), pp. 1-4.

445 FREP (2009b): p. 4; and publications of the Examination Area of Emphasis from 2007 to 2012, http://www.frep.info/pruefverfahren/pruefungsschwerpunkte_en.php (August 12, 2012, 11:00 CET).

Some limitations and problems are mentioned in FREP's annual activity reports. For instance, activity reports have highlighted errors from the complexity of IFRS and potential accounting standard improvements, as a result of the discussions between preparers, auditors and FREP examiners.[446]

3.2.5.2.8 Triangulation

Selection Methods

The selection process is certainly a mix of different methods. However, the different methods are complementary and not potential substitutes of one-another to double-check results. Thus, a method triangulation in terms of selection method is not indicated.

Examination Methods

In terms of examination, there is a certain form of triangulation in case the company does not agree on FREPs findings. At the second stage, BaFin examines the results which could be interpreted as an investigator triangulation, since there is more than one examiner involved in the examination.[447]

3.2.5.2.9 Evaluation Summary

We can conclude that the examination procedures produce objective, reliable and valid results (over all in the long run) and the methods are transparently documented, and adequately applied, as well as reflexive in a controlled and reviewed manner. Limitations are discussed to some perspectives and a triangulation is given in a sort of investigator triangulation at the second stage of the enforcement procedure. Table 3.5 clearly summarizes the results of the previous subchapters.

---

446 For instance, refer to FREP (2012), p. 8 (main causes), p. 9 (error prevention).

447 Refer to chapter 3.5.1 "Triangulation".

Table 3.5: Summary of the Assessment of the Enforcement Methodology

Criteria	Selection methods	Examination methods (incl. results' assessment methods)
Objectivity	(+/–) ■ Parts of the selection methods depend on subjective assessments (indicators and risk). ■ Over 10 years, subjectivity is more limited as the total population is examined.	(+) ■ There are at least two parties involved in the examination. ■ In 80% of the cases the examined companies agree with FREP's finding. ■ Several parties and individuals/ experts are involved (heuristic approach)
Reliability	(+/–) ■ The random sampling method is reproducible; the direct selections by indicators are difficult to reproduce ■ Over 10 years, the total population is examined, which is reproducible	(+) ■ The examination follows always the same pattern ■ A material misstatement at the first stage of enforcement procedure would probably be redetected on a repeated examination
Validity	(+) ■ It is intended to examine all PIE, the risky ones first. On the one hand, the selection methods follow a risk based approach and on the other hand it is ensured that all PIEs are examined within certain periods.	(+) ■ Examinations are intended to review whether a PIE's financial report complies with standards and law.
Transparency	(+) ■ Selection methods are thoroughly documented	(+) ■ Examination process is completely documented

Criteria	Selection methods	Examination methods (incl. results' assessment methods)
Indication / adequacy	(+) ■ There are qualitative and quantitative characteristics to be considered in the selection process. ■ For pure quantitative question the random sampling is applied, for mixed characteristics qualitative assessment are used for	(+) ■ Detecting deviations from accounting standards have a quantitative touch ■ Assessment of material misstatements requires quantitative and qualitative considerations ■ FREP applies the guidelines and methods in accordance with international standards
Reflexivity	(+) ■ Number of selections are reviewed and adjusted yearly to meet FREP's policy goals ■ Selection methods had been updated in 2009 and approved from the Ministry of Finance and the Ministry of Justice	(+) ■ Not methods but examination results are reviewed at different levels. ■ At the first stage first within FREP, than by the company (and its financial statements auditor) ■ At the second stage follows a review by BaFin and where required by a court
Discussion of limitations	(+/–) ■ The selection methods and its limitations are discussed to some extent in the CESR and FREP guidelines	(+/–) ■ Limitations to the scope of the examinations are mentioned ■ Some limitations are discussed in the annual activity reports (such as error causes, problems with standards, discussions with auditors)
Triangulation	(–) ■ No triangulation apparent relating to selection methods	(+/–) ■ In cases where BaFin examines too there is a kind of investigator triangulation

3.3 Published Reporting Errors as Audit Quality Indicator

3.3.1 Audit Failure Rates Definitions

3.3.1.1 Auditors' Absolute Failure Frequency

Starting from the point that all in the German Federal Gazette published reporting errors result from material misstatements (assumption "A2" in chapter 1.4, discussed in chapter 3.1) and that auditors have the overall objective to detect material misstatement, we assume that the German Federal Gazette published errors are not only accounting errors but also indicate auditing failures (assumption "A1" in chapter 1.4, discussed in chapter 3.2) and could therefore be used to develop a direct audit quality measurement for PIE auditors.[448]

The published reporting errors in the German Federal Gazette establish the data base, which is enriched with the information of the relevant fiscal year of error and belongs to and with the auditor, who audited the financial statements including the management report of the respective company. The information about the auditor of the financial statements for the relevant fiscal year is retrieved from the respective annual report of the examined public interest entity. Linking this data together we can obtain the absolute frequency of failures per auditor as follows:

$$AFF_{\mathrm{nT}} = \sum_{t=1}^{T} PRE_{\mathrm{tn}} \qquad (7)$$

Where:

AFF_{nT}: Absolute Frequency of Audit Failures of Auditor n over T periods
PRE_{nm}: Published Reporting Error m of Auditor n
n: 1...N: all PIE auditors involved in published reporting errors
t: $1....T$: periods of examinations

Example: The AFF of BDO in the period from mid 2005 to end 2012 is 16, which means that since FREP have started operations there have been 16 reporting errors published by BDO's PIE clients.

---

[448] A PIE auditor in Germany is an auditor or an audit firm which has audit engagements according to Sec. 319a of the HGB; a PIE itself is defined in Sec. 264d of the HGB.

3.3.1.2 Auditors' Relative Failure Frequency

The absolute frequency of audit failures per audit firm cannot be used as a measurement because audit firms vary in numbers of PIE clients. Therefore we need to put the absolute frequency in relation to a reasonable reference basis. This reasonable reference basis can be the number of PIE clients of each auditor.[449] The number of PIE clients for each PIE auditor is published in the mandatory annual transparency report of the audit firm.[450] The relative number which puts the absolute failures in relation to the number of PIE clients is called Auditor's Failure Rate (AFR) and is defined as following:

$$AFR_{\mathrm{nT}} = \frac{AFF_{\mathrm{nT}}}{\frac{1}{T}\sum_{t=1}^{T}\sum_{p=1}^{P_n} PIE_{\mathrm{np}}} \tag{8}$$

Or:

$$AFR_{\mathrm{nT}} = \frac{\sum_{t=1}^{T} PRE_{\mathrm{tn}}}{\frac{1}{T}\sum_{t=1}^{T}\sum_{p=1}^{P_n} PIE_{\mathrm{np}}} \tag{9}$$

Where:

AFR_{nT}: Auditor's Failure Rate of Auditor *i* in a given period
PRE_{nm}: Published Reporting Error *j* where auditor *n* is assigned to
PIE_{np}: Public Interest Entity *k* where auditor *n* is assigned to
AFF_{nT}: Absolute Frequency of Audit Failures of Auditor *n* over all periods
n: 1…N: all PIE auditors assigned to published reporting errors
p: 1…P_n: all PIE clients of an auditor *n*
t: 1….T: periods of examinations

Example: AFR of BDO (BDO has index n=4) after 7.5 years of examinations:[451]

$$AFR_{47} = \frac{16}{\frac{1}{4}(40+54+49+57)} = 0.32 = 32\%$$

[449] For further discussion on a reasonable reference basis, refer to chapter 3.3.3.2 "Relative failure frequencies".

[450] Sec. 55c of the WPO (Public Accountants Act).

[451] AFF = 16 refer to appendix B, average number of PIE clients is calculated from 4 periods due to lack of data, refer to BDO transparency reports 2009 (40), transparency report 2010 (54), transparency report 2011 (49) and transparency report 2012 (40).

3.3.2 Data Description

3.3.2.1 Data Basis

FREP started operations in 2005 after the Balance Sheet Control Law was enacted in December 2004. Since this date, over 800 examinations have been completed.[452] As a result of this work, 186 financial reporting errors have been published in the German Federal Gazette (refer to appendix A).[453] These 186 published reporting errors (PRE) are the initial data basis of this empirical study.

Detected Errors vs. Published Errors

Comparing the number of detected reporting errors (refer to chapter 3.2.4.1, figure 3.13) with the number of published reporting errors, there is a total difference of 6 errors in the years from 2005 to 2012 (figure 3.16).

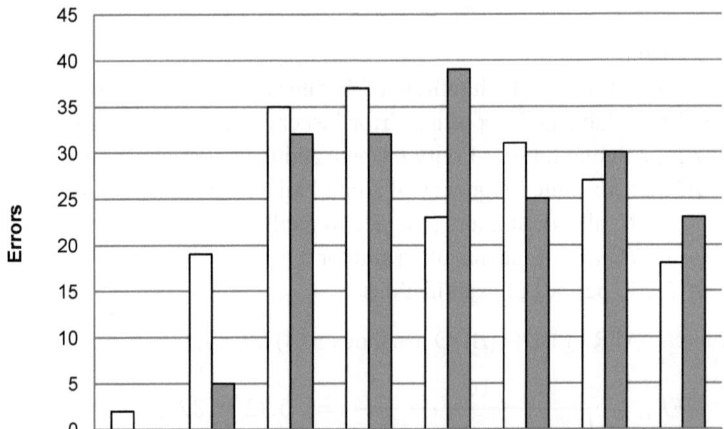

	2005	2006	2007	2008	2009	2010	2011	2012
□ Detected: 192	2	19	35	37	23	31	27	18
■ Published: 186	0	5	32	32	39	25	30	23

Figure 3.16: Detected Errors vs. Published Errors

452 In the period from July 2005 to December 2012, FREP completed in total 848 examinations, refer to chapter 3.2.4.1).

453 www.bundesanzeiger.de.

The difference arises from three aspects: (1) timing gap between the date where FREP closes the file and the date of error publication by the company and/or (2) companies' disagreement of error finding and refusal of error publication even after being ordered to publish by BaFin (at the second stage of the enforcement process) or (3) BaFin revises FREP's result and does not order the company to publish error. Hence over the total periods, the sum of all published reporting errors (PRE) is always smaller or equal to the sum of all detected reporting errors (DRE) by FREP. This fact has to be taken into account when discussing results, which are based either on published or on detected accounting errors.

3.3.2.2 Distribution of Absolute Failure Frequencies

Assigning the auditors who have served as financial statement auditors to the 186 published reporting errors, results in 61 audit firms involved.[454] On average each audit firm is burdened with 3 reporting errors. Since audit firms vary significantly in size and numbers of PIE engagements the distribution of the absolute failure frequency is quite unequal (which indicates the market concentration in PIE audit market):

- 40 audit firms have 1 failures,
- 10 audit firms have 2 failures,
- 7 audit firms have 3 failures,
- The remaining 6 audit firms have 5, 13, 16, 18, 23, and 30 failures respectively (figure 3.17).

[454] Refer to appendix B, table B.1.

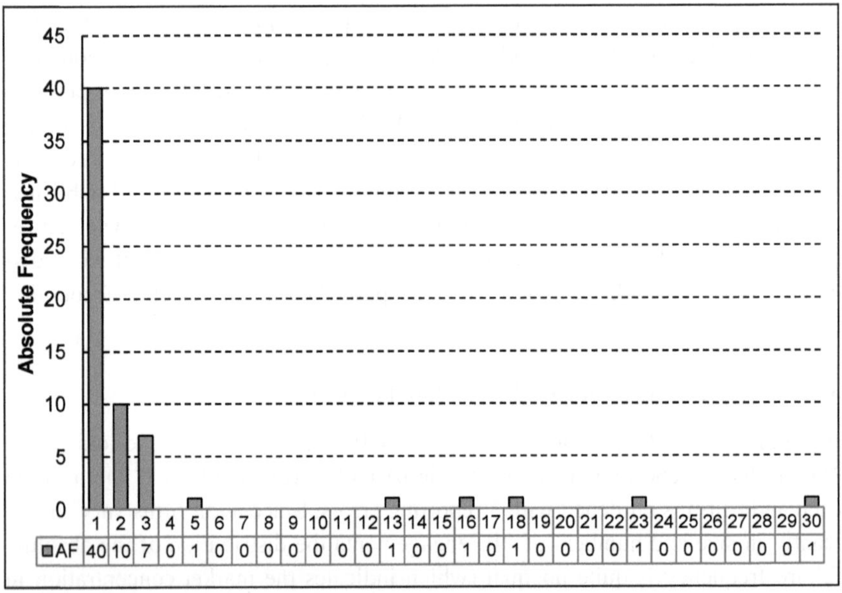

Figure 3.17: Distribution of Absolute Failures Frequencies (AFF)

3.3.2.3 PIE Market Concentration

On average for the years from 2007 to 2010, 900 PIEs had been audited by 124 PIE auditors.[455] The biggest 7 audit firms share 551 PIE clients (61.2%); the other 117 PIE auditors provide financial statement audit service for 349 clients (38.8%).[456] Table 3.6 shows the market shares of the PIE auditors. The biggest 7 PIE auditors are exhibited individually, the remaining 117 PIE auditors are grouped in the position "all others" (see table 3.6).

---

455 WPK (2011): Anbieterstruktur, Mandatsverteilung und Abschlussprüferhonorare im Wirtschaftsprüfermarkt 2010, Magazin 4/2011, p. 23; WPK (2010): Anbieterstruktur, Mandatsverteilung und Abschlussprüferhonorare im Wirtschaftsprüfermarkt 2009, Magazin 4/2010, p. 21; WPK (2009): Anbieterstruktur, Mandatsverteilung und Abschlussprüferhonorare im Wirtschaftsprüfermarkt 2008, Magazin 4/2009, p. 16; WPK (2008a): Anbieterstruktur, Mandatsverteilung und Abschlussprüferhonorare im Wirtschaftsprüfermarkt 2007, Magazin 4/2008, p. 19:

Year	2010	2009	2008	2007	2006	2005	2004
∑PIEs	855	907	923	916	872	916	971

456 The biggest 7 PIE auditors in this context are defined by the number of PIE clients. They all have more than or equal to 10 PIE clients on average in the last four years (according to their transparency reports).

Table 3.6: PIE Auditors and PIE Clients in the German Audit Market

Audit firm	PIE clients[457]	Counts	% PIE auditors	% PIE	Sum % PIE auditors	Sum % PIE
all others[458]	349.00	117	94.4%	38.8%	94.4%	38.8%
PKF	10.00	1	0.8%	1.1%	95.2%	39.9%
ESMB	17.75	1	0.8%	2.0%	96.0%	41.9%
BDO	49.25	1	0.8%	5.5%	96.8%	47.3%
Deloitte	57.75	1	0.8%	6.4%	97.6%	53.8%
E&Y	120.75	1	0.8%	13.4%	98.4%	67.2%
KPMG	145.50	1	0.8%	16.2%	99.2%	83.3%
PwC	150.00	1	0.8%	16.7%	100.0%	100.0%
	900	**124**	**100.0%**	**100.0%**		

Based on the figures in table 3.6 a market concentration can be calculated according to the following formula:[459]

$$G = \frac{2\sum_{i=1}^{n} i y_i}{n\sum_{i=1}^{n} y_i} - \frac{n+1}{n} \qquad (10)$$

Where:
G: Gini coefficient
y_i: values, indexed in non-decreasing order ($y_i \leq y_{i+1}$)
i: $1 \ldots n$: index of values, n: number of values
$0 < G \leq 0.3$: weak concentration
$0.3 < G \leq 0.7$: medium strong concentration
$0.7 < G \leq 1$: very strong concentration

Graphically the Gini coefficient is equal to the area encased between the line of equality (45 degree) and the Lorenz curve (% PIE in figure 3.18) divided by the area of the triangle (0%; 0%), (0%; 100%) and (100%; 100%).

[457] Average values based on Transparency Reports 2009–2012 of the respective audit firm.
[458] For simplification reasons we assume an uniform distribution.
[459] Bamberg/Baur (1996), p. 27 "Gini Koeffizient".

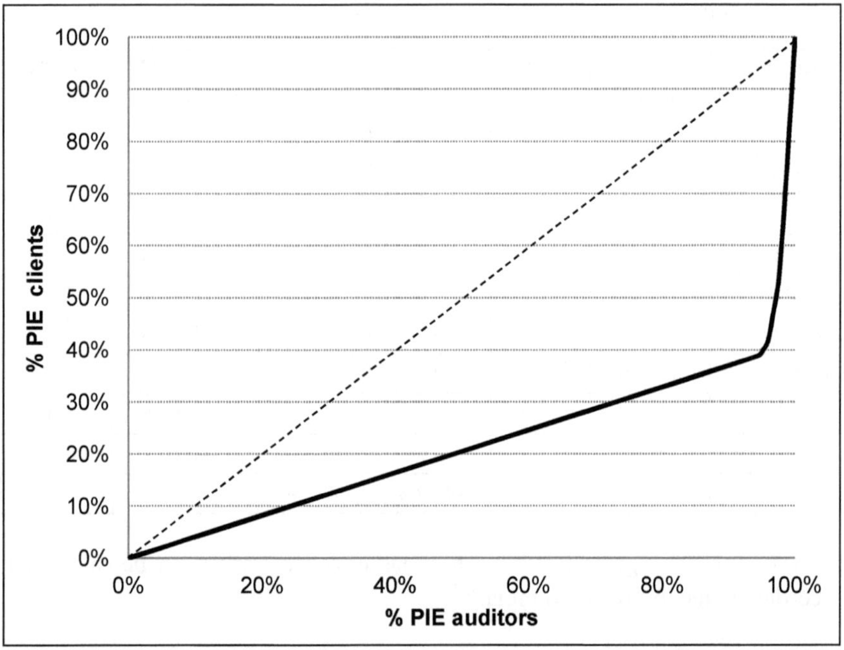

Figure 3.18: Concentration in the PIE Audit Market

The Gini coefficient in the applied case amounts to 0.57 and reflects a medium strong concentration on the PIE audit market. The 7 biggest audit firms in Germany audit 61.2% of all PIEs in Germany.[460]

3.3.2 Data analysis

3.3.2.1 Absolute Failure Frequencies

Focusing on audit firms which have an absolute failure frequency of more than or equal to 3 failures in the total period since errors have been published, we obtain a chart of 13 audit firms in figure 3.19 (data based on appendix B, table B.1).

460 The 7 biggest audit firm measured in terms of the size "PIE clients".

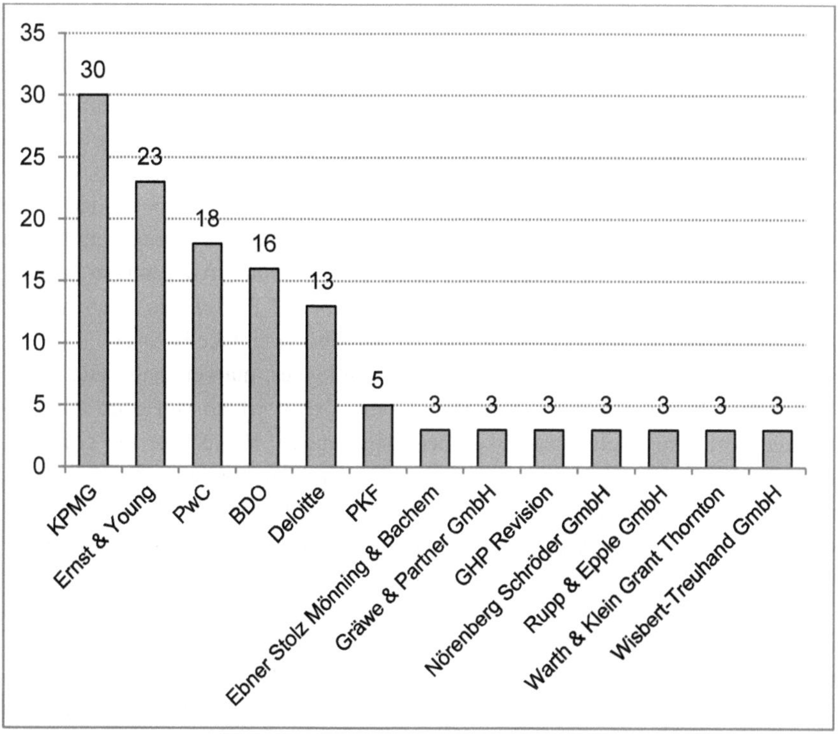

Figure 3.19: Absolute Failure Frequencies per Audit Firm (AFF ≥ 3)

Although the biggest 3 audit firms in Germany (PwC, KPMG, Ernst & Young) are comparable in terms of turnover, employees and number of PIE clients, there is a wide spread in absolute audit failure frequencies. Especially PwC, the biggest audit firm in Germany[461]; has 32% less failures than its two biggest competitors across all periods.[462] Further conclusions from absolute failure frequencies are difficult to draw due to the fact that audit firms vary in numbers of PIE clients. To address this problem, an appropriate reference basis is required.

---

461 Measured in turnover according to the financial statements of the big4 audit firms.

462 (((30+23)*1/2)-18) / ((30+23)*1/2) = 0.33.

3.3.2.2 Relative Failure Frequencies

Evidently, the most appropriate reference basis for a relative audit failure frequency would be the number of PIE clients of each audit firm examined by FREP in a given period. Unfortunately, the names of all companies which had been examined in a given time period (for instance calendar year) are not published. Only PIE clients with errors in its financial reporting are published in the German Federal Gazette. Nor FREP publishes in this respect more details than the total number of started and completed examinations in its annual activity report. Hence, we need a surrogate for the number of PIE clients of each audit firm, examined by FREP in a given period. Possible reference basis could be any size measures such as turnover, number of employees, market share, etc. of the audit firm. However, there is another reference basis, which is a good approximation to the best reference basis mentioned above. If we take the complete enforcement process, including FREP's polices and the way how FREP's selects its companies to examine, into considerations, we may consider the total number of PIE clients for each audit firm as an appropriate reference basis (refer to equation 8 in chapter 3.3.1.2).

According to its policy, FREP aims to examine all PIE entities in a period cycle. Hence, we can consider FREP's sampling and selection process as a selection approach where the sum of all samples in a complete cycle equals the whole population. For instance, for the index-listed PIEs, FREP will have examined all entities within 4 to 5 years.[463] Thus, over a 4.5-year cycle on average, we can expect that approximately all of index-listed PIEs were examined. Therefore, if we select all published reporting errors of index-listed companies in a 4.5-year period, the reference basis of all examined PIE per auditor would correspondent to all PIE clients per auditor. Obviously, the number of the examined PIE clients converges to the number of all PIEs in the course of time cycle. If an examination cycle time is passed (e.g. 4-5 years for index-listed PIEs), all PIEs are examined. In order to evaluate the appropriateness of the proposed reference basis, the measure "population coverage ratio" is introduced. The population coverage ratio is an estimation of what percentage of all PIEs had already been examined after a certain period of time. Formula 11 depicts a simplified approach to calcu-

[463] Refer to chapter 3.2.2.3 "Examination by Random Sampling".

late the portion of the whole population, which is covered by FREP's examination, after a certain period of time in a period.[464]

$$PCR(t) = \frac{t}{T_{Cycle}} \tag{11}$$

Where:
$PCR(t)$: Population Coverage Rate dependent on time period *t*
t: time passed within a cycle
T_{Cycle}: Total cycle time

Having a population (Ω_{Cycle}) which is going to be examined in the total cycle time T_{Cycle} will result in population coverage (PC) as following:

$$PC(t) = PCR(t) * \Omega_{\text{Cycle}} = \frac{t}{T_{Cycle}} \Omega_{\text{Cycle}} \tag{12}$$

APPLICATION TO THE EXAMINATION PROCESS IN GERMANY

A. POPULATION

The population of all PIEs is not uniform as there are two subgroups having different examination cycle periods: index-listed PIEs and non-index PIEs. Therefore the total population of PIEs (Ω_{total}) can be expressed by the sum of the subgroup index-listed (Ω_{index}) PIEs and the subgroup non-listed PIEs ($\Omega_{\text{non-index}}$).

$$\Omega_{\text{total}} = \Omega_{\text{index}} + \Omega_{\text{non-index}} \tag{13}$$

In Germany, there are 210 index-listed PIEs.[465] Unfortunately, the number of non-listed PIEs varies across the years. The average number of all PIEs from the years 2007 to 2010 results in 900 entities.[466] Hence, the non-listed the PIEs amounts to 690 (as an average value!).

---

[464] This fraction (equation 11) corresponds to the sampling fraction, which is defined as f = n/N where f is the sampling fraction, n is the sample size, and N is the population size (www.socialresearchmethods.net/kb/sampprob.php).

[465] By simply adding up all indexes DAX (30), MDAX (50), SDAX (100) and TechDax (30), which result in 30+50+100+30 = 210 entities.

[466] Refer to chapter 3.3.2.3 and footnote 457.

B. POPULATION COVERAGE

Correspondingly we can develop two subgroup population coverage ratios: PCR_{index} and $PCR_{non\text{-}index}$.

Population coverage ratio for index-listed PIEs[467]

$$PCR(t)_{\text{index}} = \frac{t}{T_{\text{index}}} = \frac{t}{4.5} \tag{14}$$

Population coverage for non-index PIEs[468]

$$PCR(t)_{\text{non-index}} = \frac{t}{T_{\text{non-index}}} = \frac{t}{9} \tag{15}$$

Where:
PCR(t): Population Coverage Ratio as function of time
t: Years of examinations
T: years to complete a cycle of examinations

Example: After a period of 4.5 years of examinations, FREP will have covered the index-listed population with a coverage of 1 or 100%, whereas the non-index PIEs are covered by 50%.

Since FREP started operations during 2005 (probably mid 2005), 7.5 years passed until end 2012. Hence, the calculation goes like:

For index listed:

$$PCR(7.5)_{\text{index}} = \frac{7.5}{4.5} = 1.666 = 166.7\%$$

And for non-listed:

$$PCR(7.5)_{\text{non-index}} = \frac{7.5}{9} = 0.833 = 83.3\%$$

This result means that within 7.5 years of examinations FREP has examined 83.3% of all non-listed PIEs and 166.6% of all index-listed PIEs. As a result of the different cycle times, certain examinations are double-counted in the sub-group of index-listed PIEs. The double counts can be eliminated if we count

[467] Average cycle time to complete all examinations for index-listed PIEs is 4.5 years (4 to 5 years), chapter 3.2.2.3.

[468] Average cycle time to complete all examinations for non-index PIEs is 9 years (8 to 10 years), chapter 3.2.2.3.

Table 3.7: Data Preparation for Further Analysis

Data Adjustments	PRE		Assigned auditors	
Total sum of PRE / Auditors	186		63	
Multiple counts	–28		–1	
Sum without multiple counts		153		62
PIEs not based in Germany		–11		–3
Adjusted sum of PRE/ auditors		**147**		**59**

several errors of one PIE in different years as one error count. When eliminating multiple counts we can consequently cap the population coverage ratio to a maximum of 100%. In our case the elimination of all multiple counts from the error list (appendix A) results in a new error list without the error no. #4, #33, #36, #43, #50, #56, #59, #68, #70, #74, #79, #82, #83, #90, #93, #97, #118, #120, #124, #147, #152, #153, #154, #157, #159, #165, #172, and #178.[469] Second we have also some PIEs in the error list which are not based in Germany. As this study focuses only on German auditors and German PIEs errors are also subtracted from the original list (Id. No. #29, #30, #54, #61, #66, #75, #100, #105, #115, #167, and #174). Table 3.7 shows the data preparation steps. For further study there are 147 PREs left to analyze.

After having eliminated all multiple counts, the degree of the coverage of the whole population can be calculated. We only need to weight both subgroups of population by their sizes.[470] Hence the equation for calculating $PCR(7)_{total}$ is given in equation 10.

$$PCR(t)_{\text{total}} = \frac{\Omega_{\text{index}} * PCR(t)_{\text{index}} + \Omega_{\text{non-index}} * PCR(t)_{\text{non-index}}}{\Omega_{\text{total}}} \tag{16}$$

After 7.5 years:

$$PCR(7.5)_{\text{total}} = \frac{210 * \overline{PCR}(7.5)_{\text{index}} + 690 * PC(7.5)_{\text{non-index}}}{900}$$

Remark: Since we have eliminated all multiple counts $PC(7)_{\text{index}} = 1.667$ is capped to 1 and renamed to $\overline{PCR}(7.5)_{\text{index}}$

469 Surprisingly, some PIEs have more than two counts. How can this be? The answer is, that one examination can identify an error impacting" more than one reporting year and therefore more than one set of financial statements including management reports of one and the same PIE.

470 Index-listed: 210 entities, and non-listed: 690 entities (refer to footnote 467).

$$PCR(7.5)_{\text{total}} = \frac{210 * 1 + 690 * 0.833}{900} = 0.872 = 87.2\%$$

Thus, the number of examined PIEs since FREP started operations, amounts approximately to 786 PIEs:

$$PC(7.5)_{\text{total}} = 900 * 0.872 = 786$$

Hence, 87.2% (786 PIEs from 900 PIEs) of all PIEs have approximately been examined in the past 7.5 years (mid 2005 to end 2012). This high coverage ratio is a good reason to positively assess the appropriateness of the proposed reference basis mentioned in the beginning of this subchapter.

C. SIDE CALCULATION: MARGIN OF ERROR

If we assume a onetime sample with a fraction of 87.2% of the population (sampling fraction), we can calculate the margin of error on a 99% confidence level (formula 11):[471]

$$MoE = Z\sqrt{\frac{P(1-P)(1-\frac{n}{N})}{n}} \tag{17}$$

Where:
MoE: Margin of Error (also referred to precision)
N: sample size
N: population size
P: estimated variance in population, as a decimal
(0.5 for 50-50, 0.3 for 70-30)
Z: Based on confidence level: 1.96 for 95% confidence, 1.6449 for 90% and 2.5758 for 99%

For N=900, n= 786 (87.2% of 900), P=18.7% (147/786) and Z=2.5758 (for 99% confidence level), we receive a MoE of 0.01274 = 1.27% only.[472]

$$MoE = 2.5758\sqrt{\frac{0.187(1-0.187)(1-\frac{786}{900})}{786}} = 0.0127496 = 1.27\%$$

[471] Watson, Jeff (2001): "How to Determine a Sample Size", Tipsheet #60, University Park, PA: Penn State Cooperative Extension, appendix 3 on p. 3.

[472] The result interpreted means that with a confidence of 99%, the overall AFR is in the confidence interval between 17.43% and 19.97%.

Table 3.8: Auditors' Failure Rates (Audit Firms with more than or equal to 10 PIEs Clients on Average since 2008)

Audit Firm	AFF^{*}[473]	AFF_{900}[474]	avg PIEs	AFR
KPMG	22	25.2	145.5	17.3%
E&Y	16	18.3	120.8	15.2%
PwC	16	18.3	150.0	12.2%
BDO	14	16.0	49.3	32.5%
Deloitte	11	12.6	57.8	21.8%
PKF	4	4.6	10.0	45.8%
ESMB	3	3.4	17.8	19.4%
Total	**86**	**98.5**	**551.0**	**17.9%**

Having a reduced total number of 147 published reporting errors and using the average number PIE clients for each auditor, a quite different picture in table 3.8 compared to figure 3.18 is obtained.[475]

On absolute figures KPMG is still in lead with an AFF of 22 (table 3.8). However, the gap got closer to its two big competitors in its size class (PwC and E&Y). Further, the Auditor's Failure Rate of KPMG amounts "only" to 17.3%, which is better than the average rate of the biggest 7 audit firms (17.9%) and is the third best AFR behind PwC (11.9%) and E&Y (15.6%).

In relative numbers, the medium sized audit firm, PKF, is on top with an AFR of 45.8%. This failure rate is exceptionally high, even compared to non-BigN audit firms (non-Big7 have an AFR of 20.0% on average. Also significantly out of normal range is BDO with an AFR of 32.5%.

The spread of AFRs within the 7 biggest audit firms is huge (33.6 basis points from 12.2% to 45.8%). It is worth mentioning that the biggest audit firms have the best results. Exceptionally Deloitte, which is no. 4 in Germany in terms of size, has a significantly higher AFR than the biggest 3 auditors and has the third highest AFR within the comparison of the biggest 7 (figure 3.20).

473 AFF^{*}: adjusted AFF after data has been prepared (eliminations of double counts and foreign PIEs).

474 $AFF_{900} = AFF^{*}(1/PCR(7.5)) = AFF^{*}(900/786)$.

475 In figure 3.18 the analysis is focused on all PIE auditors having more than or equal to 10 PIE clients since 2008 on average.

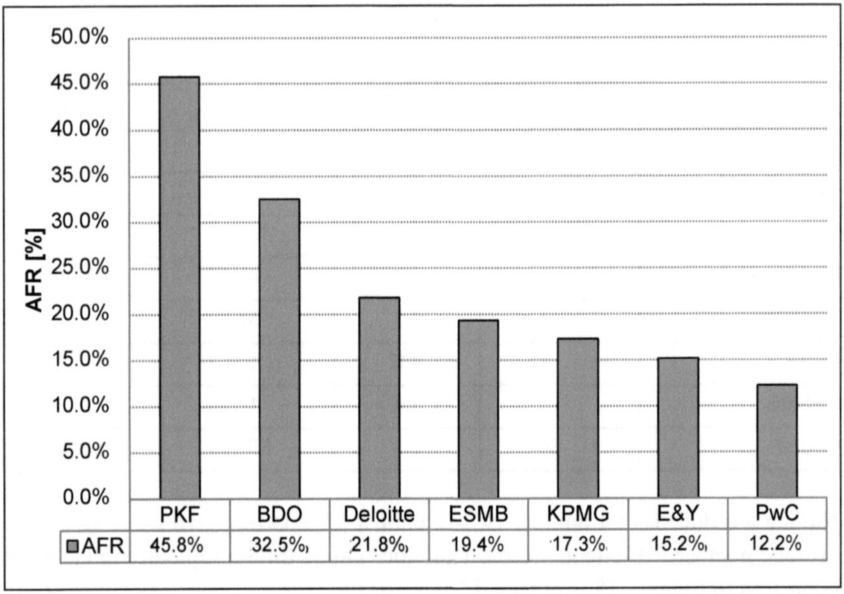

Figure 3.20: AFRs of Audit Firms having more than or equal to 10 PIE Clients since 2008 on Average

3.3.2.3 Big vs. Small Audit Firms

The question which arises from the analysis of the AFRs of the 7 biggest audit firms is whether big audit firms provide better audit quality than the smaller ones.[476] For this reason BigN Auditor Failure Rates are compared to non-BigN Audit Failures Rate for N = 1,…,7. The result is depicted in table 3.9.

---

476 This question has been researched plenty of times with different quality measurements (especially audit quality based on earnings management considerations) and with subsets of different data. For instance refer to Bauwhede, Willekens and Gaeremynck (2003): "Audit firm size, public ownership, and firms' discretionary accruals management", Chen, Lin and Zhou (2005): "Audit quality and earnings management for Taiwan IPO firms", Francis, Meydew and Sparks (1999): "The role of big6 auditors in the credible reporting of accruals", Reynolds, Deis, and Francis (2004): Professional service fees and auditor objectivity', Rahman and Ali (2006): "Board, audit committee, culture and earnings management: Malaysian evidence", Maijoor and Vanstraelen (2006): Earnings management within Europe: "the effects of member state audit environment, audit firm quality and international capital markets".

Table 3.9: Audit Failure Rates Compared BigN to the Remainder

BigN[477]	¬BigN	AFF_{900} BigN	AFF_{900} ¬BigN	PIEs BigN	PIEs ¬BigN	AFR BigN	AFR ¬BigN
0	124	0.0	168.3	0	900	0.0%	18.7%
1	123	18.3	150.0	150	750	12.2%	20.0%
2	122	43.5	124.8	296	605	14.7%	20.6%
3	121	61.8	106.5	416	484	14.9%	22.0%
4	120	74.4	93.9	474	426	15.7%	22.0%
5	119	90.4	77.9	523	377	17.3%	20.7%
6	118	93.9	74.4	541	359	17.4%	20.7%
7	117	98.5	69.8	551	349	17.9%	20.0%

The result confirms the theory that bigger audit firm provide better audit quality, since the economic independence from one single client is less (the more clients the less the portion of revenue made by one client). Further, big audit firms have more employees, which can acquire industry-specific knowledge and experience (figure 3.21).

The biggest spread is given when the Big3 are compared with to the remaining 121 audit firms (a delta of 7.1 basis points). Deloitte, no. 4 in size, has an AFR (32.5%), which is 13.8 basis points above the average of 18.7%. This downsizes the gap between the Big4 and the remaining 120 audit firms to 5.1 basis points. Including BDO to the BigN auditors, the difference of audit quality is further reduced to 2.9 basis points. The comparison between Big7 and the remainder shows that the quality gap melts to a negligible 0.3 basis points. This is mainly due to the very high failure rate of PKF.

Particularly, the theories that bigger audit firm provide better audit quality can be confirmed best for the biggest 3 audit firms (PwC, KPMG, E&Y) compared to all others audit firms in Germany.

---

[477]

Big1	PwC
Big2	PwC, KPMG
Big3	PwC, KPMG, E&Y
Big4	PwC, KPMG, E&Y, Deloitte
Big5	PwC, KPMG, E&Y, Deloitte, BDO
Big6	PwC, KPMG, E&Y, Deloitte, BDO, ESMB
Big7	PwC, KPMG, E&Y, Deloitte, BDO, ESMB, PKF.

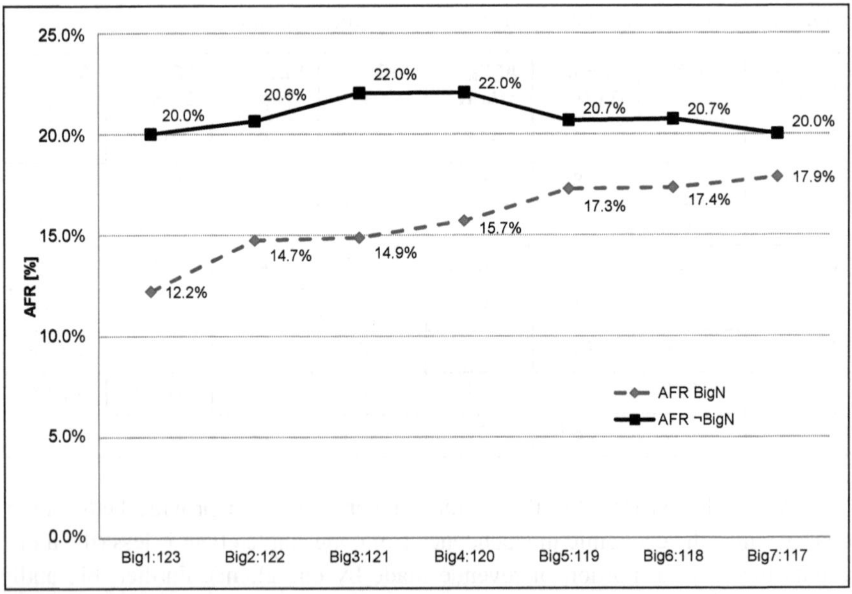

Figure 3.21: Audit Failure Rates Compared BigN to Non-BigN

3.3.3 Conclusions

Chapter three develops and applies an audit quality measurement based on published reporting errors of public interest entities in Germany.

While discussing the underlying assumptions of chapter 1.4 (A1, A2, A3), this study delivers good reasons for using published reporting errors as basis for an audit quality measurement on the audit firm level. These reasons are:

1) AFR is a direct measure of audit quality since the overall objective of the audit engagement is to detect material misstatements,
2) FREP enforcement procedure delivers reliable and consistent data, which can be used to develop an audit quality measurement system based on this data,
3) Audit quality results based on the new developed measurement are not in contradiction to contemporary theories and empirical results, and
4) All data used in this study is publicly accessible and can be reviewed by a third person at any time.

Applying the developed audit quality measurement "AFR" (Auditors' Failure Rate) chapter three reveals a huge spread in audit quality among the biggest 7 audit firms in Germany. The average failure rate over all PIEs audit firms is 17.9%.[478] The biggest 3 (PwC, KPMG, E&Y) are significantly below the average rate. This fact confirms the theory, stating that big audit firms provide better audit quality to their clients.

The second part of this dissertation (chapter four) focuses on how to explain the difference in audit quality within the PIE auditors in Germany. It tries to build connections between input factors based on audit firm characteristics such as audit skills, employee experience and client fluctuations. It first develops methods to measure selected input factors. Then, the correlation is tested between the audit quality results of chapter three with the input factors measures of chapter four. If there is a strong correlations between auditor's failure rates and input factors is verifiable, input factors can be used as explanation why some audit firm perform better than others.[479]

---

478 Refer to table 3.9.

479 "Perform better" in terms of financial reporting error prevention and measured in AFR.

4 Reporting Errors and Audit Firm Characteristics

4.1 Audit Service Production Models

4.1.1 Audit Production Function

An explanation of the audit production problem is vital for the analysis of audit inputs. Basically, a production function describes the relationship between the inputs and outputs of a production process. Inputs specify the amount of resources necessary to produce a given level of output.[480] The audit production process utilizes inputs (such as labor and technology) to obtain audit evidence in order to form the audit opinion.[481] The output of the audit service is a certain level of assurance over the audited financial statements.

Based on five assumptions,[482] O'Keefe et al. (1994) describe the auditor's decision problem as a cost minimization problem with the constraint of a fixed level of assurance.[483] Mathematically, this can be formulized as follows:

$$\text{minimize } c(h, \gamma) \tag{18}$$

$$\text{such that } \bar{q} = p(h, \gamma) \tag{19}$$

Where:

$c(\,)$ is the audit cost function

h is the vector of audit service inputs, and h_j represents the quantity of each input

γ is a vector of client firm characteristics that are exogenous to the auditor

480 Knechel/Rouse/Schellmann (2009), p. 1610.

481 Carson/Dowling (2010), p. 5.

482 "(1) The level of assurance produced by an audit firm is not directly observable. It is assumed that this assurance level is implied by the audit firm's brand name; (2) any particular audit firm produces a fixed level of assurance at a moment in time. That is, a firm's audit quality level is assumed to be fixed at any moment in time; (3) the client firm's structure is taken as predetermined; (4) a client firm's owners and managers will select an audit firm which will deliver the level of assurance demanded by the client firm; and (5) the audit firm operates in a competitive environment, motivating the firm to produce its output at minimum cost" (O'Keefe et al. 1994, Schelleman et al. 2003).

483 Hackenbrack and Knechel (1997), p. 485.

$\bar{q}$ is the level of assurance (associated with the audit firm's brand name)
p( ) is the audit production function

Obviously there might be a single combination or a bundle of combinations of inputs where the costs are minimal (services inputs h^*):

$$h^* = p^{-1}(q, \gamma) \tag{20}$$

Since audit firms operate in a competitive market the solution implies the following minimum cost level for the targeted level of assurance $\bar{q}$:

$$c(h^*, \gamma) \tag{21}$$

The vector h^* is the playground of the audit firm. Neglecting the client firm characteristics and generalizing the level of assurance γ as targeted level of assurance, the optimization problem can exemplarily be like explained.

For a targeted assurance level $\bar{q}$ (for instance an assurance level of 95%) three audit resources (resource 1 to 3), having different qualifications and different years of audit experience, are combined in an audit engagement team. The optimization function may lead to the resource mix in table 4.1, in terms of audit hours deployed, by each resource.

In this case, the required assurance level $\bar{q}$ may be reached with a minimum of costs for h_i^* ($h_1 = 20$; $h_2 = 50$; $h_3 = 200$).

The engagement costs would amount to € 11,300 for the audit.

Unfortunately, the target assurance level is not necessarily the achieved assurance level. Further, the target assurance level may not be the appropriate assurance in a given case. The quality gap should always be measured by the difference between the appropriate level and the actual achieved assurance level (figure 4.1). Further discussions on this topic can be found in Knechel (2009).[484]

Table 4.1: Example of Optimal h^* at Minimum Cost, Generating an Assurance Level $\bar{q}$

Input h*	Qualification	Experience	Hours	Cost/hour	Total
Resource 1	Certified	10 years	20	€ 90	€ 1,800
Resource 2	Certified	5 years	50	€ 70	€ 3,500
Resource 3	Not certified	1 year	200	€ 30	€ 6,000

484 Knechel (2009):Audit lessons from the Economic Crisis: "Rethinking audit quality", p. 8.

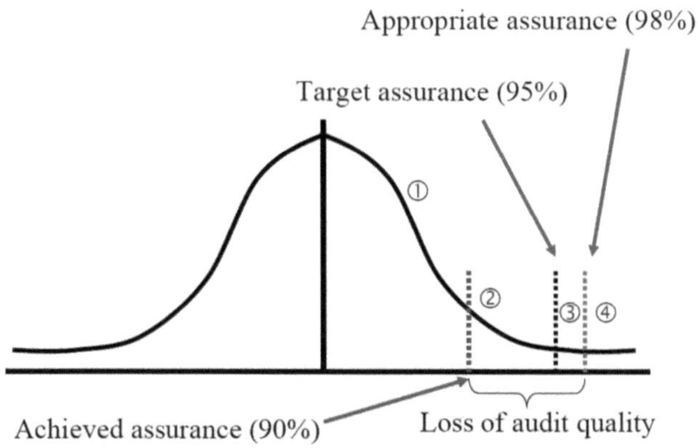

Figure 4.1: Audit Quality in Terms of Assurance Level (Source: Knechel 2009[485])

4.1.2 A Modified Audit Production Framework

Based on the theoretical literature on audit production, labor hours as inputs are converted to a certain level of assurance (representing audit quality) as output. Knechel et al. (2009) have developed a modified audit production framework. It is based on the audit production model of O'Keefe et al. (1994).

The modified framework uses an alternative output measure as a proxy for the extent of evidence gathered during the audit. Knechel et al. (2009) assume labor inputs are used in the audit process to perform audit activities, which result in the generation of audit evidence.[486] They treat evidence-gathering activities (outputs) as fixed and assume labor is varied to minimize costs. Evidence-gathering activities are, e.g. substantive testing or testing of controls. The more evidence-gathering activities are performed, the greater the likelihood that an auditor reaches a certain level of assurance (outcome).[487] Client-specific characteristics such as size, complexity and accounting quality are treated as exogenous factors and are assumed to affect audit production as a whole.

The complete picture of the relationships between inputs, outputs and outcome is exhibited in figure 4.2.

485 Knechel (2009):Audit lessons from the Economic Crisis: "Rethinking audit quality", exhibit 2, p. 20.

486 Knechel/Rouse/Schellmann (2009), p. 1610.

487 Knechel/Rouse/Schellmann (2009), p. 1611.

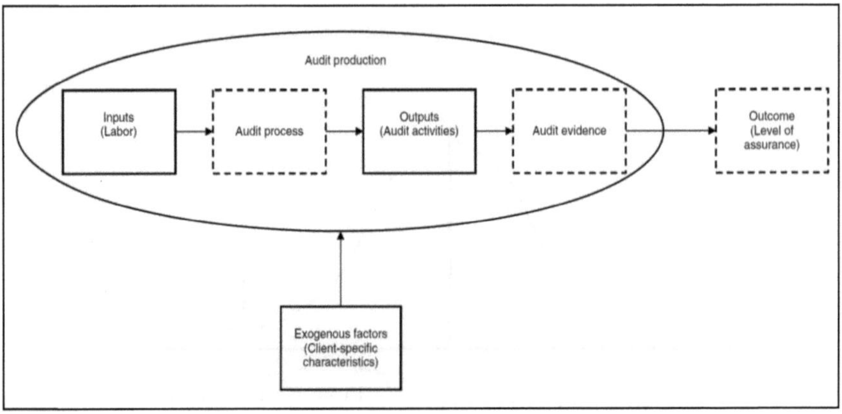

Figure 4.2: A modified Audit Production Framework (source: Knechel/Rouse/Schellmann 2009)

4.2 Audit Input Factors

4.2.1 Audit Input Factors Overview

As IAASB (2011b), UK FRC (2008), Knechel (2009), and Francis (2011) define audit inputs differently, it is necessary to explain what is meant with audit inputs in this study. In subsequent sections, four audit inputs are defined:

- Auditor's competence,
- audit effort (audit time),
- audit methodology, and
- audit support systems (figure 4.3).

Some of these audit inputs are derived from audit firm characteristics on an audit firm level, which are used in the empirical study of chapter 4.3.[488]

---

488 Refer to chapter 4.2 for the discussion of accessible and measurable audit firm characteristics.

AUDIT INPUTS	CRITERIA	INDICATORS
Auditor's competence 	Technical abilities: - Accounting knowledge - Auditing knowledge - Team/soft skills - Software, tools skills/affinity Experience: - Auditing experience - Industry experience - Client experience Objectivity, integrity & independence: - Personnel characteristics - Character, personality, nature - Moral virtues, ethics, values	• Academic degree(s) • Professional certification(s) • Training hours total and annually • Practical experience in years • Auditor's cognitive biases (questionnaire results)
Audit effort 	Audit hours per auditor and engagement Audit hours per audited client's revenue	• Deployed audit hours, derived from audit fees • Audit hours per audited client's revenue or sum of assets
Audit Methodology 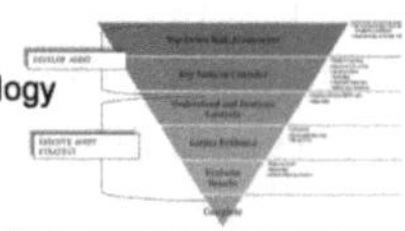	Audit approach (e.g. risk based) Audit process (e.g. top down) Audit planning Audit team organization Audit team communication Audit procedures & standards	• Appliance of International Standards on Auditing (ISA) • Audit process complexity • Quality assurance & controls • Audit committee involvement
Audit Support Systems 	Audit software Information technology Tools for testing/sampling documentation templates Communication tools	• Number of software programs and tools used to complete and document an entire audit • Software support for risk assessment and sampling

Figure 4.3: Audit Inputs, Criteria, and Indicators (source: own development)

4.2.2 Auditor's Competence and Audit Effort

4.2.2.1 Cost-Optimization Model

The main input of the audit production process is labor.[489] Labor in the sense of the audit production process, depends on both, labor quality (who is performing the audit) and labor quantity (how much time is spent to complete the audit).

Audit personnel vary in terms of technical abilities, practical experience, and attitudes. An experienced auditor may be capable of reaching a targeted assurance level in much less audit hours (audit effort) than an inexperienced auditor. Hence, labor has to be split in two components: auditor's competence and deployment of audit hours. Therefore, while looking at a complete audit engagement team, the labor resource mix has to be considered.

489 Compare to O'Keefe et al. (1994), Knechel et al. (1999).

Probably, competence and audit effort are partially substitutable in the audit production process. For simplification reasons, we assume competence equals experience; therefore the input factors would look like this:

1) audit experience, measured in years and
2) audit time, measured in hours.

A lack of audit experience can probably be compensated with increased audit effort (more audit time deployed). Being more experienced, the auditor is able to complete an audit more efficiently, which means he accomplishes the same work in fewer hours (less audit effort). Assuming that an audit firm has to reach a certain output level, e.g. an audit assurance level of 95%, there are different input factor combinations factor 1 (e.g. audit time) and factor 2 (e.g. experience), which result in the same assurance level (audit quality). Figure 4.4 shows different curves, where the assurance level is constant. These curves at different assurance levels are called isoquality curves.[490]

Isoquality curves can not only be determined in a one resource model, moreover, it can also be applied for an audit team, i.e. resource mix, where all years of experience and audit hours are summed up.

Having an isoquality curve, for instance at an assurance level of 95%, there is possibly one input factor combination, where costs are minimal. If the costs of both input components are known, the minimal audit costs can be determined (at the predetermined target assurance level).[491] For this reason, the isocost curve is needed. The isocost curve is the curve, where all input factor combinations result to the same costs. Obviously, there is an indefinite number of isocost curves, but only one, which touches the isoquality curve at one single point. Thus, the tangency point between the isoquant and the isocost curve represents the cost-minimizing input combination for "producing" the output level, that is, the targeted audit quality (assurance level e.g. 95%) with that isoquant. Figure 4.5 visualizes how the optimal input combination is determined.

490 The term "isoquality curve" is an own naming and is defined corresponding to an "isoquant" according to the classical production theory. In this respect, or instance, compare to Varian (1992), pp. 10 et seq. Since the audit service output is more reasonably measured in quality instead of quantity, a renaming from isoquant to isoquality is recommended.

491 For instance, compare to the "isocost" definition of Varian (1992), pp. 10 et seq.

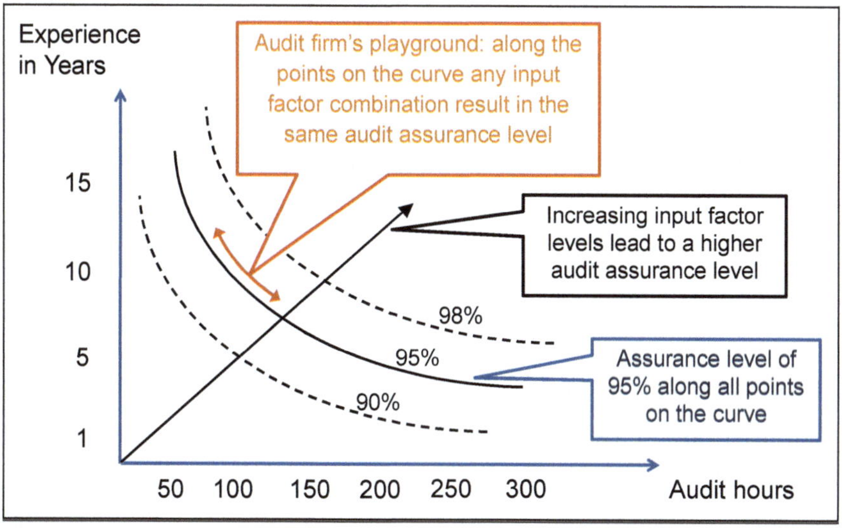

Figure 4.4: Isoquality Curves at Different Assurance Levels (source: own development)

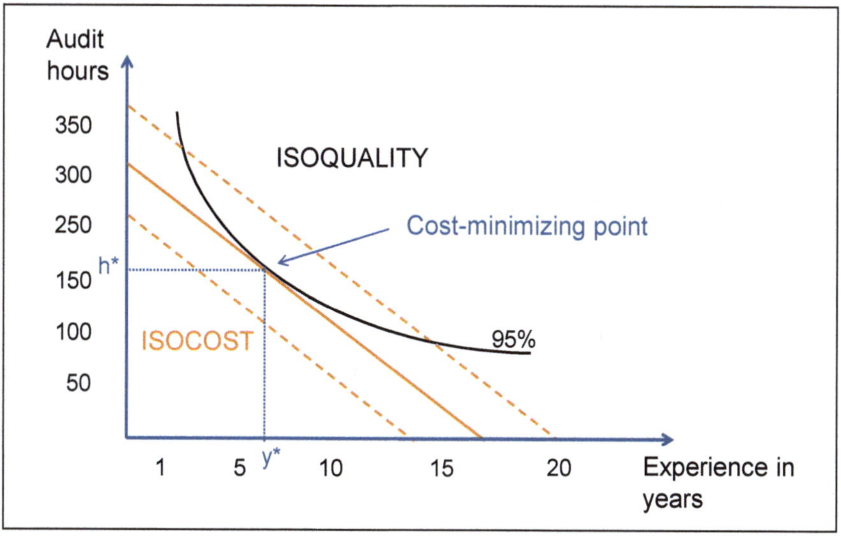

Figure 4.5: Isoqualty, Isocost, and Optimal Input Combination (source: own development[492])

492 For the underlying production theory, refer to Varian (1992), p. 51.

Formally, the optimization problem is solved by determining the equilibrium of both curves in the tangency point. At a point that minimizes costs, the slopes of both curves are equal.

Supposing that there is an audit production function $p(h, y)$ with the input factors h (audit hours) and y (experience in years), in the way that the production output is constant $\bar{q}$ (assurance level is constant):[493]

$$p(h, y) = \bar{q} \tag{22}$$

The isoquality function $p(h, y) = \bar{q}$ can be determined as function of y in the following way:[494]

$$p(h, y) = \bar{q} \overset{h=h(y)}{\Longrightarrow} h_{\bar{q}}(y) \tag{23}$$

Using the total cost function such for each cost function the total cost is constant ($\overline{TC}$) as well:

$$TC(h, y) = \overline{TC} \tag{24}$$

The isocost function $TC(h, y) = \overline{TC}$ can also be expressed as function of y:[495]

$$TC(h, y) = \overline{TC} \overset{h=h(y)}{\Longrightarrow} h_{\overline{TC}}(y) \tag{25}$$

Consequently, the optimization problem can then be solved as following:

$$\frac{\partial h_{\bar{q}}(y)}{\partial y} = \frac{\partial h_{\overline{TC}}(y)}{\partial y} \tag{26}$$

$$\Leftrightarrow \quad \frac{\partial h_{\bar{q}}(y)}{\partial y} - \frac{\partial h_{\overline{TC}}(y)}{\partial y} = 0 \tag{27}$$

4.2.2.2 Optimization Model for the Input Factors Audit Time and Experience

Concretizing this model, an isoquality curve of input factor 1 (experience in years) and input factor 2 (audit time in hours) combinations, can be determined with the following recursive function:

493 Compare to O'Keefe's audit production model, chapter 4.1.1.
494 For an example of an isoquality function, refer to the following chapter 4.2.2.2.
495 For an example of an isocost function, refer to the following chapter 4.2.2.2.

ISOQUALITY CURVE (based on recursion function)

$$h_{\bar{q}}(y):\ h_{y+1} = h_y * (1 - EG * SD^{y-1}) \tag{28}$$

Where:

h_y: Resource hours deployed for completing an audit step, audit area or an audit engagement for an audit professional with y years of experience. The recursion starts with h_1, the initially required audit hours for an audit professional with 1-year experience to complete, for instance, an audit engagement, e.g. 500 hours.

EG: (Unadjusted) Efficiency Gain rate (similar to the learning age[496]); e.g. EG = 30% means, that an employee with two years of experience is 30% more efficient than an employees with one year of experience; the efficiency rate equals 30%.

SD: Efficiency Slowdown rate. SD is an adjustment parameter to the EG. A slow down rate of 80% means, that the adjusted efficiency rate decreases with 20% annually. The adjusted EG rate ($EG * SD^{y-1}$) in this case would start with 30% in year 1, than 30% * 0.8 = 24% in year 2, 30% * 0.8* 0.8 = 19.2% and so forth.

y: Years of experience of an audit professional, for simplification reasons, only natural numbers are considered; a 0-year experience is ignored.

Mathematically, for $y, i \in \mathbb{N}\ and\ y > 1$ the recursive function can be transformed into the following product function:[497]

ISOQUALITY CURVE (based on a product function)

$$h_{\bar{q}}(y) = \left\{ \begin{array}{c|c} h_1 & y = 1 \\ h_1 \prod_{i=0}^{y} (1 - EG * SD^{i-1}) & y > 1 \end{array} \right\} \tag{29}$$

496 Refer to the learning curve model in manufacturing and the parameter a (learning percentage) in this classical equation: $Y_x = K\,x^{log_2 a}$; compare to, for instance, Chase, R. (2001). This learning curve depends on the units produced. The more units are produced, the lower the cost per unit. The problem with this function is, that it converges to zero, which does not seem realistic for professional services, such as audit services. The function used above, instead, has a limit value of about $\lim_{y\to\infty} h_{\bar{q}}(y) \approx \frac{1}{5} h_1$. This means, even if with many years of experience, some audit hours need to be spent in any case.

497 For the isoquality function in form of a product function, the derivative with respect to y cannot be calculated with standard methods. For this reason, the solution is prepared in tables and in graphics (refer to the example calculation in appendix E).

COST PER HOUR

$$c(y) = c_1(1+r)^{y-1} \tag{30}$$

Where:

$c(y)$: hourly cost rate depending of audit professionals working experience, e.g. € 60 for an audit professional with 1-year experience, € 66 for an audit professional with a 2-year experience

r: Cost increase rate for the use of a one year more experienced audit professional, the audit firm has to pay e.g. 10% more.

TOTAL COST

$$TC(y,h) = c_1(1+r)^{y-1} * h \tag{31}$$

$$\overset{h=h(y)}{\Longleftrightarrow} TC(y) = c_1(1+r)^{y-1} * h(y) \tag{32}$$

$$\overset{y=1}{\Leftrightarrow} \quad TC(y) = c_1(1+r)^{y-1} * h_1 \tag{33}$$

$$\overset{y>1}{\Leftrightarrow} \quad TC(y) = c_1(1+r)^{y-1} * h_1 \prod_{i=0}^{y}(1 - EG * SD^{i-1}) \tag{34}$$

ISOCOST

$$c_1(1+r)^{y-1} * h_{\overline{TC}}(y) = \overline{TC}$$

$$\Leftrightarrow \quad h_{\overline{TC}}(y) = \overline{TC} * \frac{1}{c_1(1+r)^{y-1}} \tag{35}$$

For a comprehensive calculation example refer to appendix D.

4.2.2.3 Auditor's Competence

Auditor's competence can be distinguished by the criteria: technical abilities, practical experience, objectivity and integrity.[498] Technical abilities basically include an advanced knowledge in auditing, accounting and taxation as well as team skills and affinity to information technology. Indicators for technical abilities are represented by the field of study (majors) and academic degrees held by the audit professional, as well as professional certifications earned. Besides pure audit certifications, additional certifications in management accounting, finance and/or information technology may signal a specialized and more profound

[498] Compare to the frameworks of IAASB (2011b) and UK FRC (2008).

knowledge in some matter and industries (e.g. an additional CFA[499] certificate additional to the audit certification when performing audits in the banking sector).

Ideally, practical experience is gathered on the job as auditor (audit experience), at different clients (client-specific experience) and in different industries (industry-specific experience). Evidently, industry specialization can also be attained by working experience in a former profession other than being auditor. Working experience could be measured in years, numbers of projects/engagements participated, or client counts in specific industries or concerning specific subject matters.

The criteria "objectivity and integrity" are affected by the auditor's cognitive biases. From well-known cognitive biases derived[500], Knapp and Knapp (2012) developed nine auditor related cognitive biases, which are likely to affect auditor's decision. Table 4.2 summarizes the typical cognitive biases of an independent auditor in audit engagements.[501]

---

499 The Chartered Financial Analyst (CFA) program offered by the CFA Institute is a qualification for finance and investment professionals particularly in the field of investment management and financial analysis of capital and financial markets (https://www.cfainstitute.org/pages/index.aspx, December 10, 2012, 14:00 CET).

500 As there are: *Bandwagon Effect*: or herd instinct, refers to people doing certain things because other people are doing them, regardless of their own beliefs; *Gambler's Fallacy (Monte Carlo Fallacy)*: also referred to "the fallacy of the maturity of chances", is the belief that if deviations from expected behavior are observed in repeated independent trials of some random process, future deviations in the opposite direction are then more likely; *Guilt by Association Fallacy*: make a negative judgment about a person or a thing, based on their relationship with other persons or things; *Illusion of Control*: is the tendency for people to overestimate their ability to control events, *Just-World Phenomenon:* refers to people's tendency to believe that the world is just and that people get what they deserve; *Ostrich Effect*: the avoidance of apparently risky situations by pretending they do not exist; *Stereotyping*: is simplified categorization about specific types of individuals or certain ways of doing things, but that belief may or may not accurately reflect reality; and *Sunk-Cost Fallacy*: Making additional (hopeless) investments because of the reasoning if one stops, all what have been invested so far would be lost (Knapp/Knapp 2012, pp. 40-41).

501 Knapp/Knapp (2012), pp. 40-45.

Table 4.2: Cognitive Biases Likely to Affect the Auditor's Professional Judgment (Knapp/ Knapp 2012[502])

Cognitive Biases	Explanation
Confirmation Bias	The tendency to search for and favor evidence that confirms one's beliefs, research hypotheses, or other expectations.
Availability Bias	A phenomenon that causes decision makers to estimate or forecast the likelihood of an event based upon how readily they can recall an example or instance of that event.
Familiarity Bias	The tendency to choose the same decision alternative in a new decision-making context that is identical or similar to a decision context faced in the past.
Anchoring and Adjustment Bias	Applies to situations in which an individual must arrive at a numerical estimate by starting from an initial value that is subsequently adjusted to arrive at the final estimated value. In such cases, the adjustments made from the initial "anchor" tend to be insufficient.
Uncertainty Aversion	The tendency for decision makers to be averse to circumstances and decision alternatives involving uncertainty.
Framing Bias	The format used to present information relevant to a decision might influence the decision alternative subsequently chosen.
Halo Bias	The tendency for one observed or known trait of a person or object to positively (or negatively) influence an individual's perception of other traits of that person or object.
Irrational Escalation	A decision maker's inclination to make irrational decisions to justify rational decisions made in the past.
False Consensus Bias	The tendency for decision makers to overestimate the degree to which other individuals agree with them.

4.2.2.4 Audit Effort

Audit effort (audit time) can be measured on audit engagement level in audit hours served. It is the effort the auditor puts in, in order to reach the necessary assurance level and to build the audit. Typically, an audit hour budget is derived from the negotiated audit fees. The higher the fees the more time the auditor can spend on the audit. Audit time can be split in two components: operative audit time and time to perform quality assurance and quality control work. Operative

502 Knapp C. and Knapp C.A. (2012), p. 42.

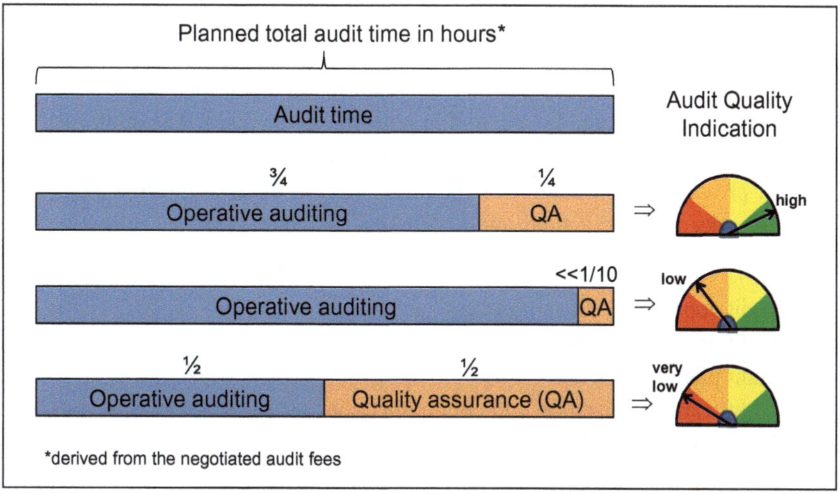

Figure 4.6: Optimal Relation between Time Spent on Operative Audit and Quality Assurance
(source: own development)

audit time is used to perform analytical procedures, substantive testing as well as control tests of the client's internal control system. Quality assurance consists in reviewing, audit milestones signing and audit report criticism. Assuming a given budget in audit hours, the more time is spent on quality assurance and control work the less time rest to perform operative audit. Hence, there is a trade-off between the time spent for operative audit and for quality assurance work. Since the total audit time is a limited due to the agreed audit fees, there must be an optimal relationship between both time components (operative auditing time and time for quality assurance work) in order to reach the targeted assurance level i.e. audit quality level. Figure 4.6 visualizes the trade-off mentioned above.[503]

4.2.3 Audit Methodology

In general, methodology in academia is the study of research methods. In particular, related to a discipline, a methodology is a body of practices, procedures,

---

503 The ratio ¾ to ¼ as optimal relation is chosen arbitrarily and has no connection to any empirical evidence.

and rules used by those who work in a discipline.[504] It is a set of working methods, which has to be followed.

Applied to the discipline of financial auditing, an audit methodology defines standards and practices to be adhered in performing the audit. The audit methodology is an inherent aspect of what the audit team does, how it does and why it does; it provides the structure for the audit team to exercise professional judgment in order to issue a final audit opinion.[505] It consists of the following elements:

- Audit approach (risk and process based)
- Audit process (top down, bottom up)
- Audit planning
- Audit team organization and communication
- Set of common tools and audit software
- Audit documentation

Exemplarily, the PwC audit approach is a top down, risk based approach, which is designed to comply with International Standards on Auditing. The approach consists of three major phases: develop, execute, and complete (figure 4.7).

In the first phase, audit risks are identified first by considering the client's business and its environment, and then by considering the key risks related to the significant accounts and relevant assertions, locations or business units and significant processes.[506]

In the second phase, the audit is conducted by understanding, evaluating and assessing the design of controls through inquiry, observation, inspection and reperformance, as well as process walkthroughs. Evidence is gathered through testing of controls and substantive testing. The results are evaluated including a reassessing of risks and the sufficiency of evidence.[507]

In the completion phase, prior to the issuance of the opinion, the financial statement is reviewed, including the adequacy and reasonableness of presentation and footnote disclosures; other audit procedures as required by professional standards will also be performed in this phase.[508]

504 Kamitz, R. (1980), p. 429.

505 Office oft he Auditor General of Canada, Assessment of the Design of the Auditor General's Quality Control System, http://www.oag-bvg.ca/internet/English/acc_rpt_e_33005.html#h10 (10:30CET, August 22, 2012).

506 PwC (2012b), pp. 12-13.

507 PwC (2012b), p. 16.

508 PwC (2012b), pp. 17-18.

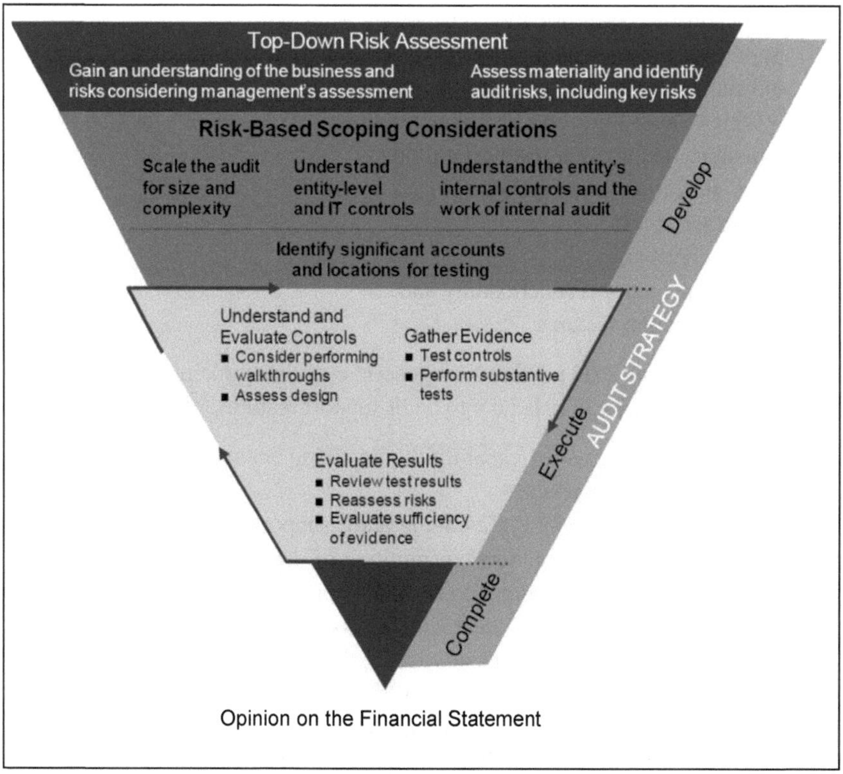

Figure 4.7: PwC Audit Approach (source: PwC 2012b[509])

4.2.4 Audit Support Systems

Audit firms deploy audit support systems to achieve efficient and effective audits.[510] These systems ensure that the firm's audit methodology is applied globally.[511] Large audit firms invest significantly in developing proprietary audit support systems for global deployment across their global network.[512] The minimum design requirements of an audit support system covers the following elements:

---

509 PwC (2012b), p. 13 and compare also to http://www.pwc.com/us/en/audit-assurance-services/financial-statement-audit.jhtml (December 15, 2012, 15:00 CET).

510 Dowling and Leech (2007), p. 92.

511 Compare also to Manson et al. (2001), Dowling and Leech (2007), Jeppesen (2007), Knechel (2007).

512 Manson et al. (2001).

- Audit software & information technology deployed,
- Appropriate documentation features (working paper templates, description and summary fields, lead schedules, etc.),
- Working paper filing and archiving features,
- Assistance features for testing/sampling,
- Work allocation functionality,
- Multi user access,
- Access controls,
- Review and sign-off functionality and,
- Communication features

Dowling and Leech (2011) define four generic enabling principles for audit support systems, which are translated into audit support features:[513]

1) Repair: System provides capabilities for fixing breakdowns; dealing with uncertainties/ contingencies
Audit support definition: An enabling audit support system contains design features that facilitate auditors' recognition of the existence of a contingency, unexpected issue or breakdown and/or provides tools to facilitate how engagement team members' deal with the issue.[514]
Software features: Context-sensitive help, diagnostics
2) Internal Transparency: Understanding of the working of local process
Audit support definition: An enabling audit support system facilitates engagement team members understanding of where their tasks fit into the engagement and the status of the engagement as it progresses.[515]
Software features: Communication tools, home page, navigator, linked information, real-time connectivity, sign-off, summary screen, work allocation
3) Global Transparency: Understanding of the working of local process
Audit support definition: An enabling audit support system promotes integration between each client's engagement at the local level and the firm's policies and methodology at the global level.[516]
Software features: Knowledge-in-context, methodology icon
4) Flexibility: Organizational members' discretion over how and the extent they use controls in the system

513 Dowling and Leech (2011), table 3, p. 37.
514 Dowling and Leech (2011), table 3, p. 37.
515 Dowling and Leech (2011), table 3, p. 37.
516 Dowling and Leech (2011), table 3, p. 37.

Audit support definition: An enabling audit support system provides users with options to tailor and use system- provided guidance to fit each engagement's characteristics.[517]

Software features: knowledge in context - prescribed substantive procedures, rationale boxes, scalability

Those audit support principles and features can be mapped to seven defined audit quality components (documentation quality, engagement supervision, knowledge development, confidence, consistency, effectiveness of service, and execution of methodology).[518]

Figure 4.8 summarizes the relationship between audit support principles, audit support software features and audit process quality components.

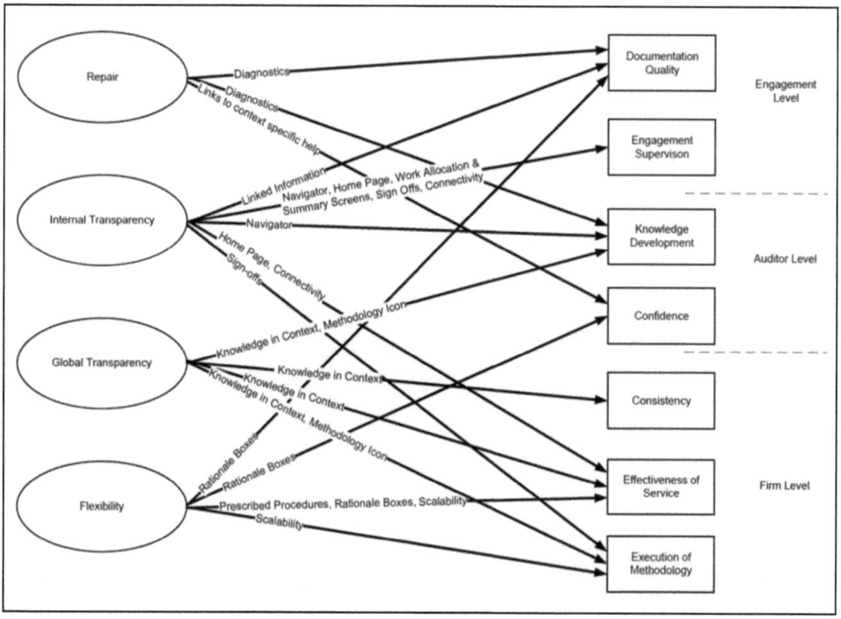

Figure 4.8: Audit Support System Design Principles Enabling Audit Process Quality (source: Dowling and Leech 2011)

517 Dowling and Leech (2011), table 3, p. 37.

518 Dowling and Leech (2011), table 3, p. 37.

4.3 Preparing and Auditing Financial Statements

4.3.1 Process Overview

The complete financial statement "production" process can be broken down into two instances: (1) preparing and (2) auditing. This split into two sub-processes makes clear, that the quality of published financial reports does not solely depend on a high quality audit. Without a robust and reliable preparation process, even good auditors cannot ensure a high quality financial reporting. Hence, the financial reporting quality depends on both performances: the preparers' and the auditors' performance. Obviously, a low preparation quality leads to higher audit risk and requires therefore a higher audit effort in order to reach an acceptable financial reporting quality.[519]

Figure 4.9 shows the financial reporting process with its sub-processes preparation and audit.

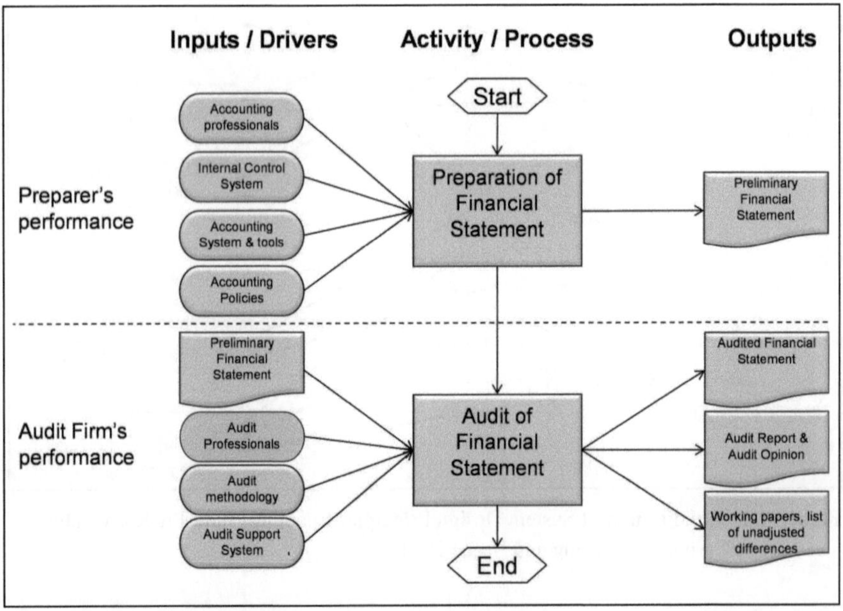

Figure 4.9: Financial Reporting Preparation and Auditing (own development)

519 Refer to chapter 2.3.4 and figure 2.6.

4.3.2 *Financial Statement Preparation*

The preparation of financial statements (both individual and consolidated) according to IFRS or other frameworks such as US-GAAP is a complex process. Most difficulties arise from the accounting for acquisitions and mergers[520], revenue recognition, segment reporting, cash flow statements, statement of shareholders' equity, and disclosures.[521] Even straightforward, but work-intensive reconciliations of intercompany transactions for a multinational reporting entity with subsidiaries in different jurisdictions and different currency zones can cause difficulties. Local financial reports need first to be currency translated and converted from local GAAP to into the parents' GAAP before they can be processed for group reporting purposes.

Corresponding to the audit production process (chapter 4.1 "audit production process"), similar inputs are used for the preparation process (chapter 4.2 "audit inputs"). The preparers' inputs are accountants, accounting policies, and an accounting software or ERP system. Furthermore, the internal controls over business processes and accounting data can also be seen as an input, or alternatively, as an endogenous driver to the preparation process. It is evident, that a deficient internal control system causes troubles while preparing the financial statements. A lack of controls may cause inconsistent, invalid and non-reconcilable data, an uncertainty in revenue recognition, misestimating and misevaluation of accruals, provisions and fair values. The same applies to the qualification and experience of the preparer's accounting personnel. Low qualifications and missing experience also increase the risk of producing misstatements. Above all, missing accounting policies and non-reliable accounting software affect the financial reporting quality as well.

4.3.3 *Audit Process*

The audit process uses the inputs, audit professionals, audit methodology, audit support systems (chapter 4.2) and the preliminary financial statement. The outputs are the audited financial statement, the audit report including the audit opinion, the summary of unadjusted differences, and working papers, which have to be filed and archived and according to professional standards. The reached financial quality level or assurance level is the outcome of the complete process

520 Refer to the complexity of IFRS 3R "Business Combinations", ASC 805, SFAS No. 141R "Business Combinations".

521 Compare to chapter 3.2.4 and figure 3.14 "most frequently identified errors 2005-2012".

according in the same way as it is seen by the modified audit production process (refer to chapter 4.2.2) of Knechel, Rouse, and Schellmann (2009). The endogenous factors in figure 4.2, also referred to as the client-specific characteristics, are concretized in figure 4.9 with the preparer's preparation process and his environment.

4.3.4 *Interactions and Iterative Process*

Ideally, the preparer has finalized his financial statement with all required components, disclosures, and supporting documentation before the auditor begins his work. In practice, this never happens (or is very rare).[522] Instead, since banks and investors urge a prompt presentation of information on management, tight timelines and reporting due dates require fast financial close, fast preparation and fast audit processes.[523] Therefore, audits are often performed simultaneously to the preparation process. As soon as reviewable parts such as inventory, accounts payable, accounts receivable, or fixed assets of the financial statement are prepared ("ready for review"), the audit can be started. It is also to be remarked that the preparation and audit process does not go straight forward in terms of "prepared – audited – completed". In contrast, the preparation and audit process in reality is cyclic and iterative, that means, it is a process of ongoing auditor's feedback and preparer's adjustments and corrections. In order to not correct every single mistake, immaterial misstatements are gathered on a list of unadjusted differences. They may be corrected in the very end after evaluating the overall materiality of the gathered deviations. Ideally, the auditor stops giving feedback when the targeted assurance level (e.g. 95%) has been reached.[524]

Figurer 4.13 shows the interaction between preparer and auditor. The outcome of this interaction is a continuously improving assurance level.

It is also very common, to split the auditor's workload into interim audit (or pre-audit) and main audit. In the interim audit, the auditor develops his audit

522 The statement refers to the author's own experience as an audit and accounting professional with a 12-year professional background.

523 For instance, compare to Bragg (2005), p. xv; or refer to Accelerating the Financial Close CFOs' Insights into the Benefits of a High-Quality Close (Source: http://www.cfoinnovation.com/system/files/Accelerating_the_Financial_Close_SAP.pdf (January 13, 2013, 14:00 CET).

524 The auditor actually stops auditing, when he has gathered enough evidence that the likelihood of the occurrence of a material misstatement is very low. This is meant with the wording "when the targeted assurance level is reached".

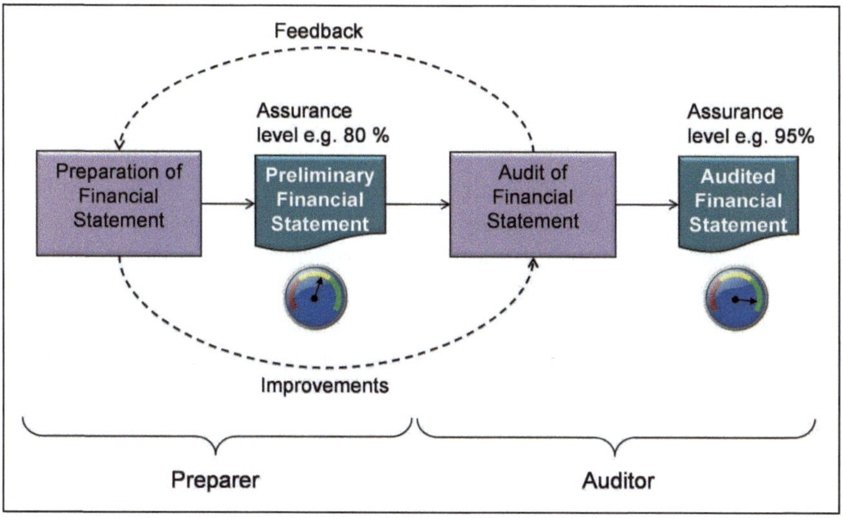

Figure 4.10: Outcome of Auditing: a Continuous Improvement of Assurance Level (source: own development)[525]

strategy while evaluating business and audit risks, derived from the client's economic and legal environments, and performs the design and effectiveness tests of the client's internal control system.[526]

4.4 Audit Firm Structure and Audit Firm Characteristics

4.4.1 Multinational Audit Firms and SMP

The global audit market can be divided in two groups: large, multinational audit firms and small- and medium-sized practices (SMP). These basic differences between both groups are the types and sizes of their clients, the service portfolio they offer, the level of specialization and the public perception.

The large, multinational audit firms tend to have large international clients. SMPs instead, operate more locally and audit predominantly small and medium-sized entities (SME). Generally, big audit firms are more specialized in terms of

---

525 Exemplarily, the assurance level of 80% in figure 4.8 is the assumed starting point of the very first preliminary financial statement figures.

526 Compare to chapter 4.2.3 "Audit Methodology" and figure 4.5 "PwC Audit Approach".

industry and service specialization. They offer a wide range of different audit services (financial statements audits, compliance audits, fraud audits, internal audits, etc.), consultancy services (valuation and strategy services, transaction services, management consulting services, business process optimization, HR services, etc.), and tax & legal services.[527] SMPs rather focus on standard financial statement audits and accounting tax services. However, SMPs may have specialists in some areas, but usually do not cover the whole range of services.

Large audit firms, such as the Big4, are structured as corporate enterprises[528], whereas small audit firms often use the legal form of society's and partnerships. The latter do not have to publish their annual reports.[529] If they do not audit PIEs, they do not need to publish transparency reports. Hence, the organizations of SMPs, firm characteristics (number of employees, audit clients and industry specialization) as well as their economic situations (gross margin, audit fees audit earned, personnel costs, and number of employees) cannot be studied.

4.4.2 Organizational Levels of Multi-National Audit Firms

When evaluating audit firms' performance in terms of audit quality, it is important to distinguish between the different organizational levels. Multinational audit firms such as the Big4 and other big ones have up to four organizational levels. On the top, there is the headquarters with central functional services such as brand development, marketing strategy, HR strategy and, last but not least, the audit methodology, including audit support systems and project management tools.

The second organizational level is often a regional grouping of countries, which could be done by continents such as "Americas" (all countries of North, South and Central America) or other useful groupings such as EMEA (Europe,

---

527 For instance, PwC: http://www.pwc.com/gx/en/global-business-services/index.jhtml, E&Y: http://www.ey.com/GL/en/Services, KPMG: http://www.kpmg.com/global/en/services/Pages/default.aspx, Deloitte: http://www.deloitte.com/view/en_GX/global/services/index.htm (all viewed on January 13, 2013, 16:00 CET).

528 Refer to the representation of the Big4 audit firms in Germany: PricewaterhouseCoopers AG (incorporation), KPMG AG (incorporation), Ernst & Young GmbH (limited liability company), Deloitte & Touche GmbH (limited liability company).

529 Non-incorporated companies (such as partnerships) only have to publish their financial statements if the two of the following criteria are met in three subsequent accounting years: total assets > € 65 million, sales > € 130 million, number of employees > 5,000 employees (Sec. 1 (1) PublG).

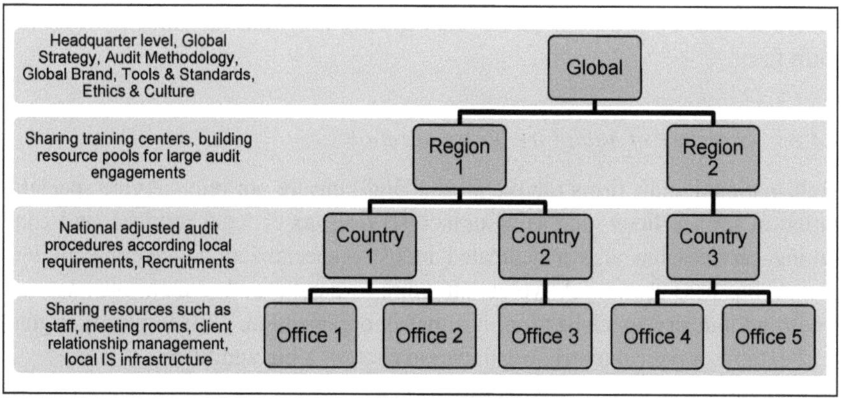

Figure 4.11: Typical Multi-National Audit Firm's Organizational Levels

Middle East, and Asia).[530] KPMG and E&Y both have also founded legal structures for Europe: KPMG Europe LLP, Ernst & Young Europe LLP.[531] On the regional level, usually information system infrastructure such as mail server and data processing facilities as well as training facilities in regional training centers are shared. For large assurance-related and consultancy engagements (implementation of internal control systems), there are also regional HR and project managers, who ensure cross-border staffing of such engagements.

On a country level, there are technical competence centers for local jurisdiction requirements (local GAAP, local tax and local legal requirements) as well as recruitment tasks and the management of a country wide learning and education center. Ideally, there is a country-wide HR management, who manages the country-wide pool of professionals.

The lowest level at the very bottom is the office level, where employees are assigned to clients and engagements are performed. HR management locally hires and fires employees. There might be also some local training facilities and experience sharing possibilities. Office sizes of big audit firms vary from only a dozen employees in small cities to several thousand employees in large cities.

On each of this level audit quality may be different. It also may vary within each level. However, on a country level, where all legal audit requirements for all offices are the same and the recruitment procedure and quality assurance

530 This is not audit firm specific. Instead, global players usually organize their markets, business units and/or organizational structure this way.

531 http://www.bundesanzeiger.de (October 10, 2012, 14:00 CET).

adhere to country-wide standards, audit quality may not vary much within the audit firm.

4.4.3 *Structure of Audit Firm's Organization*

Multi-national audit firms (above all the Big4) ensure not only service specialization in service lines such as assurance service, tax & legal services, and consulting services but also a dedicated industry specialization, covering all important business sectors. A typical structure to handle both dimensions, service types and industry specialization, is a matrix organization.[532] Exemplarily, figure 4.12 exhibits a typical matrix organization chart of a big audit firm.

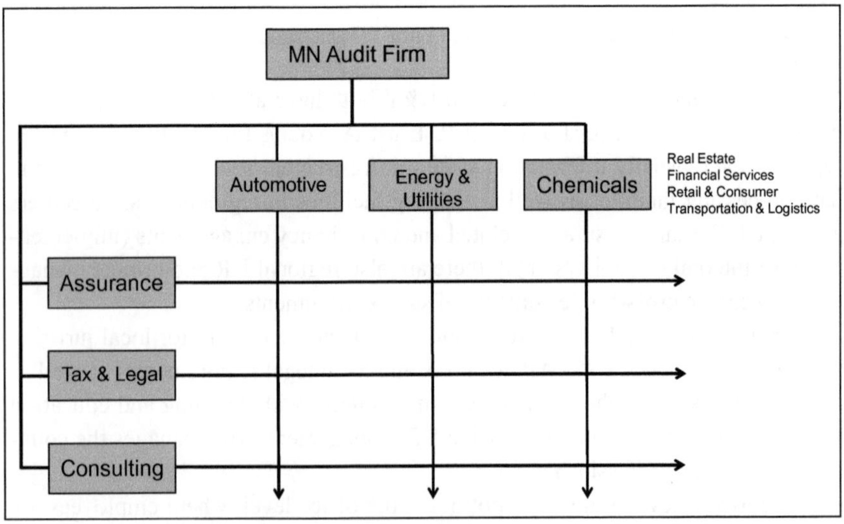

Figure 4.12: Typical Matrix Organization Example of a Big Audit Firm (source: own development[533])

---

[532] Refer to the general accessible information on the homepages of PwC, KPMG, E&Y, and Deloitte, http://www.pwc.com; http://www.ey.com; http://www.kpmg.com; http://www.deloitte.com.

[533] Refer to the general accessible information on the homepages of PwC, KPMG, E&Y, and Deloitte, http://www.pwc.com; http://www.ey.com; http://www.kpmg.com; http://www.deloitte.com.

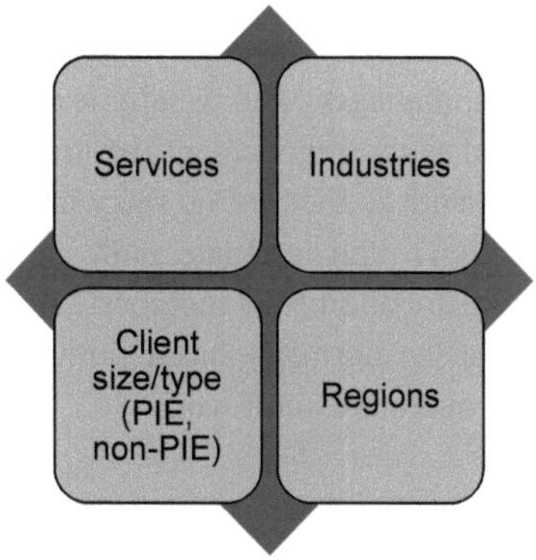

Figure 4.13: Typical Organizational Dimensions of Big Audit Firms (source: own development[534])

In multi-national and multi-regional audit firm the matrix structure is often enhanced by the dimension region (discussed above), which leads to a tensor organization. In order to complete the picture of a multinational audit firms organizational structure a fourth dimension may also be added: Client type/size.

The typical organizational dimensions of a multinational audit firms therefore are (figure 4.13):

- Services
- Industries
- Regions or countries
- Clients size and type (global players, PIEs, large non-PIEs, SME)

4.4.4 Audit Engagement Team Structure

A common audit engagement team structure, which is typically found in all audit firms identically is depicted in figure 2.12.[535]

The head of an audit assignment is represented by the engagement partner. An engagement partner is usually an owner of the audit firm, who is certified and

534 Refer to the general accessible information on the homepages of PwC, KPMG, E&Y, and Deloitte, http://www.pwc.com; http://www.ey.com; http://www.kpmg.com; http://www.deloitte.com.

535 Figure 2.11 is found in chapter 2.2.8 "Accounting and Audit Knowledge".

who has often a working experience of more than 10 years. The engagement partner takes the full responsibility of the audit engagement.

Ideally, the engagement manager, who usually is certified as well, but who is probably not as experienced as the engagement partner, is the project manager of the audit engagement. His work is focused on risky and material audit areas and he ensures adequate execution of the complete audit.

On the third level, there are audit staff members. An audit staff member may or may not be certified. He/she normally has a limited audit experience and is performing the most of the operative audit work.

4.4.5 Employee Specialization

Employees can be grouped as specialists and administrative support staff. A specialist is assigned to a service line (e.g. assurance/audit services or advisory services). Depending on the engagement and the clients, the audit specialist will gain specific industry knowledge and gather specific industry experience on the job. After some years working in the same industry, he/she will become an industry-specific audit specialist. A view to this mentioned path of specialization is shown in figure 4.14.

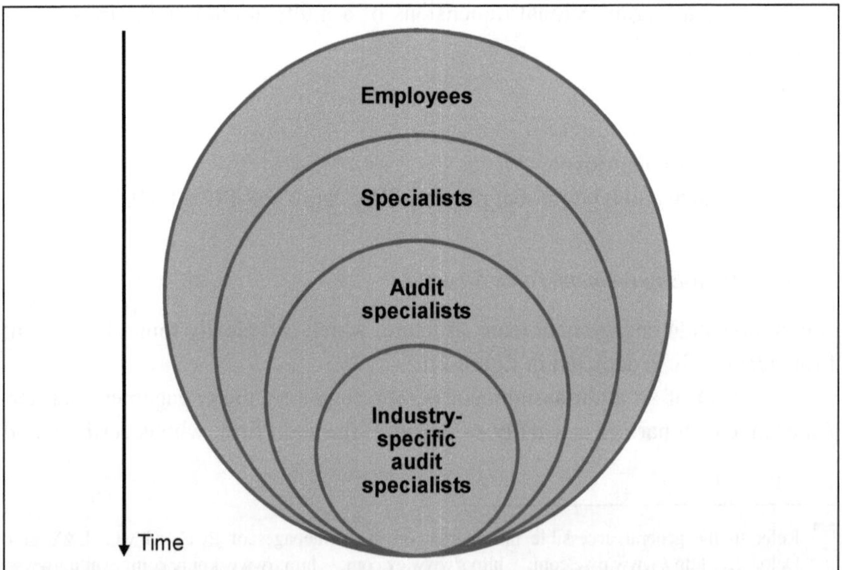

Figure 4.14: Employee Specialization (source: own development)

In addition, the audit professional may also become a subject matter expert on specific themes such as inventory valuation, impairments of real estate assets, financial assets or specific accounting standards (e.g. IFRS 3R "Business Combinations"). A voluntary switch from the audit service line to the advisory service line or vice versa may be supported by the audit firm, as knowledge spillovers probably increase service quality in both service lines.[536]

4.4.6 Accessible Audit Firm Characteristics

If audit firms have to publish both their financial statements and transparency reports, several audit firms characteristics can empirically be studied.[537] For the empirical study in chapter 4.5 the following characteristics are considered:

- Size measures in terms of turnover (total fees) and number of employees (source: financial statement)
- Breakdown of total fees in different service types (sources: financial statement, transparency report)
- Name and number of PIE clients (source: transparency report)
- Affiliated companies (source: financial statement, transparency report)
- Annual number of employees hired (not a mandatory disclosure, but is often disclosed in the notes to the financial statement, in the management discussion and analysis or in the annual report)

Since 2006, the German Chamber of Certified Public Accountants reports annually in its journals for all firms which employ more than or equal to ten certified public accountants, the number of certified public accountants per audit firm.[538]

---

536 For instance, compare to general discussions led on knowledge spillovers effects for providing both audit and non-audit services: Krishnan and Yu (2011), pp. 230 et seq., Knechel et al. (2012), pp. 60 et seq., and Walker and Hay (2011).

537 Depending on the legal form, financial statement disclosure requirements in Germany are codified either in the HGB Sec. 325 or in the PublG Sec. 1.

538 WPK (2006), WPK (2008a), WPK (2008b), WPK (2009), WPK (2010), WPK (2011).

4.5 Audit Firm Characteristics and Financial Reporting Errors

4.5.1 Working Hypothesis

Audit firms deploying a lower level of audit inputs[539] such as less experienced staff and less certified audit professionals are more likely to experience audit failures. This working hypothesis is broken down in three hypotheses, which are tested with the developed auditor's failure rate from chapter 3:[540]

[Certified audit professionals]

H1: The certified audit professional ratio has an inverse relationship to the auditor's failure rate: The lower the ratio of the number of certified audit professionals to the estimated number of employees in audit services, the higher the auditor's failure rate.

[Experience: employee's working experience and client-specific experience]

H2: Years of experience has an inverse relationship to the auditor's failure rate: the lower the years of experience of an auditor, the higher the auditor's failure rate, and

H3: Auditor turnover has a direct relationship to the auditor's failure rate: the less frequent a client changes auditors, the lower the auditor's failure rate.

Audit effort in terms of audit hours is not tested in this study. It is instead referred to the results of the empirical studies of Leventis and Caramanis (2005) as well as Caramanis and Lennox (2008), who found that audit hours as an audit effort measure is a useful proxy for audit quality, applied to the Greek audit market.[541]

The research model, with which these hypotheses are tested, is set of simple linear regressions, based on the ordinary least squares (OLS) approach.

---

539 Compare to the chapters 4.2.1, 4.2.2 and figure 4.3.

540 Compare to chapter 3.3.

541 Compare to chapter 2.3.10.

4.5.2 Research Model

The dependent variable is the auditor's failure rate (AFR), which has been developed in chapter 3 of this study. Independent variables are

CERTIFICATION:	certified audit professionals in relation to the estimated number of employees in audit services,
AVG_EXPERIENCE:	average experience in years per employee,
TTL_EXPERIENCE:	total years of experience in years of all employees, and
FLUCTUATION:	client fluctuation rate.

As employee experience and audit staff certification rate implicitly affect each other the linear regressions are performed separately (and not in one multiple regression model).[542]

4.5.3 Research Data

Due to the lack of data for the numbers of employees and the employee's turnover rate for all PIE auditors (these figures have not to be published necessarily), the regression analysis will be limited to the biggest 7 PIE auditors in Germany, where these numbers are available (refer to appendix C).

This fact definitely will weaken the statements on the results. However, it is to remark that the consciously selected sample is the most relevant one (it is about the 7 biggest PIE audit firms in the German market, which cover 61.2% of all PIE audit clients, compare to table 3.6) and the most reliable one, since AFR indicators of the selected audit firms are very reliable, because they are based on several failure counts and almost all PIE clients of these audit firms were examined by FREP in the period from 2006 to 2012 (these two dimensions are necessary to build the failure rate, compare to chapter 3).

4.5.4 Certified Audit Professionals Ratio

H1: The lower the ratio of the number of certified audit professionals to the estimated number of employees in audit services, the higher the auditor's failure rate.

542 According to the certification requirements in Germany audit professionals must have at least 3 years of working experience before they can get certified (Sec. 9 (1) of the WPO). Assuming maximum work experience of 30 years for certified audit professionals results in average work experience of 15 years.

The hypothesis above is tested with the use of the following linear regression model:

$$AFR_i = \beta_0 + \beta_1 CERTIFICATION_i + \varepsilon_i \quad (18)$$

Where:

AFR_i (Auditor's Failure Rate): Failure rate of an auditor *i* defined in chapter 3

i: 1…7: Big7 PIE auditors (more than or equal to 10 PIEs since 2008 on average)

CERTIFICATION: certified audit professionals in relation to the estimated number of employees in audit services.

β_0, β_1: Regression coefficients

ε_i: Regression residual

The certification rate calculation has tow underlying assumptions:

1) The number of employees are uniformly distributed in relation to the fees in each service type
2) 70% of all certified audit professionals work in the audit services

Data

Table 4.3: Calculation of the Certification Rate[543]

Audit Firm	Number of employees	Audit portion[544]	Employees in audit	Certified employees	Certified in audit service[545]	Certification Rate
KPMG	8361	37.9%	3166	977	684	21.6%
E&Y	6990	32.1%	2244	770	539	24.0%
PwC	8861	37.0%	3279	987	691	21.1%
BDO	1922	41.9%	805	246	172	21.4%
Deloitte	4014	33.5%	1345	384	268	20.0%
PKF	1150	30.6%	352	90	63	17.8%
ESMB	843	24.6%	207	62	43	20.8%

543 Number of employees are retrieved from financial statements (KPMG, PwC, E&Y), annual report (Deloitte, BDO) and transparency reports (PKF).

544 Calculation of audit portion, refer to appendix C.

545 Due to the of data details, it is assumed that 70% of all certified audit professionals work in the audit service line. It would not change the correlation results when choosing another constant, such as 80%, or 100%, as long as the percentage is applied equally to all audit firms.

Graphic

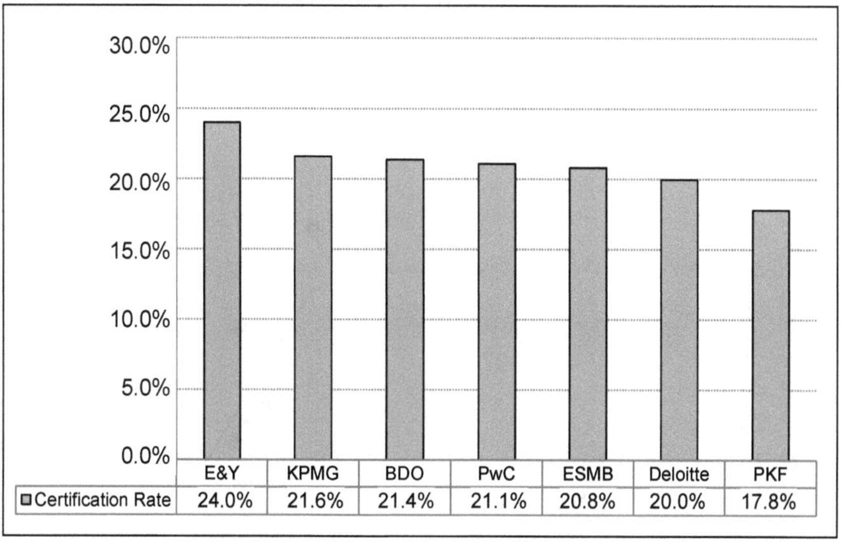

Figure 4.15: Certification Rates of Top 7 Audit Firms

Correlation Preparation Table

Table 4.4: AFR and Certification Rate (own development)[546]

Audit Firm	AFR	Certification Rate
E&Y	15.2%	24.0%
KPMG	17.3%	21.6%
BDO	32.2%	21.4%
PwC	12.2%	21.1%
ESMB	19.4%	20.8%
Deloitte	21.8%	20.0%
PKF	45.8%	17.8%

546 Number of employees are retrieved from financial statements (KPMG, PwC, E&Y), annual report (Deloitte, BDO) and transparency reports (PKF).

Data sources for number of employees stem for annual reports and/or transparency reports of the respective audit firms. The number of certified audit professionals per audit firm is annually published by the German Chamber of Public Accountants in its journals (for data details, refer to appendix C).

Correlation Results

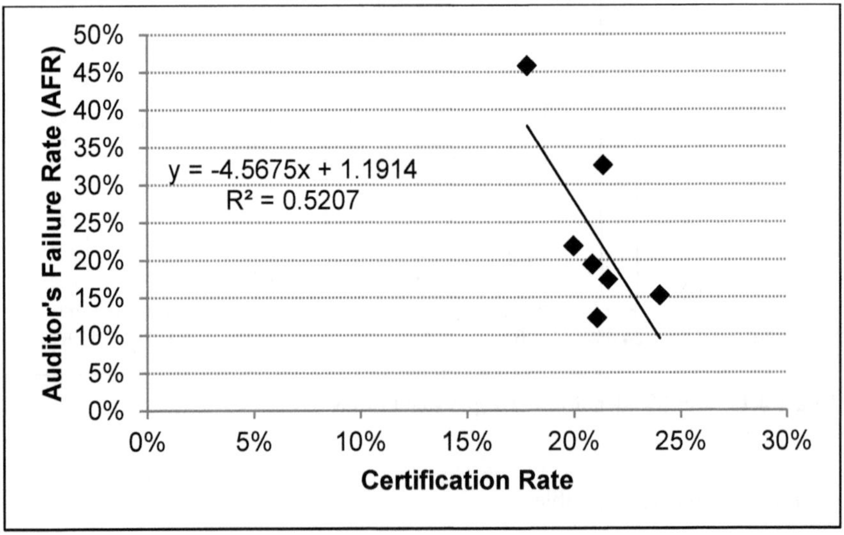

Figure 4.16: Correlation of Certification Rates with Auditor's Failure Rate of Top 7 Audit Firms

Discussion

The OLS regression results in r = -0.7216 and $R^2 = 0.5207$, which signifies a moderate correlation between both variables. Hence, the test result confirms the hypothesis: the higher the certification rate, the lower the auditor's failure rate, thus, the higher the audit quality.

It is remarkable, that the certification rates are close together between the audit firms. Five audit firms have certification rate in between the interval of 20.0% to 21.6%. The exceptions are Ernst & Young, having a very high certification rate, and PFK, having a quite low certification rate. Interestingly, PwC has a quite moderate certification rate, while the auditor's failure rate is lowest. This fact raises questions on the usability of certification rate as a quality driver.

The implicit assumption of this analysis is that certified audit professionals provide a better audit quality than non-certified audit professionals. There are different reasons why somebody works in the audit field but is not certified. The first reason could be that the audit professional has not yet met the entry requirements, i.e. misses the academic degree or the practical experience.[547] The second reason could be that the audit professional did not pass the certification examination. Not succeeding the exam means that the audit professional did not show the capabilities and competence to cover the required professional knowledge, skills values or attitudes. The third reason could be that the audit professional lost his certification license due to not fulfilling the mandatory continuous professional education requirements.

All these three reasons may be indications that non-certified professionals provide lower audit service quality than certified ones. There might also be others reasons of not being certified, which do not coercively indicate a provision a low quality of audit services. There may be some audit professionals who just don't want to take exams after finishing school and university. There might be good skilled audit professionals, holding for instance a Master of Science with accounting major and having an auditing experience of several years.

Another group of audit professionals may have problems with exam taking, because of the exam situation itself, but would fulfill all competence and capabilities requirements in their daily job. These both cases will be exceptions of the implicit assumption that certified audit professional provide better audit service than non-certified audit professionals.

In terms of auditors or audit firms competence and capabilities, certification rate is only one key performance indicator. Others would be annual training hours per audit professional, personnel characteristics (such as integrity, independence and cognitive biases) test results, and academic background.[548]

4.5.5 Employee Experience

4.5.5.1 Average of Experience per Employee

H2a: The higher the average years of experience per employee, the lower the auditor's failure rate.

[547] Compare to the audit professional phases in figure 2.11.

[548] In this context, refer to the indicators in figure 4.3.

The hypothesis above is tested with the use of the following linear regression model:

$$AFR_i = \beta_0 + \beta_1 AVG\_EXPERIENCE_i + \varepsilon_i \tag{36}$$

Where:
AFR_i (Auditor's Failure Rate): Failure rate of an auditor *i* defined in chapter 3
i: 1…4: Big4[549] auditors
AVG_EXPERIENCE: the independent variable is defined as the average experience in years per employee
β_0, β_1: Regression coefficients
ε_i: Regression Residual

Average years of experience per employee can implicitly be determined by the annual employee attrition rate.[550] Accepting two assumptions:

1) Recruited personnel had no experience before (no experienced hires), and
2) Separations occur for all employees equally. The years of experience can be calculated according the following formulas:

Total years of experience of all employees of an audit firm (refer to appendix E)

$$TYE = n \sum_{i=1}^{\frac{1}{a}-1} i = \frac{N(\frac{1}{a}-1)}{2} \tag{37}$$

Where:
TYE: Total years of employees' experience
a: employee attrition rate
N: Number of employees (head counts)
n: Number of new hired employees = $N * a$

Average years of experience per employee (AYE)

$$AYE = \frac{TYE}{N} = a \sum_{i=1}^{\frac{1}{a}-1} i = \frac{(\frac{1}{a}-1)}{2} \tag{38}$$

549 For BDO, ESMB, and PKF experience indicators could not be calculated due to lack of information.

550 In literature also referred to employee's turnover rate, fluctuation rate or hire/separation rate..

Data

Table 4.5: Number of Total Employees, Hires, Separations

Audit Firm	Em-ployees	Hires	Sepa-rations	Em-ployees	Data source	Attrition rate
Deloitte						
2009	4011	1051	366	4696	Preface to Annual Report 2009	9.1%
2010	4696	637	731	4602	Preface to Annual Report 2010	15.6%
2011	4602	840	886	4556	Preface to Annual Report 2011	19.3%
	13309	**2528**	**1983**	**13854**		**14.9%**
PwC						
2009	8870	1185	1027	9028	MDA 2009	11.6%
2010	9028	683	1038	8673	MDA 2010	11.5%
2011	8673	1550	1336	8887	MDA 2011	15.4%
	26571	**3418**	**3401**	**26588**		**12.8%**
E&Y						
2009	6315	996	432	6879	Financial Statement 2009	6.8%
2010	6879	550	653	6776	Financial Statement 2010	9.5%
2011	6776	1150	1206	6720	Financial Statement 2011	17.8%
	19970	**2696**	**2291**	**20375**		**11.5%**
KPMG						
2009	8510	730	864	8376	Financial Statement 2009	10.2%
2010	8376	800	906	8270	Financial Statement 2010	10.8%
2011	8270	1650	1482	8438	Financial Statement 2011	17.9%
	25156	**3180**	**3252**	**25084**		**12.9%**

Correlation preparation table

Table 4.6: Employee Attrition Rate and Average Years of Experience

Audit Firm	AFR	Attrition rate	Experience in years	Total years of experience
KPMG	17.3%	12.9%	3.38	28228
E&Y	15.2%	11.5%	3.85	26133
PwC	12.2%	12.8%	3.41	30188
Deloitte	21.8%	14.9%	2.86	13188

Graphic

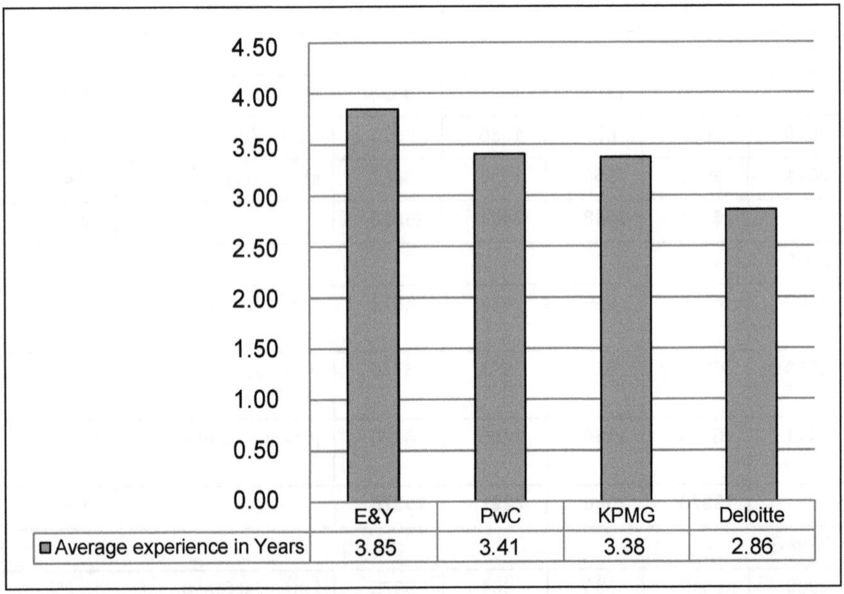

Figure 4.17: Average Experience in Years (Big4)

Correlation results

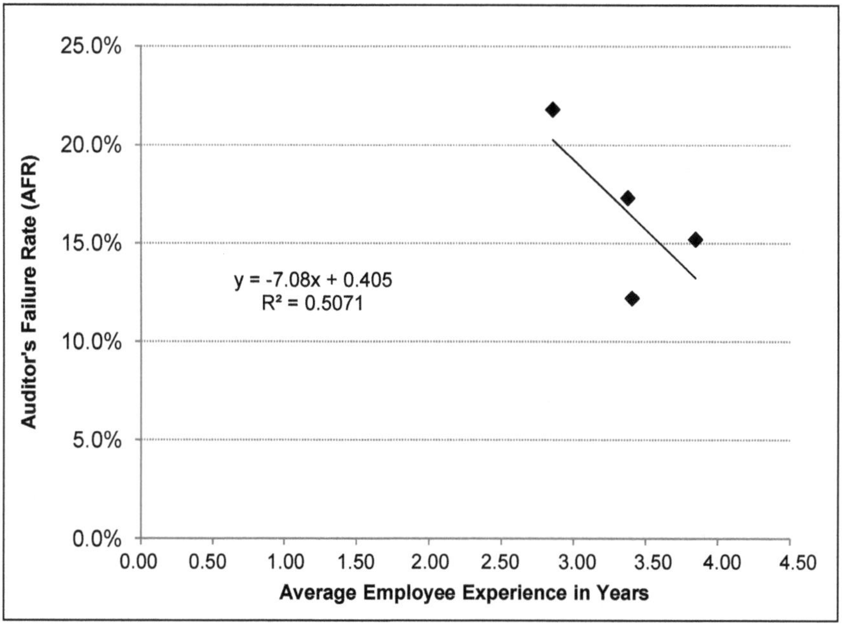

Figure 4.18: Correlation of Average Experiences in Years with Auditor's Failure Rate (Big4)

Discussion

The OLS regression results in r = -0.71626 and $R^2 = 0.5071$, which signifies a moderate correlation between both variables. Hence, the test result confirms the hypothesis: the more average years experience per employee, the lower the auditor's failure rate, thus, the higher the audit quality.

The average years of experience of PwC and KPMG are very similar. Again, Ernst & Young has the highest value, whereas Deloitte has the lowest average experience per employee. The gap between Ernst & Young's average years of experience compared to the Deloitte's average years of experience amount to almost one year. Taking into account, that the learning curve effect is highest in the first couple of years, having one year more of experience is significant. Hence, the relatively low audit failure rates of Ernst & Young can be explained compared to the relatively high auditor's failure rate of Deloitte.

The key indicator "average years of experience" is mathematically derived from the turnover rate of employees.[551] In this approach, there is no distinction between the different groups of employees (administration, auditors, specialists, managers, partners), neither within each group. So, the analysis is based on very flattened and averaged figures. However, significant different strategy in terms of human resource management may become visible using this indicator.

4.5.5.2 Total Years of Experience of all Employees

H2b: The higher the total years of experience for all employees, the lower the auditor's failure rate.

The hypothesis above is tested with the use of the following linear regression model:

$$AFR_i = \beta_0 + \beta_1 TOTAL\_EXPERIENCE_i + \varepsilon_i \tag{39}$$

Where:
AFR_i (Auditor's Failure Rate): Failure rate of an auditor *i* defined in chapter 3
i: 1…4: Big4 auditors
TTL_EXPERIENCE: the independent variable is defined as the total experience in years of all employees
β_0, β_1: Regression coefficients
ε_i: Regression Residual

Data[552]

The following figure 4.19 is based on data of table 4.6 which includes the total years of experience.

[551] Refer to appendix D.

[552] For data details, refer to chapter 4.2.4.1 "Average Years of Experience per Employee".

Graphic

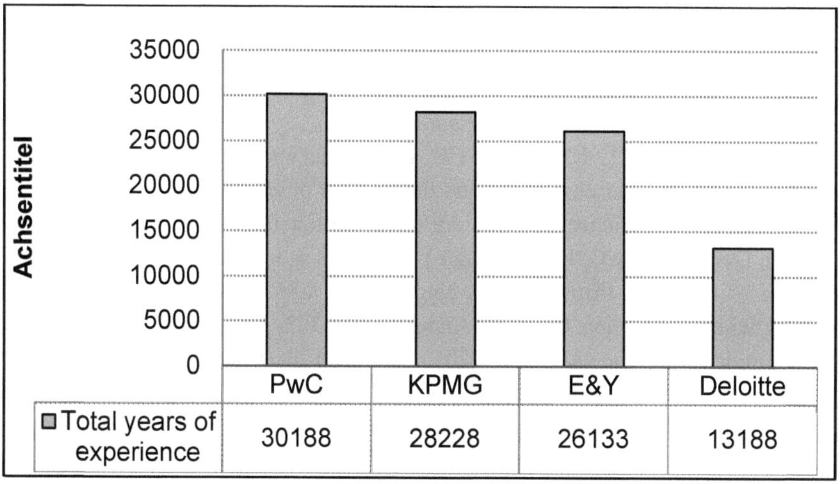

Figure 4.19: Total Years of Experience (Big4)

Correlation results

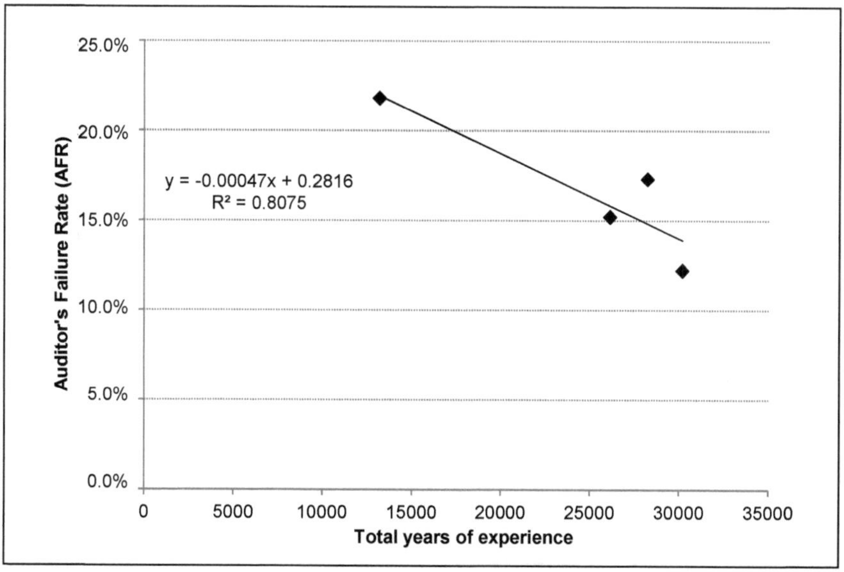

Figure 4.20: Correlation of Total Years of Experience with Auditor's Failure Rate (Big4)

Discussion

The OLS regression results in r = -0.8986 and $R^2 = 0.8075$, which signifies a strong correlation between both variables. Hence, the test result confirms the hypothesis: the more total years of experience per audit firm, the lower the auditor's failure rate, thus, the higher the audit quality.

The variable "TTL_EXPERIENCE" itself is dependent from two factors: the average experience per employees and the number of employees. Since the number of average experience of years are quite similar for the largest 3 big audit firms in Germany (PwC, KPMG, E&Y), the result is not surprising as it reflects the size of the audit firms. PwC is biggest with 8,863 employees followed by KPMG with 8,361, then Ernst & Young with 6,792, and finally Deloitte with 4,618 employees in the years 2009, 2010, and 2011 on average.[553]

For further discussion on "size" as a quality indicator, please have a look in the literature review, chapter 2.3.3 on page 38.

4.5.6 Client-Specific Experience

H3: The less frequent a client changes auditors, the lower the auditor's failure rate.

The hypothesis above is tested with the use of the following linear regression model:

$$AFR_i = \beta_0 + \beta_1 FLUCTUATION_i + \varepsilon_i \tag{40}$$

Where:
AFR_i (Auditor's Failure Rate): Failure rate of an auditor *i* defined in chapter 3
i: 1...7: Big7 PIE auditors (more than or equal to 10 PIEs since 2008 on average)
FLUCTUATION: client fluctuation rate[554]
β_0, β_1: Regression coefficients
ε_i: Regression Residual

553 Refer to the data basis of appendix C.

554 In literature also referred to client churn or turnover rate.

Data

Table 4.7: PIE Client Fluctuation Rates

	PIEs prior year	Wins	Losses	PIEs FY	Fluctu-ation	Data source
Deloitte						
2009	54	14	7	61	11.5%	TR 2009, TR 2010
2010	61	12	10	63	15.9%	TR 2011
2011	63	13	33	55	38.2%	TR 2012
	178	**39**	**38**	**179**	**21.2%**	
KPMG						
2009	140	18	17	141	12.1%	TR 2009, TR 2010
2010	141	37	41	137	29.9%	TR 2011
2011	137	25	38	124	30.6%	TR 2012
	418	**80**	**96**	**402**	**23.9%**	
PwC						
2009	151	32	27	156	17.3%	TR 2009, TR 2010
2010	156	8	17	147	11.6%	TR 2011
2011	147	21	22	146	15.1%	TR 2012
	454	**61**	**66**	**449**	**14.7%**	
E&Y						
2009	140	18	28	130	21.5%	TR 2009, TR 2010
2010	130	12	37	105	35.2%	TR 2011
2011	105	9	6	108	5.6%	TR 2012
	375	**39**	**71**	**343**	**20.7%**	
BDO						
2009	57	4	10	51	19.6%	TR 2009, TR 2010
2010	51	6	9	48	18.8%	TR 2011
2011	48	1	10	39	25.6%	TR 2012
	156	**11**	**28**	**138**	**21.0%**	
PKF						
2009	11	2	4	9	44.4%	TR 2009, TR 2010
2010	9	2	2	9	22.2%	TR 2011
2011	9	4	2	11	18.2%	TR 2012
	29	**8**	**8**	**29**	**27.6%**	
ESMB						
2009	3	17	0	20	0.0%	TR 2009, TR 2010
2010	20	12	10	22	45.5%	TR 2011
2011	22	9	7	24	29.2%	TR 2012
	45	**38**	**17**	**66**	**25.8%**	

Graphic

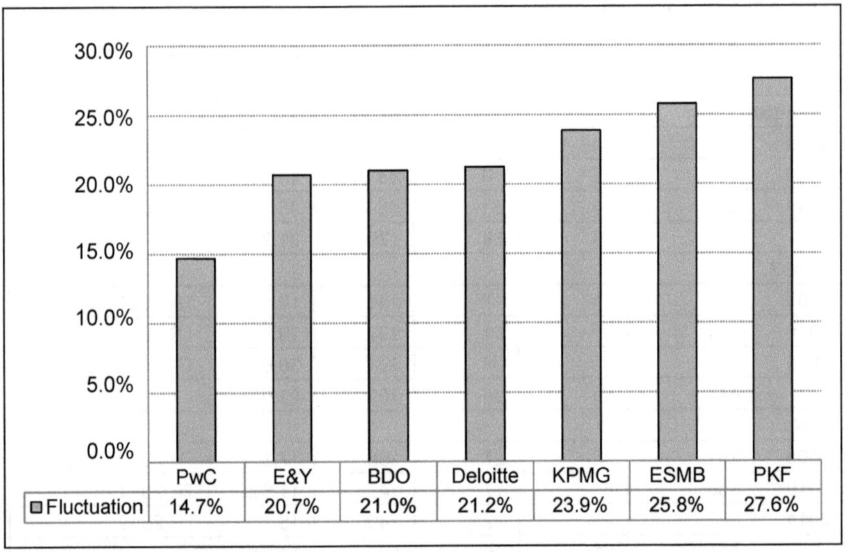

Figure 4.21: Client Fluctuation Rates

Correlation Preparation Table

Table 4.8: AFR and Client Fluctuation Rate

Audit Firm	AFR	Client Fluctuation
PwC	12.2%	14.7%
E&Y	15.2%	20.7%
BDO	21.8%	21.0%
Deloitte	34.2%	21.2%
KPMG	17.3%	23.9%
ESMB	20.4%	25.8%
PKF	48.2%	27.6%

Correlation Results

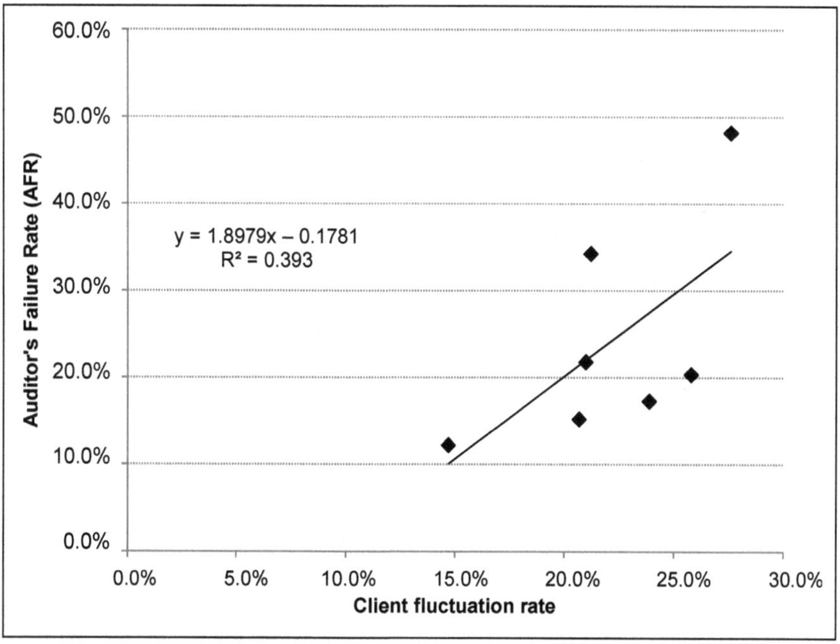

Figure 4.22: Correlation of Client Fluctuation Rate with Auditor's Failure Rate

Discussion

The OLS regression results in r = 0.6268 and R^2 = 0.393, which signifies a moderate correlation between both variables. Hence, the test result confirms the hypothesis: the lower the client fluctuation rate, the lower the auditor's failure rate, thus, the higher the audit quality.

PwC on top has a very low client fluctuation rate. The distance to the next best, Ernst & Young, is exactly 6 basis points, closely followed by BDO and Deloitte. The next firm, KPMG, is 2.7 basis points higher than Deloitte, followed by ESB another 1.9 basis points higher, then finally PKF an additional 1.8 basis points higher.

A high client fluctuation rate means low client retention and indicates a non successful client relationship management. Economically, as we have learned from chapter 2.3.4, a long auditor-client relationship maximizes auditor's profits.[555] Second, as audit failures risk is highest in the very first two years of the engagement, long term relationships augments audit quality; well-knowingly, that there are threats (familiarity and advocacy threats), which increase in the course of a long-time relationship.[556]

A low client fluctuation goes along with building a certain client expertise, which is vital in understanding client's business and client's risks. Hence, it definitely is a good quality indicator to compare audit firms in this aspect.

4.5.7 Results Summary

Although PwC has a moderate certification rate, the results in terms of experience are very good and client fluctuation is best. All factors together may explain why PwC has such a low failure rate.

Ernst & Young reaches as good results as PwC, since it has the best certification rate and the highest average years of experience, whereas client fluctuation is second best and the total experience is only ranked third. In sum, this may explain why Ernst & Young has the second lowest failure rate.

Deloitte's quality indicators are lowest within a Big4 comparison. Low certification rate, lowest experience indicators and the second highest client fluctuation rate may explain together, why Deloitte ranked last within the Big4.

The analysis over KPMG's quality indicator show moderate, but balanced results. The results are not as good as the results of PwC and Ernst & Young, but much better than the results of Deloitte. Client fluctuation is the only area, where KPMG had worse results than Deloitte.

Table 4.22 summarizes the results of the regression analysis performed.

In order to underpin the argumentations above, the results are ranked and averaged to a total rank (refer to column "Average Rank" in table 4.9). This total average rank is then being tested as an independent variable (again using a linear regression model) with the dependent variable Auditor's Failure Rate.

Figure 4.23 visualizes the correlation between both variables. The result shows a strong correlation between both variables ($r = 0.950$ and $R^2 = 0.903$).

The result indicates that the failure rates of the four tested audit firms may be well explained by the four independent variables CERTIFICATION, AVG_EXPERIENCE, TTL_EXPERIENCE, and FLUCTUATION. A multi-

555 Refer to chapter.2.3.4.

556 Refer to chapter 2.3.5.

Table 4.9: Linear Regressions Results Summary

Audit firm	AFR	Certification Rate (Big4 rank)	Average Experience (Big4 rank)	Total Experience (Big4 rank)	Client fluctuation (Big4 rank)	Average Rank (Big4 only)
PwC	**12.2%**	21.1% (3)	3.41 (2)	30188 (1)	14.7% (1)	**1.75**
E&Y	**15.2%**	24.0% (1)	3.85 (1)	26133 (3)	20.7% (2)	**1.75**
KPMG	**17.3%**	21.6% (2)	3.38 (3)	28228 (2)	23.9% (4)	**2.5**
Deloitte	**21.8%**	20.0% (4)	2.86 (4)	13188 (4)	21.8% (3)	**3.75**
BDO	**32.2%**	21.4%	N/A[557]	N/A	21.0%	**N/A**
ESMB	**19.4%**	20.8%	N/A	N/A	25.8%	**N/A**
PKF	**45.8%**	17.8%	N/A	N/A	27.6%	**N/A**
r	**N/A**	–0.7216	–0.7121	–0.8986	0.6179	**0.950**
R2	**N/A**	0.5207	0.5071	0.6268	0.393	**0.903**

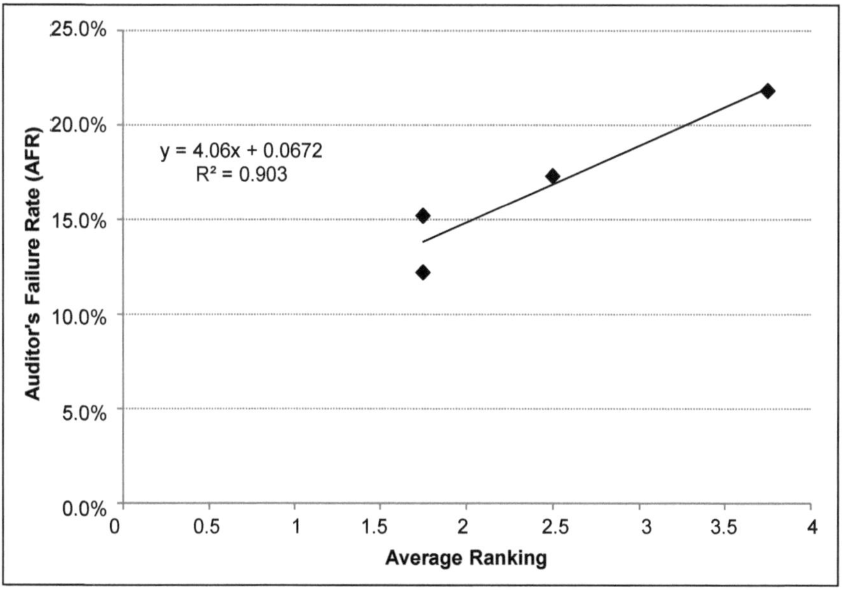

Figure 4.23: Correlation of Average Rank with AFR

557 For BDO, ESMB, and PKF experience indicators could not be calculated due to lack of information.

variate regression test of the AFR using all four variables could provide further evidence for that. However, as mentioned above, these variables might not be completely independent from each other, which impedes the researcher from doing so.[558]

[558] Refer to chapter 4.5.2 and footnote 543.

5 Summary and Conclusions

This chapter presents a summary of this study and conclusions on the empirical results. It also concludes on contributions and impacts to the research field of audit quality. In the end, it critically discusses the limitations of this study.

5.1 Conclusions on Literature Review and Current Issues

This study starts with a critical discussion of concepts, methods, and theories of prior research studies on audit quality in chapter 2. Among other things, the concept of Earnings Management, which dominates the literature about financial reporting quality is critically x-rayed. The line of thought "Earnings Management ⇒ Earnings Quality ⇒ Financial Reporting Quality ⇒ Audit Quality" is very daring in terms of conclusions on audit quality. Concluding that low earnings quality implies low financial reporting quality, which itself implies low audit quality, may be appropriate in some cases, but not in all cases. On the contrary, audit services are complex and comprise much more than solely the detection of discretionary accruals. Presentation, classification, notes on accounting estimates, reporting of going concern opinions, etc., are just as important and may not affect earnings or accruals at all.[559]

The ongoing discussion on mandatory rotation of audit firms should take into account both sides of the story: In order to find the optimal time period for switching auditors, the trade-off between high-risk audit engagements in the first two years and the increasing risk of familiarity and advocacy in a long run should be balanced. A short rotation period below 10 years would lead to multiple high risk audit engagements (engagement in the first and second year) at the same time. Risks of familiarity and advocacy are mitigated with internal mandatory rotations. Thus, a combination of mandatory internal and external rotation may have the best result to audit service quality (for instance, after 7 year an internal rotation, and after 14 years follows an external rotation).

The next theoretical subject is the quest for optimal resource mix for audit engagements under the restriction of a targeted assurance level. The fundamental

559 Refer to chapter 2.4.1.

production function of O'Keefe serves as basis for a two input factors model and the application of classical economics theory. The introduction of isoquality curves and isocost curves in this context, the connection to learning effects, and the interchangeability of audit time and experience extends the field for further empirical research. Using this model, decreasing audit fees, ceteris paribus, will directly lead to lower audit quality as both the isocost curve and isoquality curve will shift left/down in a competitive market.

5.2 Summary and Conclusions on Empirical Study

This empirical part of this study examines the association between published accounting errors and audit firm characteristics in the context of audit quality in Germany.

With the help of three major assumptions (A1, A2, A3), the audit quality measurement "Auditor's Failure Rate" is developed in the first part of chapter 3. The indicator AFR uses financial reporting errors, published in the German Federal Gazette in the period from 2006 to 2012, and the auditors' average number of PIE clients, in order to establish a proxy for audit quality on the audit firm level.[560] After having discussed the three assumptions and the method to measure, the measurement is applied to the German PIE audit market. Because of the potential for non-comparable results when assessing audit firms with few PIE clients – a single enforcement or lack thereof can change the AFR from 100% to 0% – only PIE audit firms with at least 10 clients have been analyzed under the AFR.

The results indicate a wide spread of audit quality differences among the 7 biggest audit firms in Germany.[561] The spread reaches from an auditor's failure rate of 12% (PwC) to 45% (PKF), whereas the average failure rate over all PIE auditors amounts to only to 17.9%. The biggest 3 (PwC, KPMG, and E&Y), notably 2 of them (PwC and E&Y), have markedly lower failure rates than their competitors. KPMG is slightly below average and the smallest of the Big4 in Germany, Deloitte, is well below average. In total, the empirical results go along with the theory, that bigger audit firms provide better audit quality than smaller ones.

---

560 Refer to chapter 1.4 for assumptions A1, A2, and A3.

561 "Biggest" consistently defined in terms of the number of PIE clients; refer to footnote 479.

In the second part of chapter 3, this study delivers good reasons for using published reporting errors as basis for an audit quality measurement on the audit firm level, since AFR is a direct measure of audit quality and FREP delivers – on an intersubjective view - reliable and consistent data.

In chapter 4, the AFR results are challenged with an input factors based approach. Three audit firm characteristics (employee experience, client fluctuation, and professional certification rate), are identified in order to operationalize three hypotheses (H1, H2, H3) using OLS linear regression models. As moderate to strong correlations are given, this study provides evidence that the relationships appear consistent with the theory. Therefore, the correlation tests of the 7 biggest respectively 4 biggest audit firms indicate that:

- First, the certified audit professional ratio has an inverse relationship to the auditor's failure rate: The lower the ratio of the number of certified audit professionals to the estimated number of employees in audit services, the higher the auditor's failure rate.
- Second, years of experience has an inverse relationship to the auditor's failure rate: the lower the years of experience of an auditor, the higher the auditor's failure rate.
- Third, auditor turnover has a direct relationship to the auditor's failure rate: the less frequent a client changes auditors, the lower the auditor's failure rate.

However, more work needs to be done to provide stronger evidence of the correlations between the input factor based audit firm characteristics and audit quality measured in auditor's failure rates.

Nevertheless, these three statements may explain, at least partially, the quality differences among the analyzed audit firms. PwC and E&Y both have low failure rates. This can be explained insofar as they both have the best results in terms of the evaluated input-based audit firm characteristics. They both are ranked top, since the average experience in years per employee is highest and their client fluctuation rates are lowest.[562] Within a Big4 comparison, Deloitte is ranked last, due to low certification rate, low experience, and high client fluctuation.

Extending the analysis to a Big7 comparison, reveals that PKF, which has a very high failure rate, is overall ranked last, since its employees have a very low

562 Refer to chapter 4.5.6 and table 4.9.

certification rate and its clients fluctuate more than at the other audit firms within the comparison.

5.3 Limitations and Further Research

This study is based on data from a long period of more than 7 years. In order to construct the audit quality measurement "AFR", average values are built for PIE client numbers, audit firms employees, certified professionals, etc.

Average values over a long time period have the drawback that one can never say, what the audit quality is now, or what was it in the beginning of the period, or at any point in time. Average values smoothen and balance good and bad results.

Published reporting errors may all be material, but very seldom have the same extent. Some published reporting errors are subject to a bundle of accounting issues; some others only reveal one single (material) error. Hence, there might be a way to classify the published reporting errors by severity of the material misstatements.

The data availability for this study is limited. The counts of 186 audit failures, which are reduced to only 147 in order to eliminate double counts, are not many occurrences to calculate failure rates for around 120 PIE audit firms in Germany.[563] Further, in order to indicate and to evidence correlation relationships, only 7 auditors could have been analyzed more closely.

This might not look representative at all. However, the fact that these 7 tested auditors are the biggest ones (in terms of PIE clients, they cover more than 61.2% of the PIE audit market, refer to table 3.6) and the fact, that their AFRs are most reliable (since they result from many failure counts and almost all of their PIE clients were examined by the FREP in the period from 2006 to 2012), increase the importance and reliability and the of the correlation testing results.

In order to counteract the incompleteness and limitations of publicly available information, further study could gather more audit firm specific data through questionnaires and panels. Doing so, employee experiences and employee durations could be analyzed at different organization levels (staff, manager, and partner level).

563 Actually, "only" 63 audit firms have been involved in accounting errors (refer to appendix B).

Moreover, using input-based measurements, audit quality could also be analyzed on an engagement level. For this purpose, audit time measured in audit hours per each audit professional and/or audit engagement team could be surveyed. Audit hours could even be estimated from the published audit fees by the clients, if a certain level of resource utilization and an average hourly fee rate are assumed.

Ultimately, having a data basis with more occurrences in terms of audit firm characteristics (in the best case for all PIE audit firms, instead of only 7 of them) and with additional data dimensions - variables such as industry, audit hours, fee rates, and annual training hours - may enable construction of a model for more powerful input factors correlation testing with the auditor's failure rate.

Appendix

Appendix A: Published Reporting Errors

Table A.1: 186 Reporting Errors Published between February 3, 2006 and December 31, 2012

No.	Company	Pub.date	Audit firm[564]
1	Arques Industries AG	03.02.2006	Mörtl und Kollegen GmbH
2	Allgeier Holding AG	04.08.2006	LOHR + COMPANY GmbH
3	PC-Ware Information Technologies AG	06.09.2006	Rölfs WP Partner AG
4	HAITEC AG	20.09.2006	Rupp & Epple GmbH
5	EMPRISE AG	14.12.2006	Ebner Stolz Mönning & Bachem
6	Frankfurter Sparkasse AG	03.01.2007	Sparkassen- und Giroverband
7	MTU Aero Engines Holding AG	22.01.2007	Deloitte
8	Interhyp AG	15.02.2007	Ernst & Young
9	AGOR AG	27.02.2007	Beratungs- und Prüfungsgesellschaft mbH
10	Zapf Creation AG	27.02.2007	KPMG
11	S&R Biogas Energiesysteme AG	27.03.2007	Münchner Wirtschaftsprüfungsgesellschaft GmbH
12	Mensch und Maschine Software AG	17.04.2007	AUDIT WIRTSCHAFTS-TREUHAND AG
13	Kampa AG	31.05.2007	Dr. Stückmann und Partner
14	Neue Sentimental Film AG	19.06.2007	KÖNIG WIRTSCHAFTSPRÜPFUNG GMBH
15	DEAG Deutsche Entertainment AG	26.06.2007	BDO
16	curasan AG	26.06.2007	PKF
17	OHB Technology AG	18.07.2007	BDO
18	Württembergische Lebensversiche-rung AG	20.07.2007	Deloitte
19	Schön & Cie AG i.I.	20.07.2007	PwC
20	AWD Holding AG	20.07.2007	BDO
21	Süd-Chemie AG	02.08.2007	Ernst & Young
22	Vivacon AG	06.08.2007	Ebner Stolz Mönning & Bachem
23	GESCO AG	08.08.2007	Dr. Breidenbach und Partner
24	GAG Immobilien AG	22.08.2007	Dipl.-Kfm. Hans M. Klein, Wirtschaftsprüfer
25	Action Press Holding AG	11.09.2007	Wisbert-Treuhand GmbH
26	Hageda AG	20.09.2007	Dürkop Möller und Partner
27	Dom-Brauerei AG	26.09.2007	Moses & Partner Revision und Treuhand GmbH
28	Bau-Verein zu Hamburg AG	01.10.2007	Schröder, Nörenberg + Partner GmbH
29	C.A.T. oil AG	17.10.2007	BDO
30	LBBW Bank Ireland Public Limited Company	18.10.2007	Ernst & Young

[564] Some audit firms have merged in the last of couple of years and/or are part of an audit firm group. Therefore a single name is used for: Mazars, Deloitte, BDO, PwC, Ernst & Young, KPMG, PKF, GHP Revision and RBS RoeverBroennerSusat. Behind this names there are the following legal entities listed in table A.2.

No.	Company	Pub.date	Audit firm[564]
31	Piper Generalvertretung Deutschland AG	19.10.2007	Conrad, Liprecht, Sträter
32	INDUS Holding AG	24.10.2007	Treuhand- und Revisions-AG Niederrhein
33	Bau-Verein zu Hamburg AG	25.10.2007	Schröder, Nörenberg + Partner GmbH
34	JIL SANDER AG	07.11.2007	Deloitte
35	cash.medien AG	30.11.2007	Mercurius GmbH Wirtschaftsprüfungsgesell-schaft
36	HAITEC AG	06.12.2007	Rupp & Epple GmbH
37	BBS Kraftfahrzeugtechnik AG	13.12.2007	Ernst & Young
38	HAITEC AG	15.01.2008	Rupp & Epple GmbH
39	1st RED AG	18.02.2008	Prof. Dr. Katz & Kollegen GmbH
40	LS telcom AG	22.02.2008	Ebner Stolz Mönning & Bachem
41	PA Power Automation AG	25.02.2008	PwC
42	MWG Biotech AG	28.02.2008	MDS Möhrle GmbH
43	1st RED AG	19.03.2008	Prof. Dr. Katz & Kollegen GmbH
44	SolarWorld AG	25.03.2008	BDO
45	TA TRIUMPH-ADLER AG	24.04.2008	PwC
46	Wirecard AG	24.04.2008	Control5H GmbH
47	Celesio AG	08.05.2008	PwC
48	Deutsche Wohnen AG	15.05.2008	Ernst & Young
49	LINTEC Information Technologies AG	26.05.2008	Commerzial Treuhand GmbH
50	LINTEC Information Technologies AG	26.05.2008	Commerzial Treuhand GmbH
51	Deutsche EuroShop AG	26.05.2008	BDO
52	AREAL Immobilien und Beteiligungs-AG	29.07.2008	Märkische Revision GmbH
53	Landesbank Baden-Württemberg	29.07.2008	PwC
54	Catalis SE	30.07.2008	DRV Accountants en Belastingadviseus
55	Schwarz Pharma AG	30.07.2008	Ernst & Young
56	Conergy AG	06.08.2008	Deloitte
57	Deutsche Post AG	25.08.2008	PwC
58	PONAXIS AG	28.08.2008	Gräwe & Partner GmbH
59	Deutsche Beteiligungs AG	01.09.2008	KPMG
60	Deutsche Beteiligungs AG	01.09.2008	KPMG
61	SMARTRAC N.V.	05.09.2008	KPMG
62	INTELIS AG	19.09.2008	Gräwe & Partner GmbH
63	Pongs & Zahn AG	26.09.2008	BDP Hanseatische Revisons GmbH
64	Pongs & Zahn AG	01.10.2008	Ernst & Young
65	Biofrontera AG	07.10.2008	Ernst & Young
66	Plaut AG	21.10.2008	Audit Wirtschaftsprüfungsgesellschaft m.b.H.
67	M.M.Warburg & CO Hypothekenbank AG	04.11.2008	BDO
68	Schwarz Pharma AG	10.11.2008	Ernst & Young
69	Hesse Newman Capital AG	18.11.2008	BDO
70	Plaut AG	19.01.2009	Audit Wirtschaftsprüfungsgesellschaft m.b.H.
71	STRABAG AG	22.01.2009	T&A + KPMG Austria GmbH
72	D+S europe AG	03.02.2009	Deloitte
73	ecotel communication ag	03.02.2009	Bernhard Weßendorf
74	ISRA VISION AG	05.02.2009	PKF
75	Air Berlin PLC & Co. Luftverkehrs KG	13.02.2009	KPMG
76	Conergy AG	18.03.2009	Deloitte
77	STADA Arzneimittel AG	19.03.2009	PKF
78	COLEXON Energy AG	26.03.2009	Treuökonom Beratungs-, Revisions- und TreuhandG
79	Air Berlin PLC	03.04.2009	KPMG
80	INDUS Holding AG	15.04.2009	Treuhand- und Revisions-AG Niederrhein
81	biolitec AG	20.04.2009	Mazars
82	GWB Immobilien AG	20.04.2009	GHP Revision
83	D+S europe AG	29.04.2009	Deloitte

No.	Company	Pub.date	Audit firm[564]
84	Westdeutsche ImmobilienBank AG	05.05.2009	Ernst & Young
85	Energiekontor AG	06.05.2009	TL Treuhand Leonberg GmbH
86	ISRA VISION AG	08.05.2009	PKF
87	Boetzelen Real Estate AG	08.05.2009	WBW WPG für Bau- und Wohnungswirtschaft
88	ESCADA AG	08.05.2009	BDO
89	313music JWP AG	09.06.2009	Wisbert-Treuhand GmbH
90	Curanum AG	24.06.2009	Wirtschaftstreuhand GmbH
91	Curanum AG	24.06.2009	Ernst & Young
92	Girindus AG	25.06.2009	Deloitte
93	313music JWP AG	29.06.2009	Wisbert-Treuhand GmbH
94	GESCO AG	29.06.2009	Dr. Breidenbach und Partner
95	Neschen AG	13.07.2009	ADK GmbH
96	Borussia Dortmund GmbH & Co. KG a. A.	16.07.2009	BDO
97	PIXELPARK AG	01.09.2009	KPMG
98	PIXELPARK AG	01.09.2009	KPMG
99	Praktiker Bau- u. Heimwerkermärkte Holding AG	01.09.2009	PwC
100	ETFS Metal Securities Limited	15.09.2009	Ernst & Young
101	Stadtwerke Hannover AG	21.09.2009	PwC
102	FROSTA AG	22.09.2009	Gräwe & Partner GmbH
103	ARQUANA International Print & Media AG	30.10.2009	PwC
104	3U Holding AG	27.11.2009	KPMG
105	VT Finance AG	01.12.2009	PwC
106	Merck KGaA	08.12.2009	KPMG
107	TAG Immobilien AG	21.12.2009	Nörenberg Schröder GmbH
108	Intertainment AG	21.12.2009	KPMG
109	Sanacorp Pharmaholding AG	10.02.2010	Genossenschafts-Treuhand Bayern GmbH
110	MBB Industries AG	12.03.2010	Verhülsdonk & Partner GmbH
111	Deutsche Postbank AG	14.05.2010	PwC
112	W.E.T. Automotive Systems AG	19.05.2010	KPMG
113	GfK SE	04.06.2010	KPMG
114	caatoosee ag	09.06.2010	KPMG
115	IFCO SYSTEMS N.V.	10.06.2010	Ernst & Young
116	GK Software AG	14.06.2010	Deloitte
117	Q-Cells SE	23.06.2010	KPMG
118	Q-Cells SE	23.06.2010	KPMG
119	ARBOmedia AG	30.06.2010	WAPAG
120	IFCO SYSTEMS N.V.	15.07.2010	Ernst & Young
121	Olympia Flexgroup AG	16.08.2010	Deloitte
122	MISTRAL Media AG	31.08.2010	Deloitte
123	Albis Leasing AG	31.08.2010	BDO
124	Merck KGaA	15.09.2010	KPMG
125	Porsche Automobil Holding SE	24.09.2010	Ernst & Young
126	Continental AG	08.10.2010	KPMG
127	B+S Banksysteme AG	20.10.2010	AWI TREUHAND & REVISION GMBH
128	euromicron AG communication & control technology	06.12.2010	BDO
129	TUI AG	14.12.2010	PwC
130	INTERSEROH SE	16.12.2010	KPMG
131	Sky Deutschland AG	17.12.2010	KPMG
132	MyHammer Holding AG	22.12.2010	Warth & Klein Grant Thornton
133	Infineon Technologies AG	24.12.2010	KPMG
134	SCHWÄLBCHEN MOLKEREI Jakob Berz AG	19.01.2011	TREURATIO GmbH
135	H&R WASAG AG	31.01.2011	RBS RoeverBroenerSusat

No.	Company	Pub.date	Audit firm[564]
136	zooplus AG	09.02.2011	Schaffer WP Partner GmbH
137	ELMOS Semiconductor AG	10.02.2011	Ernst & Young
138	PUMA AG Rudolf Dassler Sport	14.02.2011	PwC
139	MATERNUS-Kliniken-AG	14.02.2011	FIDES Treuhandgesellschaft KG
140	PUMA AG Rudolf Dassler Sport	14.02.2011	PwC
141	Fielmann AG	14.02.2011	RBS RoeverBroenerSusat
142	Novavisions AG	04.03.2011	PwC
143	Basler AG	18.03.2011	BDO
144	CDV Software Entertainment AG	18.03.2011	RP RICHTER GmbH
145	vwd Vereinigte Wirtschaftsdienste AG	28.03.2011	STÜTTGEN & HAEB AG
146	Schlossgartenbau- AG	04.04.2011	PwC
147	Novavisions AG	06.04.2011	PwC
148	Asian Bamboo AG	07.04.2011	Deloitte
149	HAHN-Immobilien-Beteiligungs AG	18.04.2011	Ernst & Young
150	PARK & Bellheimer AG	18.04.2011	Ernst & Young
151	sino AG	19.04.2011	Warth & Klein Grant Thornton
152	TAG Immobilien AG	02.05.2011	Nörenberg Schröder GmbH
153	INTERSEROH SE	06.05.2011	KPMG
154	TAG Immobilien AG	09.05.2011	Nörenberg Schröder GmbH
155	PETROTEC AG	17.05.2011	Rölfs WP Partner AG
156	DocCheck AG	19.05.2011	PKF
157	AREAL Immobilien und Beteiligungs-AG	28.06.2011	Märkische Revision GmbH
158	Business Media China AG	06.07.2011	BDO
159	Business Media China AG	07.07.2011	BDO
160	BKN International AG	03.08.2011	Nexia Deutschland GmbH
161	adidas AG	04.08.2011	KPMG
162	Deutsche Immobilien Holding AG	16.08.2011	KPMG
163	HSN Nordbank AG	23.09.2011	KPMG
164	Value Management & Research AG	07.02.2012	Baker Tilly Deutschland GmbH
165	MyHammer Holding AG	08.02.2012	Warth & Klein Grant Thornton
166	MLP AG	22.02.2012	Ernst & Young
167	Sanochemia Pharmazeutika AG	22.02.2012	Weiler & Weiler
168	Marbert Holding AG	22.02.2012	Mazars
169	FORIS AG	14.03.2012	Sauerland Rybka und Partner
170	Sedlmayr Grund und Immobilien KG auf Aktien	26.03.2012	KPMG
171	METRO AG	10.04.2012	KPMG
172	Norddeutsche Landesbank -Girozentrale-	24.04.2012	Ernst & Young
173	Norddeutsche Landesbank -Girozentrale-	24.04.2012	Ernst & Young
174	GAGFAH S.A.	30.04.2012	Ernst & Young
175	Beate Uhse AG	23.05.2012	Ernst & Young
176	VSM Vereinigte Schmirgel- und Maschinen-Fabriken AG	08.06.2012	Deloitte
177	GWB Immobilien AG	15.06.2012	GHP Revision
178	GWB Immobilien AG	03.07.2012	GHP Revision
179	Powerland AG	30.07.2012	BDO
180	Sedlbauer Aktiengesellschaft	06.08.2012	KPWT Kirschner Wirtschaftstreuhand
181	CCR Logistics Systems AG	03.09.2012	KPMG
182	Valovis Commercial Bank AG	18.09.2012	KPMG
183	Aurubis AG	31.10.2012	PwC
184	Deutsche Steinzeug Cremer & Breuer AG	30.11.2012	Dr. Glade, König und Partner GmbH
185	MAGNAT Real Estate AG	19.12.2012	KMPG
186	DIC Asset AG	21.12.2012	Rödl & Partner GmbH

Table A.2: Audit Firms and Legal Entities in Context with PRE

Audit Firm	Legal entity
Mazars	Mazars GmbH
	RSM Hemmelrath GmbH WPG StBG
	Mazars Hemmelrath GmbH WPG
Deloitte	Deloitte & Touche GmbH WPG
	Deloitte GmbH WPG
BDO	BDO AG WPG
	BDO AWT GmbH WPG
	AWT Horwath GmbH WPG
PwC	PricewaterhouseCoopers AG WPG
	PwC Europe AG WPG
	PwC Treuhand GmbH WPG
Ernst & Young	Ernst & Young GmbH WPG
	Ernst & Young AG WPG StBG
	Ernst & Young Deutsche Allgemeine Treuhand AG WPG StBG
	Ernst & Young S.A.
KPMG	KPMG AG WPG
	KPMG Deutsche Treuhand-Gesellschaft GmbH WPG
	KPMG Bayerische Treuhandgesellschaft AG WPG StBG
Warth & Klein Grant Thornton	Warth & Klein GmbH WPG
	Warth & Klein Grant Thornton GmbH WPG
Ebner Stolz Mönning & Bachem	Dr. Ebner, Dr. Stolz und Partner GmbH
	BFJM Bachem Fervers Janssen Mehrhoff GmbH
	Ebner Stolz Mönning Bachem GmbH & Co. KG WPG StBG
PKF	PKF Deutschland GmbH WPG
	PKF TREUROG GmbH WPG
	PKF Fasselt Partnerschaft WPG StBG
	PKF Pannell Kerr Forster GmbH WPG
Dr. Breidenbach und Partner	Dr. Breidenbach und Partner GmbH & Co. KG WPG
	Dr. Breidenbach, Dr. Güldenagel und Partner KG WPG
GHP Revision	GHP Revision GmbH WPG
	GHP Großmann & Holst Revision GmbH WPG
RBS RoeverBroennerSusat	Susat & Parner OHG WPG
	RBS RoeverBroennerSusat GmbH & Co. KG WPG StBG
	RöverBrönner GmbH & Co. KG WPG StBG
	Susat & Partner GmbH & Co. KG WPG

Appendix B: Involved Audit Firms

Table B.1: Involved Audit Firms

No.	Audit Firm	AFF
1	KPMG	30
2	Ernst & Young	23
3	PwC	18
4	BDO	16
5	Deloitte	13
6	PKF	5
7	Ebner Stolz Mönning & Bachem	3
8	Gräwe & Partner GmbH	3
9	GHP Revision	3
10	Nörenberg Schröder GmbH	3
11	Rupp & Epple GmbH	3
12	Warth & Klein Grant Thornton	3
13	Wisbert-Treuhand GmbH	3
14	Audit Wirtschaftsprüfungsgesellschaft m.b.H.	2
15	Commerzial Treuhand GmbH	2
16	Dr. Breidenbach und Partner	2
17	MÄRKISCHE REVISION GMBH	2
18	Mazars	2
19	Prof. Dr. Katz & Kollegen GmbH	2
20	Rölfs WP Partner AG	2
21	Schröder, Nörenberg + Partner GmbH	2
22	RBS RoeverBroennerSusat GmbH & Co.KG	2
23	Treuhand- und Revisions-AG Niederrhein	2
24	ADK GmbH	1
25	AUDIT WIRTSCHAFTS-TREUHAND AG	1
26	AWI TREUHAND & REVISION GMBH	1
27	Baker Tilly Deutschland GmbH	1
28	BDP Hanseatische Revisons GmbH	1
29	Beratungs- und Prüfungsgesellschaft mbH	1
30	Bernhard Weßendorf	1
31	Conrad, Liprecht, Sträter	1
32	Control5H GmbH	1
33	Dipl.-Kfm. Hans M. Klein, Wirtschaftsprüfer	1
34	Dr. Stückmann und Partner	1
35	DRV Accountants en Belastingadviseus	1
36	Dürkop Möller und Partner	1
37	FIDES Treuhandgesellschaft KG	1
38	Genossenschafts-Treuhand Bayern GmbH	1

No.	Audit Firm	AFF
39	KÖNIG WIRTSCHAFTSPRÜFUNG GMBH	1
40	KPWT Kirschner Wirtschaftstreuhand AG WPG	1
41	LOHR + COMPANY GmbH	1
42	MDS Möhrle GmbH	1
43	Mercurius GmbH Wirtschaftsprüfungsgesellschaft	1
44	Mörtl und Kollegen GmbH	1
45	Moses & Partner Revision und Treuhand GmbH	1
46	MÜNCHNER WIRTSCHAFTSPRÜFUNGSGESLLESCHAFT GMBH	1
47	Nexia Deutschland GmbH	1
48	RP RICHTER GmbH	1
49	Sauerland Rybka und Partner	1
50	Schaffer WP Partner GmbH	1
51	Sparkassen- und Giroverband	1
52	STÜTTGEN & HAEB AG	1
53	T&A + KPMG Austria GmbH	1
54	TL Treuhand Leonberg GmbH	1
55	Treuökonom Beratungs-, Revisions- und Treuhandgesellschaft mbH	1
56	TREURATIO GmbH	1
57	Verhülsdonk & Partner GmbH	1
58	WAPAG AG WPG	1
59	WBW WPG für Bau- und Wohnungswirtschaft Holup KG	1
60	Weiler & Weiler	1
61	Wirtschaftstreuhand GmbH	1
62	Rödl & Partner GmbH WPG StBG	1
63	Dr. Glade, König und Partner GmbH	1

Appendix C: Data Basis for Certification Rate Calculation

Audit portion calculation[565]

Table C.1: Certified Audit Professionals per Audit Firm (source: respective transparency reports)

ESMB	Audit	Total		Source	2008	ESM	BFJM		
2008	8.4	37.2	22.6%	TR2009	Audit	4.0	4,4		
2009	26.2	94.5	27.7%	TR2010	Total	17.8	19.4		
2010	25.8	106.0	24.4%	TR2011					
2011	27.9	121.7	22.9%	TR2012					
	88.4	359.4	24.6%						
E&Y	**Audit**	**Total**		**Source**	**KPMG**	**Audit**	**Total**		**Source**
2009	346	1087	31.9%	TR2010	2009	456	1208	37.7%	TR2010
2010	345	1055	32.7%	TR2011	2010	434	1143	37.9%	TR2011
2011	345	1088	31.7%	TR2012	2011	440	1160	37.9%	TR2012
	1036	3230	32.1%			1330	3511	37.9%	
PwC	**Audit**	**Total**		**Source**	**BDO[566]**	**Audit**	**Total**		**Source**
2009	503	1379	36.5%	TR2010	2009	66,6	166.7	39.9%	TR2010
2010	505	1336	37.8%	TR2011	2010	66.9	171.7	39.0%	TR2011
2011	528	1439	36.7%	TR2012	2011	94.4	206.2	45.8%	TR2012*2
	1536	4154	37.0%			227.9	544.6	41.9%	
Deloitte[567]	**Audit**	**Total**		**Source**	**PKF Fasselt**	**Audit**	**Total**		**Source**
2009	180	716	25.1%	TR2010	2009	16.6	57.3	29.0%	TR2010
2010	164	577	28.4%	TR2011	2010	16.8	56.3	29.8%	TR2011
2011	164	624	26.3%	TR2012	2011	16.4	58.1	28.2%	TR2012
	508	1917	26.5%			49.8	171.7	29.0%	

565 All fees in Million of €.

566 BDO changed its fiscal year; therefore figures of 2011 represent only 6 month business figures. This is why the figures were multiplied times two.

567 Deloitte Group figures from Transparency Reports.

Deloitte[568]	Audit	Total		Source	PKF DE	Audit	Total		Source
2009	174	582	29.9%	TR2010	2009	2.7	7.4	36.5%	TR2010
2010	160	444	36.0%	TR2011	2010	3.7	8.1	45.7%	TR2011
2011	158	486	32.5%	TR2012	2011	3.6	8.1	44.4%	TR2012
	492	1512	32.5%			10.0	23.6	42.4%	
Deloitte[569]	**Audit**	**Total**		**Source**	**PKF Total**	**Audit**	**Total**		**Source**
2009	180	588	30.6%	TR2010	2009	19.3	64.7	29.8%	TR2010
2010	164	447	36.7%	TR2011	2010	20.5	64.4	31.8%	TR2011
2011	164	482	34.0%	TR2012	2011	20.0	66.2	30.2%	TR2012
	508	1517	33.5%			59.8	195.3	30.6%	

Number of employees

Table C.2: Number of Employees per Audit Firm
(various sources[570])

FY	KPMG	E&Y	PwC	Deloitte[571]	BDO	ESMB	PKF
2009	8376	7096	9028	4092	1991	750	1050
2010	8270	6970	8673	4007	1896	850	1150
2011	8438	6903	8887	3942	1879	930	1250
	8361	6990	8863	4014	1922	843	1150

568 Deloitte GmbH figures (only one legal entity).

569 Deloitte Group figures minus consultancy fees (2009: 716-128; 2010: 577-130; 2011: 624-142). This is done because Deloitte is the only audit firm which did not split from its consulting firm in 2002.

570 Figures stem from annual reports and financial statements published in the federal gazette for KPMG, E&Y, PwC, Deloitte and BDO. PKF are estimated from Transparency Reports 2009, 2010 and 2011.
ESMB figures are extracted from press releases (http://www.ebnerstolz.de/de/esp/Presse/Pressemitteilungen/12791):
Press Release as of 22.05.2012: "on average about 930 employees in 2011" (http://www.ebnerstolz.de/de/esp/Presse/Pressemitteilungen/12791?subId=35164),
Press Release as of 20.04.2012: more than 950 employees,
Press Release as of 18.12.2011: more than 850 employees,
Press Release as of 18.03.2011: more than 800 employees,
Press Release as of 14.07.2010: more than 750 employees,
Press Release as 15.04.2010: round about 750 employees,
Press Release as of 18.02.2009: more than 700 employees.

571 Deloitte Group without Deloitte consulting (2009: 4696-604; 2010: 4602-595; 2011: 4556-614).

Numbers of Certified Audit Professionals ("Wirtschaftsprüfer")

Table C.3: Certified Audit Professionals per Audit Firm (source: WPK[572])

Audit Firm	average WP[573]	WPs 2010	WPs 2009	WPs 2008	WPs 2007
KPMG	977	1030	1005	945	927
E&Y	770	748	791	776	763
PwC	987	991	957	989	1010
BDO	246	240	243	248	252
Deloitte	384	420	399	367	348
PKF	90	111	92	83	72
ESMB	62	78	73	50	46

PIE clients per Audit Firm

Table C.4: PIE Clients per Audit Firm (source: respective transparency reports)

TR	PwC	E&Y	Deloitte	KPMG	BDO	ESMB	PKF
2009	151	140	52	150	57	5	11
2010	156	130	61	151	51	20	9
2011	147	105	63	147	48	22	9
2012	146	108	55	134	41	24	11

Remarks: BDO Merged with AWT in 2010

Table C.5: Break Down of BDO PIE Clients into BDO and AWT Clients

TR	BDO	AWT	SUM
2009	49	8	**57**
2010	43	8	**51**
2011	44	4	**48**
2012	39	2	**41**

572 Data basis is the annual audit market analysis of the German Chamber of Accountants published in its journals from 2006 to 2012.

573 Shortcut WP means Wirtschaftsprüfer (German CPA).

ESM merged with Bachem in 2010

Table C.6: Break Down of ESMB PIE Clients into ESM and BACHEM Clients

TR	ESM	Bachem	SUM
2009	3	2	**5**
2010	20	0	**20**
2011	22	0	**22**
2012	24	0	**24**

PKF Total Figures Consists of PKF Fasselt and PKF Deutschland

Table C.7: Break Down of PKF PIE Clients into PKF Deutschland and PKF Fasselt Clients

TR	PKF DE	Fasselt	SUM
2009	9	2	**11**
2010	6	3	**9**
2011	8	1	**9**
2012	9	2	**11**

Appendix D: Example Calculation of Isoquality Curves

Calculation Example

Example settings:

- Audit engagement, expected audit fees € 30,000
- Audit firm to select one employee from the resource pool
- Cost rate start at € 60 per hour for one year experience employee and increases by 10% for each year more experience
- An audit professional, having one year experience, will complete the audit in 500 hours at an assurance level of 95%
- Efficiency Gain rate of 30% in year 1, and
- Efficiency Slowdown rate of 80%, starting with a 2 year-experience.

Task: Select resource in order to maximize profit

Assumption: indefinite resources available having an experience between one and ten years

Solution:

1) Determining audit production isoquant by applying formula 21:

The starting point is

$$h_1 = 500$$
$$h_2 = h_1 * (1 - EG * SD^0)$$
$$h_3 = 500 * (1 - 0.3 * 0.8^0) = 350$$
$$h_3 = 350 * (1 - 0.3 * 0.8^2) = 266$$
$$h_4 = 215 * (1 - 0.3 * 0.8^3) = 215$$

...

Instead of using formula 27, the use of the product function (formula 28) leads to a direct and faster way to calculate the values. For instance, the audit hours for y=3 are determined as following:

$$h_{\bar{q}}(3) = h_1 \prod_{i=0}^{3} (1 - EG * SD^{i-1})$$

$$h_{\bar{q}}(3) = 500\,(1 - 0.3\;0.8^0)(1 - 0.3\;0.8^1)(1 - 0.3\;0.8^2) = 266$$

Table D.1: Isoquality Values: Experience in Years and Audit time in Hours (source: own development[574])

Experience [years]	Audit time [hours]
1	500
2	350
3	266
4	215
5	182
6	160
7	144
8	133
9	124
10	118

After having calculated the values, the isoquality curve can now be drawn:

Figure D.1: Isoquality Curve Based on Table E.1 (source: own development)

[574] The underlying production theory, refer to Varian (1992), p. 51.

2) Determining the cost curves

COST PER HOUR

$$c(y) = 60(1.1)^{y-1}$$

Cost per hours of an 1-year-experience audit professional: $c(1)$ = € 60
Cost per hours of an 2-year-experience audit professional: $c(2)$ = € 66
Cost per hours of an 3-year-experience audit professional: $c(3)$ = € 73

...

TOTAL COST

$$TC(y,h) = 60(1.1)^{y-1} * h(y)$$

For instance, total cost for 266 hours of an employee with a 3-year experience result in total cost of € 19,312.

$$TC(3;266) = 60\frac{€}{hour}(1+0.1)^2 * 266\ hours = €\ 19312$$

ISOCOST CURVE
Applying the isocost curve equation of formula 34, the following isocost curves are developed:

$$\overline{TC}_1 = 12000\text{:}\ h_{\overline{TC}_1}(y) = \frac{12000}{60(1.1)^{y-1}}$$

$$\overline{TC}_2 = 15293\text{:}\ h_{\overline{TC}_2}(y) = \frac{15293}{60(1.1)^{y-1}}$$

$$\overline{TC}_3 = 20000\text{:}\ h_{\overline{TC}_3}(y) = \frac{20000}{60(1.1)^{y-1}}$$

$$\overline{TC}_4 = 30000\text{:}\ h_{\overline{TC}_4}(y) = \frac{30000}{60(1.1)^{y-1}}$$

Table D.2 shows the values for each o f the isocost curves.

The isocost curves can be interpreted as budget curves; e.g. $\overline{TC}_4$: With a budget of € 30,000 all of the following input factor combinations are affordable: an 1-year experience audit professional can deploy 500 hours, an 2-year experience audit professional with 455 hours, an 3-year audit professional with 411 hours, and so on. All this combinations do not exceed the budget; they sit exactly on the affordable frontier.

Table D.2: Isoquality Curves at Different Assurance Levels (source: own development[575])

Experience [years]	Audit time [hours]	Isocost € 12000	Isocost € 15293	Isocost € 20000	Isocost € 30000
1	60	200	255	333	500
2	66	182	232	303	455
3	73	164	209	274	411
4	80	150	191	250	375
5	88	136	174	227	341
6	97	124	158	206	309
7	106	113	144	189	283
8	117	103	131	171	256
9	129	93	119	155	233
10	141	85	108	142	213

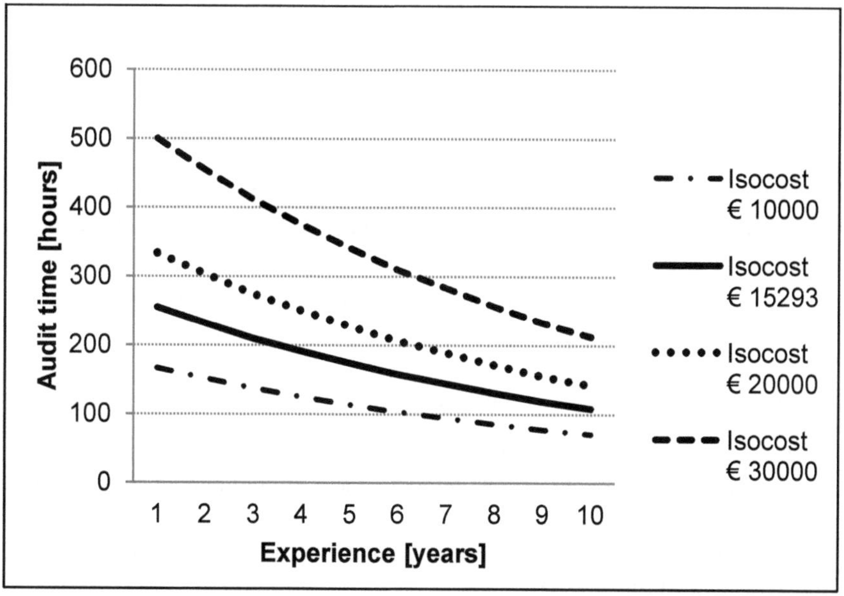

Figure D.2: Isocost Curves (source: own development)

575 The underlying production theory, refer to Varian (1992), p. 51.

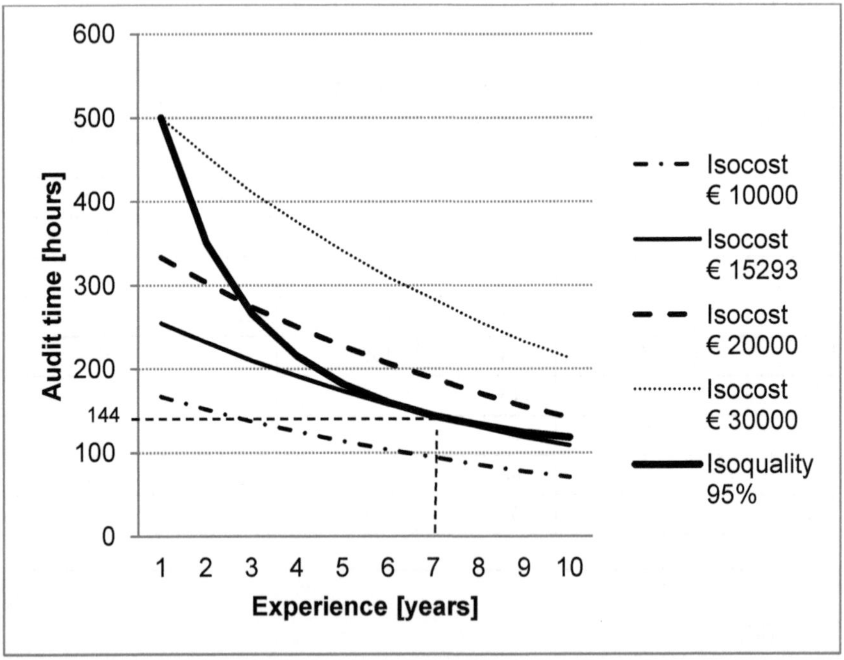

Figure D.3: Determining the Cost-Minimum Point (source: own development[576])

Adding the isoquality curve to the chart in figure D.2 there is only one isocost curve that tangentially touches the isoquant curve at one single point. In figure D.3, it is the isocost curve $h_{\overline{TC}_2}(y)$.

Hence, the cost-minimum point is 7 years and 144 hours, resulting in a minimum cost of € 15,293 (figure D.3).

Cost-minimum and profit maximum determination

Since the product function cannot be differentiated $(\partial h_{\bar{q}}(y) / \partial y)$ with standard methods (only with approximation methods), the cost minimum is determined by calculating all possible total cost values.

Applying the total cost function (formulas 30 and 31), the following table can be developed (table D.3).

[576] The underlying production theory, refer to Varian (1992), p. 51.

Table D.3: Total Audit Costs for the Given Example (source: own development)

Experience [years]	Audit time [hours]	Costs/hour	Total audit costs
1	500	60	30000
2	350	66	23100
3	266	73	19312
4	215	80	17164
5	182	88	15981
6	160	97	15419
7	144	106	15293
8	133	117	15499
9	124	129	15977
10	118	141	16690

$$TC(y) = 60(1.1)^{y-1} * h(y)$$

$$\mathrm{TC}(1) = 60 * 500 = 30000$$

$$\mathrm{TC}(2) = 66 * 350 = 23100$$

$$\mathrm{TC}(3) = 73 * 266 = 19312$$

...

A cost minimum is reached by selecting an audit professional with a 7 year experience background from the resource pool. The profit maximum amounts to € 14,707 (€ 30,000 of audit fees minus € 15,293). All other input factor combinations result in a lower profit.

Appendix E: Derivation of Formulas

Total years of experience of all employees of an audit firm (TYE)

Example: Audit firm having 10 employees (N), separation rate and hire rate is constant 20% (a), which means that every year two leaving employees are replaced by two hires.

The situation is depicted in the following sketch:

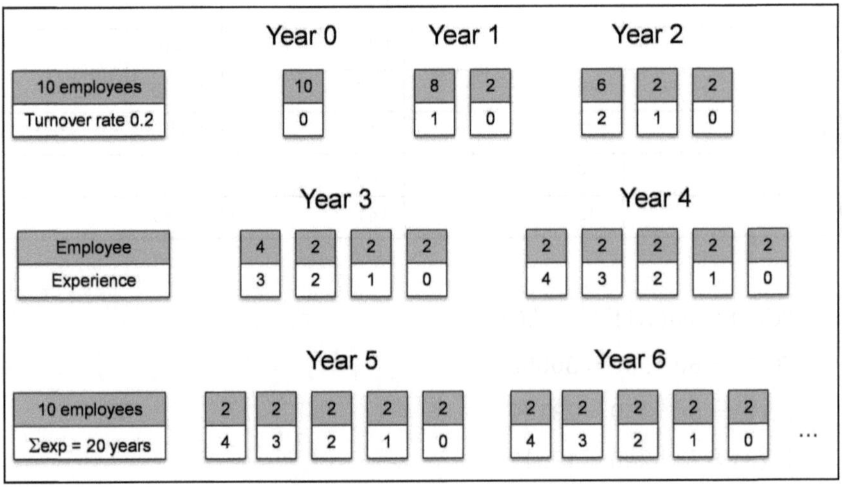

Figure E.1: Developing the Measure "Years of Experience" in an Audit Firm (source: own development)

In a steady state (in the example after 4 years), the employees can be grouped into 1/0.2 = 5 groups (in general in 1/a groups), each group has 2 employees (N*a). Group 1, which represent new hires, have 0 years of experience, group 2, which includes employees hired one year ago, have 1 year times 2 employees that means 2 years of experience, group 3 has in total 4 years of experience, group 4 has 3 * 2 = 6 years of experience, and group 5 has in total 4 * 2 = 8 years of experience. In sum all employees together have 0 + 2 + 4 + 6 + 8 = 20 years of experience.

This can be transformed in a general sum formula:

$$TYE = Na\sum_{i=1}^{\frac{1}{a}-1} i = 10 * 0.2\sum_{i=1}^{\frac{1}{0.2}-1} i = 2(1+2+3+4) = 2+4+6+8 = 20$$

Applying the Gauß formula of "the sum of the first n natural numbers"

$$1 + 2 + 3 + \cdots + n = \sum_{k=1}^{n} k = \frac{n(n+1)}{2} \qquad \text{(E.1)}$$

The formula can be simplified as follows:

$$TYE = n \sum_{i=1}^{\frac{1}{a}-1} i = \frac{N(\frac{1}{a}-1)}{2}$$

Applied to the example above:

$$TYE = Nh \sum_{i=1}^{\frac{1}{a}-1} i = \frac{N(\frac{1}{a}-1)}{2} = \frac{10(\frac{1}{0.2}-1)}{2} = \frac{10(4)}{2} = 20$$

Average years of experience of an employee of an audit firm (AYE)

$$AYE = \frac{TYE}{N} = n \sum_{i=1}^{\frac{1}{a}-1} i = \frac{(\frac{1}{a}-1)}{2} \qquad \text{(E.2)}$$

References

Abbott, L.J., and G.F. Peters (2002): Audit committee characteristics and financial misstatement: A study of the efficacy of certain blue ribbon committee recommendations, Working paper, University of Memphis.

Abbott, L. J., Parker, S. & Peters, G. F. (2006): 'Earnings management, litigation risk, and asymmetric audit fee responses', Auditing: A Journal of Practice & Theory, Vol. 25, No. 1, pp. 85–98.

Acuitas (2012): inc.'s survey of fair value audit deficiencies, April 2012, http://www.acuitasinc.com/documents/Survey_of_Fair_Value_Audit_Deficiencies_for_Big_Four_Audit_Firms_as_Reported_in_the_Wall_Street_Journal.pdf (Aug 21, 2012, 15:00 CET).

Agrawal, A. & Chadha, S. (2005): 'Corporate governance and accounting scandals', Journal of Law and Economics, Vol. 48, pp. 371–406.

Akerlof, George A. (1970): "The Market for 'Lemons': Quality Uncertainty and the Market Mechanism". Quarterly Journal of Economics (The MIT Press), Volume 84 (3), pp. 488–500.

Aldhizer/Miller/Moraglio (1995): Common contributes of audit quality. Journal of Accountancy, Vol. 179 (January), p. 61-68.

Antle, R., Gordon, E., Narayanamoorthy, G. & Zhou, L. (2006): 'The joint determination of audit fees, non-audit fees, and abnormal accruals', Review of Quantitative Finance and Accounting, Vol. 27, pp. 235–66.

Arrow, K. J. (1985): The Economics of Agency, In: Pratt, J., Zeckhauser, R., J.: Principals and Agents: The Structure of Business, Boston 1985, pp. 37–51.

Audit Analytics (2010): "Audit Fees and Non-Audit Fees – A Seven Year Trend", March 2010. For purchase online at: http://www.auditanalytics.com (July 14, 2011, 18:00 CET).

Audit Analytics (2012): "Financial restatements: A ten year comparison." April 2012. For purchase online at: http://www.auditanalytics.com (Downloaded: Aug 14, 2012, 11:00 CET).

Baldauf, Steckel and Steller (2012): The influence of Audit Risk and Materiality Guidelines on Auditors Materiality Assessment, American Accounting Association, Annual Meeting in August 4-8, 2012, Washington D.C.

Balsam, S., Krishnan, J. and Yang, J. S (2003): Auditor Industry Specialization and Earnings Quality. Auditing: A Journal of Practice & Theory, September 2003. Available at SSRN: http://ssrn.com/abstract=436260 or http://dx.doi.org/10.2139/ssrn.436260.

Bamberg and Baur (1996): Statistik, Oldenbourg Verlag, 9th Edition 1996, ISBN 3-486-23520-6.

Bauer, Michael (2004): Die Unabhängigkeit des Abschlussprüfers im Zusammenhang mit dem gleichzeitigen Angebot von Beratungsleistungen beim Prüfungsmandanten – Eine empirische Analyse; Universität Würzburg, available at (download July 11, 2011): http://opus.bibliothek.uni-wuerzburg.de/volltexte/2005/1491/pdf/Dissertation_Bauer_UB.pdf.

Bauwhede, H. V., Willekens, M. & Gaeremynck, A. (2003), "Audit firm size, public ownership, and firms' discretionary accruals management", The International Journal of Accounting, Vol. 38, pp. 1–22.

Bauwhede, H. V. & Willekens, M. (2004): "Evidence on (the lack of) audit-quality differentiation in the private client segment of the Belgian audit market", European Accounting Review, Vol. 13, No. 3, pp. 501–522.

BDO (2009): Transparenzbericht 2009, BDO AG WPG, March 2009, http://www.bdo.de.

BDO (2010): Transparenzbericht 2010, BDO AG WPG, March 2010, http://www.bdo.de.

BDO (2011a): Transparenzbericht 2011, BDO AG WPG, March 2011, http://www.bdo.de.

BDO (2011b): Transparenzbericht 2011, BDO AWT GmbH WPG, March 2011, http://www.bdo.de.

BDO (2012a): Transparenzbericht 2012, BDO AG WPG, March 2012, http://www.bdo.de.

BDO (2012b): Transparenzbericht 2012, BDO AWT GmbH WPG, March 2012, http://www.bdo.de.

Bedard, J., Chi M., Graham L, and J. Shanteau (1993). Expertise in Auditing; Discussion. Auditing: A Journal of Practice and Theory, Vol. 12 (1993), pp. 21-56.

Bedard, J.C, K. M. Johnstone, and E. F. Smith (2010): Audit Quality Indicators: A Status Update on Possible Public Disclosures and Insights from Audit Practice, Current Issues in Auditing: June 2010, Vol. 4, No. 1, pp. C12-C19.

Berger/Zemper (2012): Comment on Sec. 342b of the HGB, Haufe-HGB-Kommentar, 3rd Edition 2012, pp. 2607-2627.

Bonner, S. E., Palmrose, Z.-V. and Young, S. M. (1998): Fraud Type and Auditor Litigation: An Analysis of SEC Accounting and Auditing Enforcement Releases The Accounting Review Vol. 73, No. 4 (Oct., 1998), pp. 503-532.

Bragg, Steven M. (2005): A Guide To Closing The Books Quickly, First edition, John Wiley & Sons, Inc., ISBN 0-471-70897-6.

Bundestag (2004): Drucksache 15/4055 as of October 27, 2004. Beschlussempfehlung und Bericht des Rechtsausschusses (6. Ausschuss) zu dem Gesetzesentwurf der Bundesregierung –Drucksache 15/2421 – Entwurf eines Gesetzes zur Kontrolle von Unternehmensabschlüssen (Bilanzkontrollgesetz – BilKoG).

Bundesministerium der Justiz (2004), Press release as of October 29, 2004: „Bundestag verabschiedet Bilanzrechtsreformgesetz und Bilanzkontrollgesetz“, http://www.standardsetter.de/drsc/docs/press_releases/presse_BilReG%20und%20BilKoG_291004.pdf.

Caramanis C. and Lennox, C. (2008): Audit effort and earnings management. Journal of Accounting and Economics 45 (2008) 116–138.

Carcello, J. V, T. L. Neal, and R. A. Riley (2002): Board characteristics and audit fees. Contemporary Accounting Research, Volume 19, No. 3, pp. 365–384.

Carson, E. and Dowling (2010): The production of audit services: the relationship between audit support system design and audit pricing by global audit firm networks, May 2010, http://www.afaanz.org/openconf/2010/modules/request.php?module=OC_program&action=view.php&id=82 (download 17:30 CET, November 23, 2012).

Catanach Jr, A.H., and Walker, P.L. (1999): The International debate over mandatory auditor rotation: a conceptual research framework, Journal of International Accounting, Auditing & Taxation, Volume 8, Issue 1, pp. 43-66.

CAQ (2008): Report of the Major Public Company audit firms to the Department the Treasury Advisory Committee on the Auditing Profession, Center for Audit Quality, January 23, 2008.

Chase, Richard B. (2001): Operations management for competitive advantage, ninth edition, International edition: McGraw Hill/ Irwin, ISBN 0-07-118030-3.

Chen, K. Y., Lin, K-L. & Zhou, J. (2005), ‘Audit quality and earnings management for Taiwan IPO firms’, Managerial Auditing Journal, Volume 20, Issue 1, pp. 86–104.

Chow, C. W. and Rice, S. J. (1982): Qualified audit opinions and auditor switching, The Accounting Review, Volume 57, No. 2, pp. 326-335.

Chung, H. and S. Kallapur (2003): Client Importance, Non-audit Services, and Abnormal Accruals, The Accounting Review, Volume 78, No. 4, pp. 931-955.

Copley, P. and Doucet, M. (1993): The impact of Competition on the Quality of Governmental Audits, Journal of Auditing, Spring 1993, pp. 88-98.

Carcello, J., D. Hermanson, T. Neal, and R. Riley (2002): Board characteristics and audit fees. Contemporary Accounting Research, Volume 19, Issue 3, pp. 365–384.

Carcello, J.V. and Nagy, A.L. (2004): Audit firm tenure and fraudulent financial reporting, Auditing Journal of Practice and Theory, Volume 23, Issue 2, pp. 55–69.

Crabtree, A. D., Brandon, D.M., and Maher, J.J. (2006): The impact of auditor tenure on initial bond ratings, Advanced in Accounting, Volume 22, pp. 97-121.

DCGC (2010): Deutscher Corporate Governance Kodex, Regierungskommission, May 26, 2010.

DeAngelo, L. E. (1981a): “Auditor Size and Audit Quality”, Journal of Accounting and Economics. Vol. 3, Issue 3, pp. 183-199.

DeAngelo, L. E. (1981b): “Auditor independence, low balling, and disclosure regulations”, Journal of Accounting and Economics. Vol. 3, Issue 3, pp. 113-127.

DeAngelo, L. E. (1986). “Accounting Numbers as Market Valuation Substitutes: A Study of Management Buyouts of Public Shareholders.”, The Accounting Review 61, pp. 400-420.

Dechow, P.M., R.G. Sloan, and A.P. Sweeney (1995: “Detecting Earnings Management” The Accounting Review 70, pp: 193-225.

DeFond, M. (1992): The Association Between Changes in Client Firm Agency Costs and Auditor Switching. Auditing, Volume 11, No. 1, pp. 16-31.

DeFond, M. and K.R. Subramanyam. (1998): Auditor changes and discretionary accruals. Journal of Accounting & Economics, Volume 25, No. 1, pp. 35-67.

DeFond, M., J.R. Francis, and T.J. Wong (2000): Auditor industry specialization and market segmentation: Evidence from Hong Kong. Auditing: A Journal of Practice and Theory 19 (Spring), pp. 1-17.

DeFond, M., K. Raghunandan and K. R. Subramanyam (2002): Do Non-Audit Service Fees Impair Auditor Independence? Evidence from Going Concern Audit Opinions. *Journal of Accounting Research*, Volume 40, No. 4, pp. 1247-1273.

Deloitte (2010): Transparenzbericht 2010, Deloitte & Touche WPG, March 2010, http://www.deloitte.com/view/de_DE/de/index.htm.

Deloitte (2011): Transparenzbericht 2011, Deloitte & Touche WPG, March 2011, http://www.deloitte.com/view/de_DE/de/index.htm.

Deloitte (2012): Transparenzbericht 2012, Deloitte & Touche WPG, March 2012, http://www.deloitte.com/view/de_DE/de/index.htm.

De Poorter, Ingrid (2008): Auditor’s liability towards third parties within the EU: A comparative study between the United Kingdom, the Netherlands, Germany and Belgium1 Journal of International Commercial Law and Technology Vol. 3, Issue 1 (2008), pp. 68-75.

Denzin, N.K. (1989): The Research Act: A Theoretical Introduction to Sociological Methods. 3rd Edition. Prentice Hall, Englewood Cliffs, NJ [1970] 1989, ISBN 0-13-774381-5.

Dowling, C. and S. Leech (2007): Audit support systems and decision aids: Current practice and opportunities for future research, International Journal of Accounting Information Systems, Vol. 8 (2007), pp. 92–116.

Dowling, C. (2009): Appropriate Audit Support System Use: The Influence of Auditor, Audit Team, and Firm Factors. The Accounting Review, Volume 84, No. 3, pp. 771-810.

Dowling, C. and Leech, S. A. (2011): Enabling Audit Process Quality Through Audit Support System Design (August 17, 2011). Available at SSRN: http://ssrn.com/abstract=1918602.

Ellrott/Aicher (2006): Prüfstelle für Rechnungslegung, Beck'scher Bilanzkommentar, 6th Edition 2006, comment on Sec. 342b of the HGB, pp. 2295-2313.

Ernst & Young (2009): Transparenzbericht 2009, Ernst & Young GmbH WPG, March 2009, http://www.ey.com/DE/de/Home/Home.

Ernst & Young (2010): Transparenzbericht 2010, Ernst & Young GmbH WPG, March 2010, http://www.ey.com/DE/de/Home/Home.

Ernst & Young (2011): Transparenzbericht 2011, Ernst & Young GmbH WPG, March 2011, http://www.ey.com/DE/de/Home/Home.

Ernst & Young (2012): Transparenzbericht 2012, Ernst & Young GmbH WPG, March 2012, http://www.ey.com/DE/de/Home/Home.

ESMA (2003): CESR Standard No. 1 on Financial Information – Enforcement of Standards on Financial Information in Europe, March 12, 2003, Ref.: CESR/03-073. http://www.esma.europa.eu/documents/overview/10.

ESMA (2004): CESR Standard No. 2 on Financial Information – Coordination of Enforcement Activities, April 2004, Ref.: CESR/03-317c. Available at: http://www.esma.europa.eu/documents/overview/10.

ESMA (2005): Enforcement of Standards on Financial Information – CESR Guidelines on Application of Selection Methods, October 2005, Ref.: CESR/05-547, available only by request, not public accessible.

ESMA (2011): Consultation Paper, Considerations of materiality in financial reporting, European Securities and Markets Authority, November 9, 2011, available at: http://www.esma.europa.eu/system/files/2011_373_.pdf (September 3, 2012).

ESMB (2009): Transparenzbericht 2009, Ebner Stolz Mönning Bachem GmbH & Co. KG WPG, March 2009, http://www.ebnerstolz.de/.

ESMB (2010): Transparenzbericht 2010, Ebner Stolz Mönning Bachem GmbH & Co. KG WPG, March 2010, http://www.ebnerstolz.de/.

ESMB (2011): Transparenzbericht 2011, Ebner Stolz Mönning Bachem GmbH & Co. KG WPG, March 2011, http://www.ebnerstolz.de/.

ESMB (2012): Transparenzbericht 2012, Ebner Stolz Mönning Bachem GmbH & Co. KG WPG, March 2012, http://www.ebnerstolz.de/.

European Commission (2002), Commission Recommendation of May 16, 2002 (notified under document number C(2002), 1873, 2002/590/EC.

European Commission (2004), DIRECTIVE 2004/109/EC OF THE EUROPEAN PARLIAMENT AND OF THE COUNCIL of 15 December 2004 on the harmonisation of transparency requirements in relation to information about issuers whose securities are admitted to trading on a regulated market and amending Directive 2001/34/EC.

European Commission (2006a): Directive 2006/43/EC of the European Parliament and of the Council of 17 May 2006 on statutory audits of annual accounts and consolidated accounts, amending Council Directives 78/660/EEC and 83/349/EEC and repealing Council Directive 84/253/EEC.

European Commission (2006b): Statutory Auditors' Independence in the EU: A Set of Fundamental Principles, Commission Recommendation, 2002/590/EC, May 16, 2002.

European Commission (2010): Green Paper „Audit Policy: Lessons Learned from the Crisis", October 13, 2010, European Commission, http://ec.europa.eu/internal_market/consultations/docs/2010/audit/green_paper_audit_en.pdf.

European Commission (2011): Proposal for a REGULATION OF THE EUROPEAN PARLIAMENT AND OF THE COUNCIL on specific requirements regarding statutory audit of public-interest entities, COM (2011) 779/3.

Fairchild, R. (2008): Auditor tenure, managerial fraud and report qualification: a behavioural game-theoretic approach. International Journal Behavioural Accounting and Finance, Volume 1, Issue 1, pp. 23–37.

FASB (2008): Statement of Financial Accounting Concepts No. 2, "Qualitative Characteristics of Accounting Information" Original Pronouncements as amended, Financial Accounting Standards Board, 2008, Replaced by Statement of Financial Accounting Concepts No. 8.

FASB (2010): Statement of Financial Accounting Concepts No. 8, "Conceptual Framework for Financial Reporting" Replacement of FASB Concepts Statements No. 1 and No. 2, September 2010.

Francis, Jere R. (1984): The Effect of Audit Firm Size on Audit Prices: A Study of the Australian Market, Journal of Accounting & Economics, Volume 6 (1984), No. 2, S. 133–151.

Francis, J. R. and J. Krishnan (1999): Accounting accruals and auditor reporting conservatism, Contemporary Accounting Research, Volume 16, No. 1, pp. 135-165.

Francis, Jere R. (2004): What do we know about audit quality? The British Accounting Review, Vol. 36, Issue 4, December 2004, p. 345-368.

Francis, J. R., Maydew, E. L. & Sparks, H. C. (1999), 'The role of big 6 auditors in the credible reporting of accruals', Auditing: A Journal of Practice & Theory, Vol. 18, No. 2, pp. 17–34.

Francis, Jere R. (2011): „A Framework for Understanding and Researching Audit Quality", Auditing: A Journal of Practice & Theory, Vol. 30, Issue 2, May 2011, pp. 125-152.

Frankel R, Johnson M, Nelson K (2002): The relation between auditors' fees for non-audit services and earnings quality. Account Review 77, pp. 71–105.

FREP (2005): Code of Procedures of the enforcement panel, Financial Reporting Enforcement Panel, August 2005, available at: http://www.frep.info/pruefverfahren/verfahrensregelungen_en.php.

FREP (2006): Annual Activity Report 2005, FREP Presidential Board, Financial Reporting Enforcement Panel, Berlin, February 6, 2012, available at: http://www.frep.info/presse/taetigkeitsberichte_en.php.

FREP (2007): Annual Activity Report 2006, FREP Presidential Board, Financial Reporting Enforcement Panel, Berlin, February 2007, available at: http://www.frep.info/presse/taetigkeitsberichte_en.php.

FREP (2008): Annual Activity Report 2007, FREP Presidential Board, Financial Reporting Enforcement Panel, Berlin, January 14, 2008, available at: http://www.frep.info/presse/taetigkeitsberichte_en.php.

FREP (2009a): Grundsätze für die stichprobenartige Prüfung gemäß § 342b Abs. 2 Satz 3 Nr. 3 HGB, beschlossen von der Prüfstelle und Erteilung des Einvernehmens durch das Bundesministerium der Justiz und das Bundesministerium der Finanzen am 20. April 2009, available at: http://www.frep.info/pruefverfahren/ablauf_eines_pruefverfahrens_en.php.

FREP (2009b): Information relating to the Examination Process of the Financial Reporting Enforcement Panel, October 2009, available at: http://www.frep.info/pruefverfahren/ablauf_eines_pruefverfahrens_en.php.

FREP (2009c): Examination Process (Graphic Chart), Financial Reporting Enforcement Panel, October 2009, available at http://www.frep.info/pruefverfahren/ablauf_eines_pruefverfahrens_en.php.

FREP (2009d): Annual Activity Report 2008, FREP Presidential Board, Financial Reporting Enforcement Panel, Berlin, January 28, 2009, available at: http://www.frep.info/presse/taetigkeitsberichte_en.php.

FREP (2010): Annual Activity Report 2009, FREP Presidential Board, Financial Reporting Enforcement Panel, Berlin, February 4, 2010, available at: http://www.frep.info/presse/taetigkeitsberichte_en.php.

FREP (2011): Annual Activity Report 2010, FREP Presidential Board, Financial Reporting Enforcement Panel, Berlin, January 20, 2011, available at: http://www.frep.info/presse/taetigkeitsberichte_en.php.

FREP (2012): Annual Activity Report 2011, FREP Presidential Board, Financial Reporting Enforcement Panel, Berlin, January 18, 2012, available at: http://www.frep.info/presse/taetigkeitsberichte_en.php.

FREP (2013): Annual Activity Report 2012, FREP Presidential Board, Financial Reporting Enforcement Panel, Berlin, January 29, 2013, available at: http://www.frep.info/presse/taetigkeitsberichte_en.php.

FRC (2008a): The Audit Quality Framework, UK Financial Reporting Council (FRC), February 2008, and available at: http://www.frc.org.uk/getattachment/79a53c7d-1289-4a9f-bb84-5c9829fb964a/The-Audit-Quality-Framework-(1).aspx.

FRC (2008b): APB Ethical Standards, Glossary of Terms, UK Financial Reporting Council (FRC), revised April 2008, and available at: http://www.frc.org.uk/get attachment/38e65797-f3c7-4c0e-8d64-7123ce1c0ecd/Glossary-2008.aspx

Gabler Verlag (Herausgeber), Gabler Wirtschaftslexikon, online in the Internet: http:// wirtschaftslexikon.gabler.de/.

GAO (2002): Financial Statement Restatements – Trends, Market, Impacts, Regulatory Responses, and Remaining Challenges, Report to the Chairman, Committee on Banking, Housing, and Urban Affairs, U.S. Senate, U.S. General Accounting Office, Report No. GAO-03-138, October 2002, Washington D.C., Government Printing Office.

GAO (2003): Public Accounting Firms: Required Study on the Potential Effects of Mandatory Audit Firm Rotation, U.S. Government Accountability Office, Report No. GAO-04-216, November 2003, Washington D.C., Government Printing Office, http://www.gao.gov/new.items/d04216.pdf.

GAO (2006): Financial Restatements Update of Public Company Trends, Market Impacts, and Regulatory Enforcement Activities, U.S. Government Accountability Office, Report No. GAO-06-678, July 2006, Washington D.C., Government Printing Office

Geiger, M. and D. Rama. (2006): Audit Firm Size and Going-Concern Reporting Accuracy. Accounting Horizons, Vol. 20, No. 1, pp. 1-17.

Gelhausen, H.F. and Hönsch H (2005): Das neue Enforcement-Verfahren für Jahres- und Konzernabschlüsse, in: Die Aktiengesellschaft. Vol. 50 (2005), pp. 511-529.

Gramling, A. and D. Stone (2000): A review and evaluation of industry concentration, specialization, experience and knowledge research in auditing. Working paper, University of Illinois.

Groner, R., Groner M. and Bischof W.F. (editors) (1983): Methods of Heuristics, Laurence Erlbaum Associates, Inc. ISBN 0-89859-251-8.

Herzig, N., Watrin, C. (1995): Obligatorische Rotation des Wirtschaftsprüfers – ein Weg zur Verbesserung der externen Unternehmenskontrolle, Zeitschrift für betriebswirtschaftliche Forschung 1995, Heft 9, pp. 775-804.

Hackenbrack, K., and. Knechel, W.R. (1996): Resource allocation decisions in audit engagements, Contemporary Accounting Research, Volume 14 (Fall), pp. 481-499.

Hay, D. C., Knechel, W. R. & Wong, N. (2006): 'Audit fees: a meta-analysis of the effect of supply and demand attributes', Contemporary Accounting Research, Vol. 23, No. 1, 141–91.

Healy, P. M. (1985): "The Effect of Bonus Schemes on Accounting Decisions." Journal of Accounting and Economics 7, pp. 85-107.

Healy, P. M. & Wahlen, J. M. (1999): 'A review of the earnings management literature and its implications for standard setting', Accounting Horizons, Volume 13, No. 4, pp. 365–83.

Hennes, K., A. Leone, and B. Miller (2011): Accounting Restatements and Auditor Accountability Working paper, American Accounting Association, Annual Meeting Midyear 2004.

Hennrichs, Joachim (2004): Fehlerhafte Bilanzen, Enforcement und Aktienrecht, ZHR – Zeitschrift für das gesamte Handels und Wirtschaftsrecht 2004, pp. 383-413.

Hennrichs, Joachim (2009): Fehlerbegriff und Fehlerbeurteilung im Enforcement-verfahren, DStR 2009, pp. 1446-1452.

Hoitash, R., Markelevich, A. & Barragato, C. A. (2007): 'Auditor fees and audit quality', Managerial Auditing Journal, Vol. 22, No. 8, pp. 761–786.

Holland, Ray (1999): Reflexivity. Journal "Human Relations", Vol. 52, No. 4, pp. 463, April 1999.

Huang, H.-W, Ch.-Ch. Lee and Ena Rose-Green (2010): The Association between Audit Fees and Subsequent Client Litigation, Journal of Forensic & Investigative Accounting, Vol. 2 (2010), Issue 2, pp. 105-126.

IASB Framework (1989): Framework for the Preparation and Presentation of Financial Statements, approved by the IASC Board in April 1989 for publication in July 1989, and adopted by the IASB in April 2001. Annex of "Comments concerning certain Articles of the Regulation (EC) No 1606/2002 of the European Parliament and of the Council of 19 July 2002 on the application of international accounting standards and the Fourth Council Directive 78/660/EEC of 25 July 1978 and the Seventh Council Directive 83/349/EEC of 13 June 1983 on accounting.

IASB Conceptual Framework (2010): Conceptual Framework for Financial Reporting, International Accounting Standards Board, September 2010, www.ifrs.org.

IAASB (2011): International Audit Quality: an IAASB perspective, International Auditing and Assurance Standards Board (IAASB), January 2011 http://www.ifac.org/sites/default/files/publications/files/audit-quality-an-iaasb-per.pdf.

IAASB (2012a): Audit Quality: An International Framework, Draft Paper, Version 1, The International Auditing and Assurance Standards Board (IAASB), August 2012, available at (download on October 10, 2012): https://www.ifac.org/sites/default/files/meetings/files/20120911-IAASBCAG-Agenda_Item_B1-Draft_AQ_Frame work-V1.pdf.

IAASB (2012b): Handbook of International Quality Control, Auditing Review, Other Assurance, and Related Services Pronouncements, International Auditing and Assurance Board, Volume 1, Edition 2012.

ICAI (2005): Revised Guidance Note on Independence of Auditors, issued by the Council of the Institute of Chartered Accountants of India, Journal: The Charted Accountant, February 2005, pp. 1090-1098, http://www.icai.org/resource_file/10485 feb051090-98.pdf (14:00 CET, October, 12 2012).

IDW (2012): Response to "ESMA Consultation Paper: Considerations of Materiality in Financial Reporting", March 9, 2012, Institut der Wirtschaftsprüfer (IDW), http://www.idw.de/idw/download/ESAM_Consultation_Paper_OTC_IDWStell.pdf?id=622208&property=Datei (September 6, 2012, 12:00 CET).

IESBA (2012): Handbook of the Code of Ethics for Professional Accountants, International Ethics Standards Board for Accountants, Edition 2012.

IMA (2008): Accounting Control Assessment Standards: The Missing Piece of the Restatement Puzzle, Institute of Management Accountants Discussion Paper, February 2008, available at: http://sec.gov/comments/265-24/26524-41.pdf.

Ioannidis (2007): Limitations are not properly acknowledged in the scientific literature, Journal of Clinical Epidemiology, Volume 60 (2007), pp. 324-329.

Ittelson, T. (2009): Financial Statements: A Step-by-Step Guide to Understanding and Creating Financial Reports, Career Press, 2009.

Jenkins, J.G. and D. J. Lowe (1999): Auditors as advocates for their clients: perceptions of the auditor-client relationship, Journal of Applied Business Research, Volume 15, No. 2, pp. 73-78, 1999.

Jeong, S. W. & Rho, J. (2004): 'Big six auditors and audit quality: the Korean evidence', The International Journal of Accounting, Vol. 39, pp. 175–96.

Johnson, V., Khurana, I. & J. Reynolds. (2002): Audit-Firm Tenure and the Quality of Financial Reports. Contemporary Accounting Research, Volume 19, Issue 4, 637–660.

Jones, J. (1991): "Earnings Management During Import Relief Investigations." Journal of Accounting Research 29, pp. 193-228.

Kamitz, R. (1980): Methode/Methodologie. In: J. Speck (Hrsg.): Handbuch wissenschaftstheoretischer Begriffe. Bd. 2, UTB 967, Göttingen 1980, pp. 429–433.

Kessler, Anke (2012): Frontiers in Microeconomics: The Economics of Contracts and Information Asymmetric Information and Market Failure, CGDE Course, Dresden, August 20-22, 2012, http://cgde.wifa.uni-leipzig.de/Program/1adselection.pdf (January 15, 2013, 16:00 CET).

Kleining, G., and Witt, H. (2000): The Qualitative Heuristic Approach: A Methodology for Discovery in Psychology and Social Science. Rediscovering the Method of Introspection as an Example, in: Forum: Qualitative Social Research, Sozialforschung, Volume 1, No. 1, Art. 13, January 2000.

Kinney, W. and L. McDaniel (1989): Characteristics of firms correcting previously reported quarterly earnings, Journal of Accounting and Economics, Volume 11, Issue 1, pp. 71-93.

Kinney, W. R., and Libby, R. (2002): Discussion of the relation between auditors' fees for nonaudit services and earnings management, The Accounting Review 77 (Supplement), pp. 107-114.

Kilgore, A., Radich, R., Harrison, G. (2011): The Relative Importance of Audit Quality Attributes, Australian Accounting Review, Volume 21, Issue 3, pp. 253–265, September 2011.

Kirk, J. and Miller, M. L. (1986): Reliability and validity in qualitative research, Beverly Hills, Sage Publications, 1986.

Knapp, M. C. and C. A. Knapp (2012): Cognitive Biases in Audit Engagements – Errors in Judgment and Strategies for Prevention, The CPA Journal, June 2012, pp. 40-45.

Knechel, W. R. (2007): The Business Risk Audit: Origins, Obstacles and Opportunities, Accounting, Organizations and Society, Volume 32, pp. 383-408.

Knechel, W. R. (2009): "Audit lessons from the economic crisis: rethinking audit quality", Inaugural Lecture, open access publications from Maastricht University, urn: nbn:nl:ui:27-20860, Maastricht University.

Knechel W. R., Rouse, P., and C. Schelleman (2009): A Modified Audit Production Framework: Evaluating the Relative Efficiency of Audit Engagements. The Accounting Review: September 2009, Vol. 84, No. 5, pp. 1607-1638.

Knechel, R. W., D. S. Sharma, V. D. Sharma (2012): Non-Audit Services and Knowledge Spillovers: Evidence from New Zealand, Journal of Business Finance & Accounting, Volume 39, Issue 1-2, pp. 60–81, January/February 2012.

Köhler, A. G., Marten, K.-U., Ratzinger, N. V. S., Wagner, M. (2010): Prüfungshonorare in Deutschland – Determinanten und Implikationen“. In: Zeitschrift für Betriebswirtschaft, 2010, pp. 5-29.

Köhler, Annette (2012): Pflichtrotaton auf dem deutschen Prüfungsmarkt – Eine Szenarioanalyse, Die Wirtschaftsprüfung 9 (2012), pp. 477-481.

KPMG (2009): Transparenzbericht 2009, KPMG AG Wirtschaftsprüfungsgeesellschaft, March 2010, http://www.kpmg.de.

KPMG (2010): Transparenzbericht 2010, KPMG AG Wirtschaftsprüfungsgeesellschaft, March 2010, http://www.kpmg.de.

KPMG (2011): Transparenzbericht 2011, KPMG AG Wirtschaftsprüfungsgeesellschaft, March 2012, http://www.kpmg.de.

KPMG (2012a): Transparenzbericht 2012, KPMG AG Wirtschaftsprüfungsgesellschaft, March 2012, http://www.kpmg.de.

KPMG (2012b): Transparenzbericht 2012, KPMG Bayerische Treuhandgesellschaft AG WPG StBG, March, 2012, http://www.kpmg.de.

Krauss, P., Pronobis, P. and Zülch, H. (2010): Unexpected Audit Fees and Audit Quality: Do Audit Fee Premiums Trigger Error Announcements and Earnings Management? (June 17, 2010). Available at SSRN: http://ssrn.com/abstract=1626186 or http://dx.doi.org/10.2139/ssrn.1626186 (August 30, 2012, 12:30 CET).

Krishnan, J. and J. Krishnan (1997): The role of economic trade-offs in the audit opinion decision: an empirical analysis. Journal of Accounting, Auditing and Finance, 17: 565–586.

Krishnan, J. and Schauer P. C. (2001): “Differences in Quality among Audit firms”, Journal of Accountancy, Vol. 192 (2), p. 85.

Krishnan, Gopal V. (2003): “Does Big 6 Auditor Industry Expertise Constrain Earnings Management?”, Accounting Horizons, Supplement 2003, pp. 1-16.

Krishnan, G. V. and Yu, Wei (2011) "Further evidence on knowledge spillover and the joint determination of audit and non-audit fees", Managerial Auditing Journal, Vol. 26 Iss: 3, pp. 230–247.

Kwon, S. Y., Ch. Y. Lim, and P. M.-S. Tan (2007): Legal Systems and Earnings Quality: The Role of Auditor Industry Specialization. AUDITING: A Journal of Practice & Theory: November 2007, Vol. 26, No. 2, pp. 25-55.

Lawrence, A., Minutti, M. and Zhang, P. (2007): A Study on the Adequacy of Non-Big 4 Audits, Rotman School of Management, University of Toronto, download: http://www.rotman.utoronto.ca/accounting/zhang.doc.

Leffson, Ulrich (1988): Wirtschaftsprüfung, 4. Auflage, Wiesbaden 1988, Verlag Gabler.

Lennox, C. (1999): Are large auditors more accurate than small auditors? Accounting and Business Research, Volume 29, Issue 3, pp. 217–227.

Leventis, S. and C. Caramanis (2005): Determinants of audit time as a proxy of audit quality, Managerial Auditing Journal, Volume 20, No. 5, 2005, pp. 460-478.

Lin, W. and Hwang, M. I. (2010): Audit Quality, Corporate Governance, and Earnings Management: A Meta-Analysis, International Journal of Auditing, Volume 14, 2010, pp. 57–77.

Lu, T. and Sivaramakrishnan, K. (2009): Mandatory audit firm rotation: fresh look vs. poor knowledge. Journal of Accounting and Public Policy, Volume 28, pp. 71–91.

Lys, T. and R.L. Watts (1994): Lawsuits against auditors, Journal of Accounting Research, Supplement, Volume 32, Issue 3 (Supplement), p. 65-93.

McKee, T. E. and Eilifsen, A. (2000). “Current materiality guidance for auditors”, The CPA Journal, Volume 70, No. 7, pp. 54-57.

Maijoor, S. J. & Vanstraelen, A. (2006): ‘Earnings management within Europe: the effects of member state audit environment, audit firm quality and international capital markets’, Accounting and Business Research, Vol. 36, No. 1, pp. 33–52.

Mansi, S., W. Maxwell and D. Miller (2004): Does Auditor Quality and Tenure Matter to Investors? Evidence from the Bond Market, Journal of Accounting Research, Volume 42, No. 4, pp. 755-793.

Manson, S., S. McCartney and M. Sherer (2001): Audit Automation as Control within Audit Firms, Accounting, Auditing & Accountability Journal, Volume 14, Issue 1, pp. 109-130.

Mareva, M. (2010): Zur Entwicklung des Enforcement in Deutschland, Studienarbeit, Grin-Verlag, January 18, 2010.

Messier, W. F. (2003): Auditing & Assurance Services – A systematic Approach, Volume 3, McGraw-Hill, Irwin.

Meyer, M.J., Rigsby, J.T. and Boone, J. (2007): The impact of auditor–client relationships on the reversal of first-time audit qualifications. Managerial Auditing Journal, Volume 22, Issue 1, pp. 53–79.

Montoya del Corte, Garcia and Laviada (2010): "Effective use of qualitative materiality factors: evidence from Spain" in: Managerial Auditing Journal, Vol. 25 No. 5, 2010, pp. 458-483.

Myers, J.N., Myers, L.A., and Omer, C.T. (2003): Exploring the term of the auditor-client relationship and the quality of earnings: A case for mandatory auditor rotation. The Accounting Review, Volume 78, Issue 3, pp. 779-799.

Niehus, R.J. (2002): Corporate Governance: Das Honorar und der Abschlussprüfer – Stärkung der Unabhängigkeit durch Offenlegung?, in: Die Wirtschaftsprüfung, 55. Jg., 2002, pp. 616-625.

Niemann, W. (2004): Prüfungsqualität. In: Beck'sches StB-Handbuch 2004/2005, herausgegeben von: Pelka, Jürgen und Niemann Walter: C.H. Beck, Kapitel D. Jahresabschlussprüfung, Rz. 202-212.

O'Keefe, T.B., Simunic, D.A., and M.T. Stein (1994): The Production of Audit Services: Evidence from a major public accounting firm, Journal of Accounting Research 32, (Autumn), pp. 241-261.

Palmrose, Z.-V (1986): Audit Fees and Auditor Size: Further Evidence, Journal of Accounting Research Vol. 24, No. 1 (Spring 1986), pp. 97-110.

Palmrose, Z.-V. (1988): An Analysis of Auditor Litigation and Audit Service Quality, The Accounting Review, Vol. 63, No. 1 (January 1988), pp. 55-73.

Palmrose, Z.-V. and Scholz, S. (2000): Restated financial statements and auditor litigation. Working paper, University of Southern California, October 2000, Available at SSRN: http://ssrn.com/abstract=248455 or http://dx.doi.org/10.2139/ssrn.248455 (March 15, 2012, 15:00 CET).

Paulitschek, P. (2009): Aufsicht über den Berufsstand der Wirtschaftsprüfer in Deutschland – eine agencytheoretische Betrachtung, Auditing and Accounting Studies, Gabler Edition Wisschschaft, 1st edition 2009.

PCAOB (2011): Concept Release on Auditor Independence and Audit Firm Rotation; Notice of roundtable, PCAOB Release No. 2011-006, August 16, 2011, http://pcaobus.org/Rules/Rulemaking/Docket037/Release_2011-006.pdf (March 15, 2012, 15:00 CET).

Peemöller, Volker H. (2012): Gebührenordnung für Abschlussprüfer – ein Ansatz zur Qualitätssicherung, WPK Magazin 1/2011, pp. 37-42.

Picot, A., Dietl, H., Franck, E. (2005): Organisation – Eine ökonomische Perspektive, 4. Auflage, Stuttgart.

PKF Deutschland (2010): Transparenzbericht 2010, PKF Deutschland GmbH WPG, March 2010, http://www.pkf.de.

PKF Deutschland (2011): Transparenzbericht 2011, PKF Deutschland GmbH WPG, March 2011, http://www.pkf.de.

PKF Deutschland (2012): Transparenzbericht 2012, PKF Deutschland GmbH WPG, March 2012, http://www.pkf.de.

PKF Fasselt (2010): Transparenzbericht 2012, PKF Deutschland GmbH WPG, March 2010, http://www.pkf-fasselt.de.

PKF Fasselt (2011): Transparenzbericht 2012, PKF Deutschland GmbH WPG, March 2011, http://www.pkf-fasselt.de.

PKF Fasselt (2012): Transparenzbericht 2012, PKF Deutschland GmbH WPG, March 2012, http://www.pkf-fasselt.de.

Plumlee, M. A. and Yohn, T. L. (2009): An Analysis of the Underlying Causes Attributed to Restatements (June 9, 2009). Available at SSRN: http://ssrn.com/abstract= 1104189 or http://dx.doi.org/10.2139/ssrn.1104189.

PwC (2009a): Erfahrungen mit DPR-Prüfungen, Ergebnisse einer Umfrage unter Führungskräften im Rechnungswesen kapitalmarktorientierter Unternehmen, PricewaterhouseCoopers AG Wirtschaftsprüfungs-gesellschaft und Deutsches Aktieninstitut e.V., September 2009.

PwC (2009b): Transparenzbericht 2009, PricewaterhouseCoopers Germany, March 2009, http://www.pwc.de.

PwC (2010): Transparenzbericht 2010, PricewaterhouseCoopers Germany, March 2010, http://www.pwc.de.

PwC (2011): Transparenzbericht 2011, PricewaterhouseCoopers Germany, March 2011, http://www.pwc.de

PwC (2012a): Transparenzbericht 2012, PricewaterhouseCoopers Germany, March 2012, http://www.pwc.de.

PwC (2011b): University of California, Audit and Communication Plan, PwC, June 30, 2011, http://regents.universityofcalifornia.edu/regmeet/mar12/a2attach3.pdf (October 15, 2012, 11:00 CET).

Quick, R. (1996): The legal liability of auditors in Germany, European Accounting Review, Volume 5, Issue 3, 1996, pp. 507-521.

Raghunandan, K. and D. Rama (1999): Auditor resignations and the market for audit services. Auditing, Volume 18, No.1, pp. 124-134.

Raghunandan, K., Read, W. J. & Whisenant, J. S. (2003): 'Initial evidence on the association between nonaudit fees and restated financial statements', Accounting Horizons, Vol. 17, pp. 223–234.

Rahman, R. A. and Ali, F. H. M. (2006): 'Board, audit committee, culture and earnings management: Malaysian evidence', Managerial Auditing Journal, Vol. 21, No. 7, pp. 783–804.

Reynolds, J. K., Deis, D. R. & Francis, J. R. (2004): 'Professional service fees and auditor objectivity', Auditing: A Journal of Practice & Theory, Vol. 23, No. 1, pp. 29–52.

Rollins, T. P. and Bremser, W.G. (1997): The SEC's enforcements actions against auditors: an auditor reputation and institutional theory perspective, Critical Perspectives on Accounting, Volume 8, Issue 3, June 1997, pp. 191-206, ISSN 1045-2354.

Rüchardt, F. A. (1995): Qualitätsmanagement in der Wirtschaftsprüfung: Konzeption eines Qualitätsmanagements für Abschlussprüfer unter Berücksichtigung haftungsrechtlicher Aspekte: Reihe: Schriftenreihe zum Finanz-, Prüfungs- und Rechnungswesen, Band 9, München VVF 1995.

Schauer, P. (2002): "The Effects of Industry Specialization on Audit Quality: An Examination using Bid-Ask Spreads", Journal of Accounting and Finance Research, Volume 10, No. 1, pp.76-86.

Schelleman, C.C.M., and Maijoor, S.J. (2003): Benchmarking the Production of Audit Services: An Efficiency Frontier Approach, Working paper, Universiteit Maastricht.

Scherl, J. B. (1994): Evolution of Auditor Liability to noncontractual third parties: balancing the equities and weighing the consequences The American University Law Review, Volume 44, 1994, pp. 255-289.

Schipper, K. (1989): 'Commentary on earnings management', Accounting Horizons, Volume 3, pp. 1–102.

Schmidt, Sutherland, van Schalkwyk, Lowe and Bockmann (2011): Monitoring and enforcement of financial reporting standards in South Africa and Germany: A comparative assessment, Namibia Law Journal, Volume 3 Issue 1, January 2011.

Schurz, G. (2005): Einführung in die Wissenschaftstheorie, Wissenschaftliche Buchgesellschaft, 2. Auflage, April 20057.

SEC (1999): SEC Staff Accounting Bulletin No. 99 – Materiality, Securities and Exchange Commission Washington D.C.: Available at http://www.Sec.gov/interps/account/sab99.htm (August 30, 2012, 12:30 CET).

SEC (2001): Final Rules: Revision of the Commission's Auditor Independence Requirements, RIN 3235-AH91, Effective date: February 5, 2001, www.sec.gov/rules/final/33-7919.htm (August 30, 2012, 12:30 CET).

Shockley, R. (1981). Perceptions of auditors' independence: an empirical analysis. The Accounting Review, Volume 56, Issue 4, pp. 785–800.

Simunic, D.A. (1980): "The pricing of audit services: theory and evidence", Journal of Accounting Research, Vol. 18 No. 1, pp. 161-90.

Sipple, B. and Glemser, M. (2012): Die Rotation des Abschlussprüfers im europäischen Vergleich, Die Wirtschaftsprüfung 16 (2012), pp. 875-881.

Siregar, S. V., F. Amarullah, A. Wibowo and V. Anggraita (2012): "Audit Tenure, Auditor Rotation, and Audit Quality: The Case of Indonesia", Asian Journal of Business and Accounting, Volume 5, No. 1, 2012, pp. 55-74, ISSN 1985-4064.

SOX (2002): The Sarbanes-Oxley Act of 2002. Public Law No. 107-204. Washington, D.C.: Government Printing Office.

Titman, S. and Trueman, B. (1986): "Information Quality and the Valuation of New Issues", Journal of Accounting and Economics. Vol. 8, No. 2, pp. 159-172.

U.S. Department of Treasury (2008), Advisory Committee on the Auditing Profession, Final Report, October 2008, http://www.treasury.gov/about/organizational-structure/offices/Documents/final-report.pdf.

Walker, A. and Hay, David (2011): Non-Audit Services and Knowledge Spillovers: An Investigation of the Audit Report Lag (May 25, 2011). Available at SSRN: http://ssrn.com/abstract=1852836 or http://dx.doi.org/10.2139/ssrn.1852836 (January 13, 2013, 17:30 CET).

Watson, J. (2001): How to Determine a Sample Size: Tipsheet #60, University Park, PA: Penn State Cooperative Extension. Available at: http://www.extension.psu.edu/evaluation/pdf/TS60.pdf (August 30, 2012, 12:30 CET).

Wiemann, D. (2011): Prüfungsqualität des Abschlussprüfers, Einfluss der Mandatsdauer auf die Bilanzpolitik beim Mandanten, Gabler Verlag, 1. Auflage 2011.

Wild, A. (2010): Fee cutting and fee premium of German auditors, Die Betriebswirtschaft, Schäffer-Poeschel, ZDBID: 213053-1, ISSN: 03427064, Volume 70 (2010), Issue 6, pp. 513-527.

Woodland, A. and Reynolds, K. (2003): Restatements and audit quality. Working paper. American Accounting Association, Annual Meeting Midyear 2004. Available at: http://raw.rutgers.edu/raw/aaa/audit/midyear/04midyear/2004%20Midyear%20Auditing%20Meeting.

Wooten, T. C. (2003), "Research about Audit Quality", CPA Journal, Vol. 73, Issue 1, January 2003, pp. 48-64.

WPK (2006): Anbieterstruktur und Mandatsverteilung im Wirtschaftsprüfermarkt 2006, WPK Magazin 4/2006, pp. 13-17.

WPK (2008a): Anbieterstruktur und Mandatsverteilung im Wirtschaftsprüfermarkt 2006, WPK Magazin 1/2008, pp. 6-11.

WPK (2008b): Anbieterstruktur, Mandatsverteilung und Abschlussprüferhonorare im Wirtschaftsprüfermarkt 2007, WPK Magazin 4/2008, pp. 14-22.

WPK (2009): Anbieterstruktur, Mandatsverteilung und Abschlussprüferhonorare im Wirtschaftsprüfermarkt 2008, WPK Magazin 4/2009, pp. 11-19.

WPK (2010): Anbieterstruktur, Mandatsverteilung und Abschlussprüferhonorare im Wirtschaftsprüfermarkt 2009, WPK Magazin 4/2010, pp. 16-24.

WPK (2011): Anbieterstruktur, Mandatsverteilung und Abschlussprüferhonorare im Wirtschaftsprüfermarkt 2010, WPK Magazin 4/2011, pp. 17-27.

WPK (2012a): Ergebnisse der Honorarumfrage 2010/2011, Aus der Arbeit der WPK, WPK Magazin 2/2012, p. 16, available also online: http://www.wpk.de/praxis hinweise/honorarumfrage.asp (August 30, 2012, 12:30 CET).

WPK (2012b): Gebührenordnung für gesetzliche Abschlussprüfungen – Schreiben der WPK an den Deutschen Bundestag, Aus der Arbeit der WPK, WPK Magazin 2/2012, p. 17.

Van Dijk, M. (1998): Litigation and audit quality; Rijksuniversiteit Groningen / SOM Research Reports, http://som.eldoc.ub.rug.nl/FILES/reports/1995-1999/themeC/1998/98C42/98c42.pdf (August 14, 2012, 9:00 CET).

Varian, Hal R. (1992): Microeconomic Analysis, third edition, W. W. Norton & Company, Inc., ISBN 0-393-95735-7.

Velte, Patrick (2012): Stärkung der Qualität der Abschlussprüfung durch die externe Rotationspflicht? – Eine Reflexion der empirischen Prüfungsforschung vor dem Hintergrund des Verordnungsentwurfs der EU-Kommission vom 30.11.2011, Die Wirtschaftsprüfung 6 (2012), pp. 317-323.

Velte, P. and Stiglbauer M. (2012): Impact of Auditor and Audit Firm Rotation on Accounting and Audit Quality: A Critical Analysis of the EC Regulation Draft, International conference "Improving financial institutions: the proper balance between regulation and governance", Helsinki, April 19, 2012.

Venkataraman, R., J. P. Weber, and M. Willenborg (2008): Litigation Risk, Audit Quality, and Audit Fees: Evidence from Initial Public Offerings. The Accounting Review: September 2008, Vol. 83, No. 5, pp. 1315-1345.

Yang, Junfeng (2011): Industry Expertise and Audit Quality Literature Review and Analysis, M & D Forum, 2011, pp. 156-160, available at: http://www.seiofblue mountain.com/upload/product/201111/2011kjxid4.pdf (August 10, 2012, 9:00 CET).

Zülch, Hoffmann (2005): Das deutsche Enforcement-Modell des Bilanzkontrollgesetzes – Ausgestaltung und Implikationen für Rechnungslegung und Abschlussprüfung, in: Steuern und Bilanzen 2005, Issue 1, pp. 1-9.

Zülch, Hoffmann (2010): Rechtsprechung zum Rechnungslegungs-Enforcement in Deutschland – ein erster Überblick, DStR 2010, pp. 945-951.

MIX
Papier aus verantwortungsvollen Quellen
Paper from responsible sources
FSC® C105338

If you have any concerns about our products,
you can contact us on
ProductSafety@springernature.com

In case Publisher is established outside the EU,
the EU authorized representative is:
Springer Nature Customer Service Center GmbH
Europaplatz 3, 69115 Heidelberg, Germany

Printed by Libri Plureos GmbH
in Hamburg, Germany